D0207956

# Medical Issues
## and the
## Eating Disorders

### THE INTERFACE

BRUNNER/MAZEL
EATING DISORDERS MONOGRAPH SERIES
*Series Editors*
PAUL E. GARFINKEL, M.D.
DAVID M. GARNER, PH.D.

FLORENCE A. MOORE LIBRARY OF MEDICINE
MEDICAL COLLEGE OF PENNSYLVANIA

BRUNNER/MAZEL EATING DISORDERS MONOGRAPH SERIES NO. 7

DREXEL UNIVERSITY
HEALTH SCIENCES LIBRARIES
HAHNEMANN LIBRARY

# *Medical Issues and the Eating Disorders*

## THE INTERFACE

*Edited by*
## ALLAN S. KAPLAN
M.SC., M.D., FRCP(C)
## PAUL E. GARFINKEL
M.SC., M.D., FRCP(C)

**BRUNNER/MAZEL** *Publishers* • NEW YORK

WM
175
M489
1993

Library of Congress Cataloging-in-Publication Data
Medical Issues and the eating disorders : the interface / edited by
Allan S. Kaplan, Paul E. Garfinkel.
     p.     cm.—(Brunner/Mazel eating disorders monograph series ;
no. 7)
   Includes bibliographical references and index.
   ISBN 0-87630-681-4
   1. Eating disorders—Physiological aspects.   I. Kaplan, Allan S.
II. Garfinkel, Paul E.
   [DNLM:   1. Eating Disorders.      W1 BR917D v. 7 / WM 175
M489]
RC552.E18M445    1993
616.85'26—dc20
DNLM/DLC
for Library of Congress                                    92-48961
                                                                CIP

Copyright © 1993 by Brunner/Mazel, Inc.

All rights reserved. No part of this book may be
reproduced by any process whatsoever without
the written permission of the copyright owner.

*Published by*
BRUNNER/MAZEL, INC.
19 Union Square West
New York, New York 10003

Manufactured in the United States of America

10   9   8   7   6   5   4   3   2   1

For Rochelle
and our children
Jesse, Zekiel, and Alisha

and

For Dorothy
and our children
Jonathan, Stephen, and Joshua

7.25.94 Ritter $26.93

HCD8 46U

# Contents

# Introduction

"A young woman thus afflicted, her clothes scarcely hanging together on her anatomy, her pulse slow and slack, her temperature two degrees below the normal mean, her bowels closed, her hair like that of a corpse dry and lustreless, her face and limbs ashy and cold, her hollow eyes the only vivid thing about her . . . . This wan creature whose daily food might lie on a crown piece, will be busy yet on what funds God only knows." (Allbutt 1910, p. 398)

There are clear and compelling reasons for publishing this monograph, despite a surfeit of books on eating disorders published in the past decade. These previous texts have provided overviews of anorexia and bulimia nervosa and have dealt specifically with the sociocultural aspects of these disorders, their psychobiology, and their psychological and pharmacotherapeutic management. However, there remains a need for a comprehensive clinically oriented medical text on the eating disorders for clinicians. Such a text would bring together a large body of disparate literature on the biomedical variables relevant to the understanding and treatment of anorexia and bulimia nervosa.

*Medical Issues and the Eating Disorders: The Interface* has been prepared to fill this void. It is intended as a reference text not only for psychiatric physicians and medical colleagues in other specialties who are likely to encounter these patients but also for nonphysician clinicians, including psychologists, nutritionists, and other health professionals who may not be familiar with these issues. More than any other psychiatric disorder, anorexia and bulimia nervosa are conditions in which a disturbed psyche directly contributes to a disturbed soma. This psychosomatic link is clearly demonstrated by the disturbingly high mortality of these conditions, approaching 18% in some studies (Theander, 1985; Ratnasuriya, Eisler, Szmukler, & Russell, 1991). A significant percentage of the mortality is directly attributable to the physical complications that accompany these disorders. Familiarity with these medical aspects becomes crucial for any clinician, regardless of orientation or discipline, who treats these patients. Such an understanding provides the necessary tools for the competent and comprehensive care of patients with anorexia and bulimia nervosa, and could potentially contribute to prevention of these disorders. These biomedical variables, however, must always be considered within the wider context of sociological and psychological parameters that have been clearly delineated (Garfinkel & Garner, 1982).

This monograph reviews issues relevant to assessment, etiology, and treatment. Following a review of the medical and nutritional assessment of patients are two chapters that deal with diagnostic issues: a description of those medical conditions that have as part of their presentation a disturbance in eating behavior or weight and a review of the unique issues relevant to the obese bulimic. The monograph then details the medical and dental complications that arise in eating disorder patients and discusses more specifically the reproductive, neuroendocrine, neurotransmitter, and metabolic disturbances that can occur. A review of the genetics of these conditions follows, as well as a description of the mechanisms by which a chronic medical illness, such as diabetes mellitus, interacts with anorexia and bulimia nervosa. It concludes with a chapter dedicated to the medical management of the hospitalized patient, including pharmacotherapeutic treatments.

A comment about obesity is in order. It is our philosophy that obesity alone is neither a psychiatric disorder nor an eating disorder; it is not implicitly associated with a disturbance in psychological functioning or in eating behavior. Pathophysiologically, we consider obesity to be a multideterminedmetabolic disorder, encompassing a diverse patient population, with a genetic predisposition playing an important role in its genesis. We have therefore not included in this text the substantial and important literature on medical illness and obesity. However, we have focused on issues specific and relevant to the obese bulimic patient. This is a patient population that heretofore has been somewhat neglected by clinicians and investigators working in the eating disorders community, but which is now receiving closer attention as the DSM-IV Eating Disorders Work Group considers inclusion of a new diagnosis, binge eating disorder, in the DSM-IV (Spitzer et al., 1992).

Finally, the chapters in this book raise a number of questions that will require further research in the decade to come. What is the specific role of the various neuropeptides and neurohormones in the regulation of eating behavior? Which as yet undiscovered neuroregulators remain to be elucidated? What are the mechanisms for bone abnormalities found in anorexia and bulimia nervosa? What is the specific hypothalamic disturbance that is responsible for menstrual abnormalities in these patients? What is the true nature of the genetic contribution to the development of an eating disorder? What is the evidence for the validity of the proposed binge eating disorder, and what may be unique about those patients that may affect their treatment and outcome differently than the treatment of a normal weight or underweight patient with bulimia nervosa? What is the effect of concomitant medical illness on long-term outcome? These and other relevant questions will likely be the subject of much scientific inquiry and scholarly work in the next decade as we continue to struggle to improve our understanding and treatment for these enigmatic and disabling conditions.

*November 1992*                                             ALLAN S. KAPLAN
                                                            PAUL E. GARFINKEL

## REFERENCES

Allbutt, T. C. (1910). Neuroses of the stomach and of other parts of the abdomen. In T. C. Allbutt & H. D. Rolleston (Eds.), *System of medicine*, p. 398. London: The Macmillan Company.

Garfinkel, P. E., & Garner, D. M. (1982). *Anorexia nervosa, a multidemensional perspective*. New York: Brunner Mazel.

Ratnasuriya, R. H., Eisler, I., Szmukler, G. F., & Russell, G. F. (1991). Anorexia nervosa: Outcome and prognostic factors after 20 years. *British Journal of Psychiatry, 158,* 495–502.

Spitzer, R. L., Devlin, M., Walsh, B. T., Hasin, D., Wing R., Marous, M., Stunkard, A., Wadden, T., Yanouski, S., Agras, S., Mitchell, J., & Nonas, C. (1992). Binge eating disorder: A multisite field trial of the diagnostic criteria. *International Journal of Eating Disorders, 11,* 191–508.

Theander, S. (1985). Outcome and prognosis in anorexia nervosa and bulimia: Some results of previous investigations, compared with those of a Swedish long term study. *Journal of Psychiatric Research, 19,* 493–508

# Acknowledgments

We would like to thank our distinguished colleagues for their contributions to this book. Their clear conceptualizations and prompt attention to detail facilitated the editorial task. We would also like to thank Ms. Kathy Muich for her technical assistance in typing and coordinating parts of the manuscript.

# Contributors

**Richard M. Black, Ph.D., B.Sc., Psych.**
Assistant Professor of Nutritional Sciences; Research Associate, Department of Psychiatry, The Toronto Hospital, Toronto, Ontario, Canada.

**Denis Daneman, M.B., B.Ch., FRCP(C)**
Chief, Division of Endocrinology, Hospital for Sick Children; Associate Professor of Pediatrics, University of Toronto, Toronto, Ontario, Canada.

**Caroline Davis, Ph.D.**
Research Associate, Department of Psychiatry, The Toronto Hospital; Associate Professor, Department of Physical Education, York University, North York, Ontario, Canada.

**Janet deGroot, M.D., FRCP(C)**
Staff Psychiatrist, The Toronto Hospital; Assistant Professor of Psychiatry, University of Toronto, Toronto, Ontario, Canada.

**Martina de Zwaan, M.D.**
Department of Psychiatry, University of Minnesota, Minneapolis, Minnesota.

**Paul E. Garfinkel, M.Sc., M.D., FRCP(C)**
Director and Psychiatrist-in-Chief, Clarke Institute of Psychiatry; Professor and Chairman, Department of Psychiatry, University of Toronto, Toronto, Ontario, Canada.

**David S. Goldbloom, M.D., FRCP(C)**
Staff Psychiatrist, The Toronto Hospital; Associate Professor of Psychiatry, University of Toronto, Toronto, Ontario, Canada.

**Allan S. Kaplan, M.Sc., M.D., FRCP(C)**
Director, Eating Disorder Day Centre; Associate Professor of Psychiatry, University of Toronto, Toronto, Ontario, Canada.

**Mark Katz, M.D.**
Fellow in Psychiatry, The Toronto Hospital, Toronto, Ontario, Canada.

**Sidney H. Kennedy, M.D., FRCP(C)**
Head, Eating Disorder Program; Director, Psychiatry Research, The Toronto Hospital; Associate Professor of Psychiatry, University of Toronto, Toronto, Ontario, Canada.

**R. John McComb, B.D.S., M.Sc., FRCD(C)**
Dentist-in-Chief, The Toronto Hospital; Associate Professor of Oral Pathology, Faculty of Dentistry, University of Toronto, Toronto, Ontario, Canada.

**James E. Mitchell, M.D.**
Professor of Psychiatry; Director, Division of Adult Psychiatry, University of Minnesota, Minneapolis, Minnesota.

**Gary Rodin, M.D., FRCP(C)**
Psychiatrist-in-Chief, The Toronto Hospital; Associate Professor of Psychiatry, University of Toronto, Toronto, Ontario, Canada.

**Colin Shapiro, B.Sc. (Hon), M.B.B.Ch., M.D., Ph.D., MRC. Psych., FRCP(C)**
Professor of Psychiatry, University of Toronto, Toronto, Ontario, Canada.

**G. Terence Wilson, Ph.D.**
Oscar K. Buros Professor of Psychology, Graduate School of Applied and Professional Psychology, Rutgers University, Piscataway, New Jersey.

**D. Blake Woodside, M.Sc., M.D., FRCP(C)**
Staff Psychiatrist, Eating Disorder Day Centre, The Toronto Hospital; Assistant Professor of Psychiatry, University of Toronto, Toronto, Ontario, Canada.

# Medical Issues and the Eating Disorders

## THE INTERFACE

# 1

# Medical and Nutritional Assessment

## Allan S. Kaplan
### M.SC., M.D., FRCP(C)

The eating disorders anorexia nervosa and bulimia nervosa are complex psychosomatic illnesses. Underlying biological diatheses related to the regulation of mood, hunger, satiety, weight control, and metabolism, combined with psychological and sociocultural vulnerabilities, place an individual at risk for developing an eating disorder. The clinical manifestation of the affected individual's attempt to deal with these underlying vulnerabilities often begins with an intense loathing of the body followed by caloric restriction, ostensibly in the pursuit of a thinner body shape. This behavior creates a vicious circle of weight loss and/or starvation, with behavioral and psychological sequelae that perpetuate the disorder.

The medical sequelae that result from starvation, weight loss, bingeing, and purging are manifold and necessitate a thorough medical and nutritional assessment. This chapter will review the essential components of such an assessment. The specific areas that should be enquired about are listed in Table 1.1.

## WEIGHT HISTORY

Several aspects of weight history are essential information. The patient's current weight, preferably obtained by objective weighing in a hospital gown and not by self-report, needs to be established. Patients with anorexia and bulimia nervosa are often unreliable in their self-estimation of

1

**TABLE 1.1.**
**Components of an Eating Disorder Assessment**

I. Weight
    A.   Current (BMI)
    B.   Highest ever
    C.   Lowest ever
    D.   Premorbid
    E.   Perceived ideal
    F.   Menstrual threshold
II. Body Image
    A.   Attitudes and feelings re: overall size
    B.   Attitudes and feelings re: specific body parts
    C.   Cosmetic procedures
III. Means of Weight Control
    A.   Caloric Intake
        1. Number of calories
        2. Number of meals
        3. Binge episodes
           a. Frequency
           b. Time of day or night
           c. Amount of food consumed
           d. Type of food consumed
           e. Subjective experience
           f. Associated behaviors—stealing, rumination, pica
        4. Idiosyncratic nutritional beliefs and practices
    B.   Purging behaviors
        1. Vomiting (ipecac)
        2. Laxatives
        3. Drugs to control weight
           a. Diet pills
           b. Diuretics
           c. Caffeine
           d. Thyroid
    C.   Exercise
        1. Type
        2. Amount
IV. Physical and Laboratory Examination
    A.   Review of systems (especially cardiovascular, gastrointestinal, endocrine, gynecologic, dermatologic)
    B.   Physical complications
    C.   Laboratory investigations
        1. Routine
           a. CBC
           b. Electrolytes
           c. BUN
           d. Creatinine

2. If indicated
   a. EKG (weight loss, hypokalemia, ipecac)
   b. Liver function (weight loss, alcohol abuse
   c. CPK (abusing ipecac)
   d. Amylase (gastrointestinal symptoms)
   e. Calcium, phosphorus (chronic amenorrhea or fractures)
   f. Endoscopic or roentgenographic exam (blood loss)

V. Initial feedback
   A. Cessation of dieting behavior
   B. Regular intake of adequate calories (2,000–3,000 calories/day)
   C. Proscription of laxatives, diet pills, diuretics
   D. If underweight, cessation of exercise

VI. Medical indications for immediate hospitalization
   A. Severe fluid and electrolyte disturbance (i.e., K < 2.5 m mol/L)
   B. Cardiac complications
      1. Arrhythmia or conduction disturbance (i.e., QT prolongation)
      2. Cardiomyopathy (ipecac)
   C. Acute rapid weight loss
   D. Acute pancreatitis or gastric dilatation
   E. Convulsions

VII. Ongoing medical management
   A. Close monitoring of weight, fluid and electrolyte and cardiac status
   B. Psychiatric consultation
   C. Dental consultation
   D. Nutrition consultation
   E. Periodic hospitalization
      1. Crisis intervention for medical or psychiatric reasons
      2. In a specialized unit to treat the eating disorder

---

body weight. It is helpful to express weight in terms of height, through the establishment of the patient's body mass index (BMI), expressed as kilogram/meter$^2$. Because it corrects for height and is highly correlated with direct measures of body fat, BMI represents a more accurate nutritional assessment than does total body weight (Marliss, 1987). The clinician should attempt to establish the patient's premorbid weight as well; this is the weight the patient maintained prior to the attempt to alter body weight or shape. This weight provides a crude approximation of the patient's natural weight; that is, the weight that is genetically determined for physiological homeostasis. There is evidence that for patients with bulimia nervosa, this is often significantly above matched population mean weights for age and height (Garner, Garfinkel, & O'Shaughnessy, 1985). In contrast, patients with anorexia nervosa without bulimia tend not to be premorbidly over average weight (Garfinkel, Moldofsky, & Garner,

1980). For patients who develop an eating disorder in adolescence, prior to the closing of skeletal epiphyses, there is no reliable way of establishing such a premorbid weight. This weight can be estimated by adjusting the average weight for height and age according to familial patterns of weight. The premorbid or set point weight should be adjusted upward if there is a clear childhood or family history of obesity.

Additional noteworthy weights must be established. The patient's menstrual threshold, that is, the weight at which amenorrhea or oligomenorrhea occurs, should be noted. This threshold, usually around 85% of matched population mean weight (Frisch & McArthur, 1974) for individuals who begin at normal weight, is often a phobic weight beyond which a patient must pass in order to be fully nutritionally rehabilitated. The degree of weight fluctuation also needs to be established, with both the highest and lowest adult weights noted. Interestingly, patients with bulimia nervosa have as much weight fluctuation over their lifetime as do patients with anorexia nervosa (Garner & Fairburn, 1988). Finally, the patient's wished for or desired weight, when compared to the premorbid weight, provides some measure of the patient's drive for thinness and the degree of psychological work required for the patient to begin to tolerate and eventually accept a healthy body weight.

## BODY IMAGE

An evaluation of patients' feelings and attitudes about their bodies is important. This should include enquiry about the degree of body dissatisfaction, with emphasis on both overall size and specific body parts that the patient may particularly loathe. Attempts to change body shape through procedures such as liposuction or cosmetic surgery are not uncommon in eating disorder patients (Yates, Shisslak, Allender, & Wolman, 1988). There is a suggestion that such operations are risky in these patients, as they often have unrealistic expectations from the surgery and may be dissatisfied with the results. In essence, such patients are attempting to deal surgically with a psychological disturbance. Enquiry about a possible eating disorder should occur with any young woman who persistently seeks cosmetic surgery when there is no obvious clinical reason for it. Finally, sociocultural pressures to be thin, such as involvement in dance or modeling, should be assessed. It may be necessary for the clinician to recommend that the patient cease such activities as part of recovery from the disorder.

## MEANS OF WEIGHT CONTROL

A thorough investigation of the means by which a patient is controlling body weight is an essential part of the initial assessment. These behaviors are often experienced by the patient as embarrassing or shameful and, as such, they are not readily divulged or volunteered. Specific questions need to be asked about general eating behavior and the degree of caloric restriction, purging behaviors, the intake of various drugs, and the degree of exercise in any patient suspected of having an eating disorder.

### Eating Behavior and Caloric Intake

The number of calories eaten during the course of the day and the number of meals, snacks, and other eating episodes need to be carefully documented. It is also useful as part of a nutritional assessment to review the variety of commercial diets that have been pursued (e.g., Weight Watchers, TOPS, Nutrisystem, Pritiken, Fit for Life, Optifast, liquid protein diets). Self-imposed caloric restriction in the pursuit of a thinner shape is characteristic of anorexia nervosa. Patients with anorexia nervosa commonly consume diets low in carbohydrate and fat, with the proportion of energy obtained from macronutrients higher from protein and lower from total and concentrated carbohydrates than in the diets of controls (Thibault & Roberge, 1987; Huse & Lucas, 1984). In addition, anorexics tend to consume less calcium, thiamine, riboflavin, niacin, and ascorbic acid than controls (Thibault & Roberge, 1987). Low plasma zinc and copper and elevated serum cholesterol have been observed in anorexia nervosa patients (Schwabe, Lippe, Chang, Pops, & Yager, 1981).

Noteworthy is the observation that bulimic patients do not follow normal eating patterns even when they are not bingeing (Woell, Fichter, & Pirke, 1989). They report intermittent caloric restriction, eating fewer meals and abstaining from food more frequently when hungry than controls (Mitchell, Hatsukami, & Eckert, 1985). Studies have demonstrated that bulimic patients, much like anorexic patients, have elevated levels of plasma beta-hydroxybutyric acid and free fatty acids and lower levels of $T_3$ and glucose compared to normal weight controls (Pirke, Pahl, Schweiger, & Warnhuff, 1985). These are biochemical indices of starvation that suggest that bulimic patients are intermittently in a starved state during the course of their illness. This emphasizes the importance of documenting food intake in bulimics between binges.

The frequency and timing of binge episodes as well as the quantity of food consumed and quality of the subjective experience should be clearly documented. An objective binge episode requires the consumption of a large amount of food in a discreet period of time, accompanied by a feeling of being out of control. Patients may subjectively report bingeing but may not consume what would objectively be considered a large number of calories (Dilsaver, 1988).

Compositional analysis of the macronutrient content of binge and nonbinge foods in bulimics reveals that the former tend to be low in protein, high in refined carbohydrate, and high in fat. The latter tend to be devoid of fat and refined carbohydrates (Kales, 1990). Similar macronutrient composition of binges has been reported across earlier studies (Krissileff, Walsh, Kral, & Cassidy, 1986; Kaye, Gwirtsman, Genge, Weiss, & Jimerson, 1986; Mitchell & Laine, 1985). However, the macronutrient composition of binges in these laboratories closely resembles the nutritional content of freely selected human diets (Krissileff & Van Itallie, 1982). Studies have consistently demonstrated that the most pronounced difference in macronutrients between the so-called safe (nonbinge) and forbidden (binge) foods for bulimics is in fat content (Kales, 1990). Interestingly, although not surprisingly, bulimics report a taste aversion for high-fat foods (Drewnowski, Bellisle, Aimez, & Remy, 1987).

An evaluation of idiosyncratic beliefs and practices around food should be made. These may include the practice of vegetarianism, the intake of multiple vitamin and mineral supplements, specific food phobias, distorted attitudes about macronutrients, and the belief that the patient is suffering from a variety of disorders such as food allergies, lactose intolerance, or hypoglycemia. The relationship between these conditions and eating disorders will be discussed later in this chapter. It is noteworthy that patients with eating disorders, despite being well-informed about the caloric content of food, are often misinformed about the physiology of digestion and the body's handling of nutrients (Beumont et al., 1981). Nutritional beliefs that may have started with a germ of fact become distorted beyond recognition in the service of maintaining a restrictive caloric intake. For example, the admonition of health professionals to limit fat intake to approximately 30% of total calories may become, for the eating disorder patient, a license to follow a totally fat-free diet (Winocur, 1990). The suggestion to vary protein sources in order to reduce cholesterol levels may be taken by the eating disorder patient as license to eliminate meat of all types. An important part of the initial assessment is to provide patients with an accurate and balanced view of nutrition, which will help modify distortions about food, energy intake, and body weight. This is best accomplished by having the patient meet with a nutritionist who is experienced in the treatment of eating disorders.

It is important to emphasize that a significant part of the disturbed eating behavior prominent in both anorexia and bulimia nervosa is not specific to the disorder but is directly attributable to the effects of starvation. This includes the patient's preoccupation with food, peculiar eating rituals, food-related dreams, involvement in food-related occupations, and even disturbed hunger and satiety cues leading to increased hunger after eating and binge eating. All of these symptoms were exhibited by 36 young, healthy, psychologically normal men who were experimentally starved at the University of Minnesota during World War II (Keys, Brozek, Henschel, Mickelsen, & Taylor, 1950). These men exhibited disturbances in eating behavior, cognitions, perception, and mood, as well as sleep and sexual behavior, that are common in patients with eating disorders. These observations accentuate the importance of nutritional rehabilitation for the psychological recovery from anorexia and bulimia nervosa. Attempting to treat an underweight or starved patient psychologically, without attention to refeeding, is akin to trying psychologically to convince an intoxicated alcoholic to stop drinking. Improved nutritional status is a necessary prerequisite for successful psychological intervention.

## Purging Behaviors

### Vomiting

A variety of different methods of purging are utilized by patients with eating disorders. Vomiting is the commonest form of purging, with between 53% and 94% of bulimics across studies reporting self-induced vomiting and 10% reporting vomiting at least once per day (Mitchell, Hatsukami, & Eckert, 1985; see Chapter 4 this volume). The prevalence of self-induced vomiting in patients with anorexia nervosa is lower but still occurs in approximately 25% of patients studied (Garfinkel & Garner, 1982). Ipecac abuse has been reported in patients with eating disorders to facilitate vomiting (Palmer & Guay, 1986). The dangers of this practice are discussed in Chapter 4. Clinicians should be careful to distinguish between self-induced vomiting and other forms of psychogenic vomiting such as that which occurs in conversion disorder (Garfinkel, Kaplan, Garner, & Darby, 1983).

*Laxatives*

Laxative use is a particularly dangerous form of purging because of its effect on fluid and electrolyte balance (see Chapter 4). Patients tend to abuse stimulant-type laxatives (Ex-lax or Correctol) rather than bulk-forming (Metamucil), fecal lubricant (mineral oil), or saline (Milk of Magnesia) laxatives. The prevalence of daily laxative abuse has been reported to be as high as 20% in patients with bulimia nervosa (Mitchell et al., 1985). Fairburn and Cooper (1984) reported that up to 75% of patients had at some point used laxatives. This contrasts with approximately 20% of patients with anorexia nervosa without bulimia reporting any laxative use (Garfinkel & Garner, 1982). The presence of unexplained metabolic acidosis in an otherwise healthy young woman should raise the suspicion of laxative misuse and an underlying eating disorder.

*Drugs to Control Weight*

Patients with eating disorders ingest a large number of drugs in an attempt to control their weight. As many as 25% of a cohort of bulimic patients reported having used diet pills at least once a day for an extended period of time (Mitchell et al., 1985). Patients with anorexia and bulimia nervosa may also abuse thyroid in an attempt to increase their basal metabolic rate and in the process to facilitate weight loss. In one study, approximately 7% of patients with eating disorders were found to have at one point abused thyroid to facilitate weight loss (Woodside, Walfish, Kaplan, & Kennedy, 1991). Caffeine, usually in the form of beverages such as coffee or diet cola, is also ingested in large quantities because of its appetite suppressant, diuretic, and stimulant effects (Fahy & Treasure, 1991). Diuretics are often misused by patients with eating disorders. Such patients often request diuretics from family physicians for what they describe as "premenstrual bloating." Such a request in a young adult female should raise the suspicion of an eating disorder. Despite the fact that the use of diuretics is contraindicated in patients with eating disorders, one study found 10% of bulimic patients to be using diuretics daily (Mitchell et al., 1985).

*Exercise*

Excessive exercise is a behavior that is common amongst patients with anorexia nervosa, and less so in those with bulimia nervosa. Often it is a behavior that is overlooked or even encouraged by physicians or therapists who are unaware of the critical and often detrimental role exercise plays in weight control. Eating disorder patients typically choose socially isolating and solitary forms of exercise such as jogging or aerobics. Such exercise tends to be excessive, in part because there are no built-in restraints on its limits such as might occur when the exercise is competitive and social. On the other hand, studies have documented the importance of a regular exercise pattern in the process of recovery, specifically for the prevention of osteoporosis in emaciated anorexics (Rigotti, Neer, Skates, Herzog, & Nussbaum, 1991; Rigotti, Nussbaum, & Herzog, 1984) and to help facilitate normal bowel habits. The issue of exercise is discussed more fully in Chapter 7. Suffice it to say that the clinician should be prepared to determine the extent of exercise and to proscribe all exercise during the initial nutritional rehabilitation of an underweight patient. Later, when the patient is more stable, a moderate exercise program that is competitive and social may be reintroduced.

## PHYSICAL EXAMINATION

The initial assessment of a patient must include a thorough physical examination. This should be done either by the psychiatrist or by a physician who is involved in the care of the patient and is closely collaborating with the therapist.

There are two distinct reasons for conducting a physical examination. One is to elicit the signs related to the complications of anorexia or bulimia nervosa, and in the process to begin to stabilize patients medically. The second is to confront patients with objective evidence that their disordered eating behavior has adversely affected their physical health. The importance of conducting a thorough physical examination is underscored by the findings of one study (Hall, Hoffman, & Beresford, 1989) that reported that of several hundred patients with eating disorders, 39% of the anorexic and 32% of the bulimic patients suffered from a significant medical complication requiring treatment. Ten percent of the group required admission to the medical intensive care unit. The majority of these medical problems were undiagnosed at the time of hospital admission. This information is particularly relevant and sobering for physicians in light of the long-term mortality rate reported to be as high as 18% in patients with anorexia nervosa (Theander, 1985; Ratnasuriya, Eisler, Szmukler, & Russell, 1991).

The physical examination should cover all organ systems, with specific attention to dermatologic (Gupta, Gupta, & Haberman, 1987), gastrointestinal (Cuellar & Van Thiel, 1986), cardiovascular (Schocken,

Holloway, & Powers, 1989), and endocrine (Kaplan & Garfinkel, 1988) function. Common physical signs of bulimia nervosa include bilateral parotid gland enlargement, calluses on the dorsum of the hand as a result of irritation by the teeth during repeated vomiting (the so-called Russell's sign), perimolysis (see Chapter 5), periorbital petechiae, and perioral irritation of the skin as a result of acidic stomach contents irritating the area around the mouth. In patients with anorexia nervosa, there is obvious emaciation sometimes accompanied by thinning of scalp hair, lanugo hair growth, and a yellowish hue to the skin (due to carotinemia), as well as the clinical effects of down-regulation of the autonomic nervous system manifested by bradycardia, hypotension, and hypothermia. A detailed description of the signs and symptoms and medical complications that commonly occur in eating disorders is found in Chapter 4.

## LABORATORY INVESTIGATION

Initial laboratory investigation should routinely include serum electrolytes, creatinine, blood urea nitrogen (BUN), and a complete blood count (CBC). In addition, an electrocardiogram is required in any patient who is abusing ipecac, who has lost a significant amount of weight, who may have hypokalemia, or who has signs and symptoms attributable to the cardiovascular system. Liver enzymes should be checked in patients who have lost weight rapidly or who are chronically emaciated, as hepatic damage can result from hepatic wasting and fatty deposition in the liver (Cuellar & Van Thiel, 1986). Patients who have experienced gastrointestinal bleeding should have their stool examined for blood and should undergo radiographic and/or endoscopic procedures if there is evidence of significant blood loss. A serum amylase is recommended for patients who have significant abdominal symptomatology, although the hyperamylasemia that is found in eating disorder patients tends to be primarily salivary rather than pancreatic in origin (Kaplan, 1987). Serum calcium and phosphate should routinely be ordered in patients who are chronically amenorrheic and/or emaciated. Consideration should be given to referring such patients for bone density studies if there has been evidence of unexplained or repeated fractures with poor healing (Biller, Saxe, & Herzog, 1989).

Although most appropriately utilized as a research tool, the assessment of resting metabolic rate may help to document the effects of weight loss and caloric restriction on energy expenditure and assist in planning a refeeding program for the patient. Studies (Devlin, Walsh, & Kral, 1990;

Altemus et al., 1991) have shown that patients with bulimia nervosa have lowered metabolic rates compared to controls. This issue is explored more fully in Chapter 7. In addition, assessment of body composition through anthropometric measurements such as skin fold thickness and total body electrical conductivity are more sophisticated techniques to assess the nutritional status of patients (Presta et al., 1983).

## ONGOING MANAGEMENT

Following the initial assessment, it is essential for the physician to provide specific feedback to the patient that includes an unequivocal statement regarding the need for cessation of dieting behavior and the importance of the regular intake of an adequate amount of calories. For the underweight patient, this should begin at 1,500 calories and be gradually increased to between 2,000 and 3,000 calories from three meals and two snacks per day. Considerable variation in this amount occurs, depending on the individual patient and on the need for weight maintenance or weight gain; consultation with an experienced nutritionist is helpful. In the day hospital program for eating disorders at Toronto General Hospital, we have developed a useful exchange system, the Food Group System for eating disorders, similar to the Diabetic Food Groups. In this system, foods are grouped according to type, and are chosen on that basis rather than for specific caloric content. Such a system discourages the choice of particular foods based on their being lowest in calories and therefore "safe," and encourages an acceptance of a wider range of foods. This system has been described more fully elsewhere (Winocur, 1990); it is a helpful tool in the outpatient nutritional management of eating disorder patients.

It is incumbent on the physician to clearly proscribe the use of laxatives, diuretics, and diet pills, emphasizing that these substances have no beneficial role in weight control. Unless there is evidence of physiological dependence and a risk of serious withdrawal effects from the use of prescribed or illicit weight-reducing substances, diet pills as well as diuretics and laxatives should be stopped abruptly. This may need to be done in the hospital. Patients often require reassurance and support to accomplish this as there can be considerable fluid and feces retention and subsequent distress because of the resulting weight gain after stopping diuretics and laxatives. The use of bulk-forming laxatives such as Metamucil should be encouraged during this process.

Ongoing management of patients requires considerable clinical skill. These patients need close medical monitoring of their weight and their fluid, electrolyte, and cardiovascular status. Dental consultation may also be required during the course of treatment (see Chapter 5).

Not infrequently, patients with eating disorders require hospitalization to deal with their medical instability. Indications for hospital admission vary but include acute weight loss, usually more than 25% of original body weight, or potassium levels under 2.5 mmL/L accompanied by electrocardiographic changes. The use of ipecac with cardiac enzyme changes, severe dehydration, acute abdominal symptoms that may indicate gastric dilatation or pancreatitis, and the presence of convulsions are all indications for immediate medical intervention and hospitalization. Chapter 11 describes more fully the issues related to the management of the hospitalized patient.

## MISDIAGNOSIS OF MEDICAL ILLNESS IN EATING DISORDER PATIENTS

Patients with eating disorders often present to physicians with a multitude of symptoms and complaints that are directly attributable to their underlying disturbed eating behavior. However, such patients may be reluctant to disclose the exact nature of their weight regulation behaviors; clinicians then investigate these symptoms without being aware of their underlying causes. As a result, such patients may receive misdiagnoses that lead to interventions that often perpetuate or exacerbate the underlying eating problems. For example, the nondisclosing laxative-abusing patient who presents with complaints of intermittent diarrhea and constipation may be diagnosed as having either lactose intolerance or irritable bowel syndrome. Chronic laxative abuse can induce a temporary state of lactose intolerance; however, the primary treatment for such a condition is not the prescription of a restricted, lactose-free diet, but the proscription of the laxatives themselves.

Patients not infrequently present to physicians with abdominal pain accompanied by an elevated serum amylase. This clinical picture is often thought to signal pancreatitis, when in fact, the hyperamylasemia is often salivary rather than pancreatic in origin and results from enlarged salivary glands due to overeating, vomiting, or other undetermined causes. The treatment of illnesses such as pancreatitis includes the prescription of a restricted diet that is likely to make the eating disorder worse. A further example includes hypoglycemia, which, when it occurs in patients with anorexia and bulimia nervosa, is usually a direct result of depletion of hepatic glycogen stores secondary to starvation and not necessarily related to a primary defect in carbohydrate metabolism. However, diabetes mellitus and bulimia nervosa can occur together; the issues that arise in the management of such patients are discussed in Chapter 9. Iatrogenesis can also occur as a result of patients with anorexia nervosa being misdiagnosed as having hypothyroidism. The pattern of thyroid indices found in anorexia nervosa is low normal $T_4$, decreased serum $T_3$, increased reverse $T_3$, and normal thyroid-stimulating hormone (TSH). This is a pattern that occurs in states of malnutrition and low carbohydrate intake or chronic illness and is a physiological adaptation to starvation (Chopra, 1983). There is no role for treating these laboratory findings with thyroid replacement. Such hormone therapy often is abused by patients in order to further weight loss.

Patients with anorexia and bulimia nervosa are not infrequently diagnosed as having premenstrual syndrome. Such a diagnosis can lead to a restrictive diet or the prescription of inappropriate drugs that can interfere with normal eating and weight gain. An exacerbation of what seems like premenstrual symptoms, such as dysphoria and bloating, may result from an increase in disordered eating behavior at this time rather than from an underlying primary gynecologic or hormonal disturbance. Mitral valve prolapse also has been found to occur at increased rates in patients with anorexia nervosa and bulimia nervosa (Johnson et al., 1986). The most likely explanation for this finding is a change in the geometry of the mitral valve secondary to weight loss and hemodynamic alterations. The definitive treatment for this condition is the restoration of normal geometry and cardiovascular hemodynamics through weight gain and rehydration rather than the prescription of antiarrhythmic drugs.

Patients with eating disorders can be labeled by physicians as suffering from a wide range of nondescript conditions such as systemic candidiasis, food allergies, and chronic fatigue syndrome. Although requiring further study, it may be that symptoms attributable to these conditions actually result from or are exacerbated by chaotic eating patterns. Such diagnoses, however, are often used by the patient as an excuse to restrict caloric intake. The diagnosis of an eating disorder should be entertained in any young adult female who presents with vague, nonspecific signs and symptoms that are not easily explained. Through a careful and meticulous history and physical examination, the diagnosis of an eating disorder will be confirmed, appropriate investigations and treatment will be instituted, and iatrogenesis will be prevented.

## REFERENCES

Altemus, M., Hetherington, M., Flood, M., Licinio, J., Nelson, M., Bernat, A., & Gold, P. (1991). Decrease in resting metabolic rate during abstinence from bulimic behavior. *American Journal of Psychiatry, 148,* 1071–1072.

Beumont, P. J. V., Chambers, T. L., Rouse, L., et al. (1981). The diet composition and nutritional knowledge of patients with anorexia nervosa. *Journal of Human Nutrition, 35,* 265–273.

Biller, B. M., Saxe, V., & Herzog, D. B. (1989). Mechanisms of osteoporosis in adult and adolescent women with anorexia nervosa. *Journal of Clinical Endocrinology and Metabolism, 68,* 548–551.

Chopra, I. J. (1983). Thyroid function in nonthyroidal illnesses. *Annals of Internal Medicine, 98,* 946–957.

Cuellar, R. E., & Van Thiel, D. H. (1986). Gastrointestinal complications of the eating disorders anorexia nervosa and bulimia nervosa. *American Journal of Gastroenterology, 81,* 1113–1124.

Devlin, M. J., Walsh, T., & Kral, J. G. (1990). Metabolic abnormalities in bulimia nervosa. *Archives of General Psychiatry, 47,* 144–148.

Dilsaver, S. C. (1988). Bulimia: When is a binge a binge? *Journal of the American Medical Association, 259,* 45.

Drewnowski, A., Bellisle, F., Aimez, P., & Remy, B. (1987). Taste and bulimia. *Physiology and Behaviour, 41,* 621–626.

Fahy, T., & Treasure, J. (1991). Caffeine abuse in bulimia nervosa. *International Journal of Eating Disorders, 10,* 373–377.

Fairburn, D., & Cooper, P. (1984). The clinical features of bulimia nervosa. *British Journal of Psychiatry, 144,* 238–246.

Frisch, R. E., & McArthur, J. W. (1974). Menstrual cycles: Fatness as a determinant of minimum weight for height necessary for their maintenance or onset. *Science, 185,* 949–951.

Garfinkel, P. E., & Garner, D. M. (1982). *Anorexia nervosa: A multidimensional perspective.* New York: Brunner/Mazel.

Garfinkel, P. E., Kaplan, A. S., Garner, D. M., & Darby, P. L. (1983). The differentiation of vomiting and weight loss as a conversion disorder from anorexia nervosa. *American Journal of Psychiatry, 140,* 1019–1022.

Garfinkel, P. E., Moldofsky, H., & Garner, D. M. (1980). The heterogeneity of anorexia nervosa. *Archives of General Psychiatry, 37,* 1036–1040.

Garner, D. M., & Fairburn, C. G. (1988). The relationship between anorexia nervosa and bulimia nervosa: Diagnostic implications. In D. M. Garner & P. E. Garfinkel (Eds.), *Diagnostic issues in anorexia nervosa and bulimia nervosa*. New York: Brunner/Mazel.

Garner, D. M., Garfinkel, P. E., & O'Shaughnessy, M. (1985). The validity of distinction between bulimia with and without anorexia nervosa. *American Journal of Psychiatry, 142*, 581–587.

Gupta, M. A., Gupta, A. K., & Haberman, H. F. (1987). Dermatologic sign in anorexia nervosa and bulimia nervosa. *Archives of Dermatology, 123*, 1386–1390.

Hall, R. C., Hoffman, R. S., & Beresford, T. P. (1989). Physical illness encountered in patients with eating disorders. *Psychosomatics, 30*, 174–191.

Huse, D. M., & Lucas, A. R. (1984). Dietary patterns in anorexia nervosa. *American Journal of Clinical Nutrition, 40*, 251–254.

Johnson, G. L., Humphries, L. L., Shirley, P. B., et al. (1986). Mitral valve prolapse in patients with anorexia nervosa and bulimia. *Archives of Internal Medicine, 146*, 1525–1529.

Kales, E. F. (1990). Macronutrient analysis of binge eating in bulimia. *Physiology and Behaviour, 48*, 837–840.

Kaplan, A. S. (1987). Hyperamylasemia and bulimia: A clinical review. *International Journal of Eating Disorders, 6*, 537–543.

Kaplan, A. S., & Garfinkel, P. E. (1988). Neuroendocrinology of anorexia nervosa. In R. Collu, G. Brown, & R. Van Loon (Eds.), *Clinical neuroendocrinology*. Boston: Blackwell Scientific Publications.

Kaye, W. H., Gwirtsman, H., Genge, D. T., Weiss, S. R., & Jimerson, D. C. (1986). Relationship of mood alterations to bingeing behaviour in bulimia. *British Journal of Psychiatry, 149*, 479–485.

Keys, A., Brozek, J., Henschel, A., Mickelsen, O., & Taylor, H. L. (1950). *The biology of human starvation (Vol. 1)*. Minneapolis: University of Minnesota Press.

Krissileff, H. R., & Van Itallie, T. B. (1982). Physiology of the control of food intake. *Annual Review of Nutrition, 2*, 371–418.

Krissileff, H. R., Walsh, B. T., Kral, J. G., & Cassidy, S. M. (1986). Laboratory studies of eating behaviour in women with bulimia. *Physiology and Behaviour, 38*, 563–570.

Marliss, E. B. (1987). Current concepts concerning corpulence. *Rapport, 2*, 1–2.

Mitchell, J. E. (1990). *Bulimia nervosa*. Minneapolis: University of Minnesota Press.

Mitchell, J. E., Hatsukami, D., & Eckert, E. D. (1985). Characteristics of 275 patients with bulimia. *American Journal of Psychiatry, 142*, 482–485.

Mitchell, J. E., & Laine, D. C. (1985). Monitored binge eating behaviour in patients with bulimia. *International Journal of Eating Disorders, 4*, 177–183.

Palmer, E. P., & Guay, A. T. (1986). Reversible myopathy secondary to abuse of ipecac in patients with major eating disorders. *New England Journal of Medicine, 313,* 1457–1459.

Pirke, K. M., Pahl, J., Schweiger, V., & Warnhuff, M. (1985). Metabolic and endocrine indices of starvation in bulimia. A comparison of anorexia nervosa. *Psychiatry Research, 15,* 33–39.

Presta, E., Wang, J., Harrison, G. G., Bjorntorp, P., Harker, W. H., & Van Itallie, T. B. (1983). Measurement of total body electrical conductivity: A new method for estimation of body composition. *American Journal of Clinical Nutrition, 37,* 735–739.

Ratnasuriya, R. H., Eisler, I., Szmukler, G. F., & Russell, G. F. (1991). Anorexia nervosa: Outcome and prognostic factors after 20 years. *British Journal of Psychiatry, 158,* 495–502.

Rigotti, N. A., Neer, R. M., Skates, S. J., Herzog, D. B., & Nussbaum, S. R. (1991). The clinical course of osteoporosis in anorexia nervosa. *Journal of the American Medical Association, 265,* 1133–1138.

Rigotti, N. A., Nussbaum, S. R., & Herzog, D. B. (1984). Osteoporosis in women with anorexia nervosa. *New England Journal of Medicine, 311,* 1601.

Schocken, D. D., Holloway, D., & Powers, P. (1989). Weight loss and the heart: Affects of anorexia nervosa and starvation. *Archives of Internal Medicine, 149,* 877–881.

Schwabe, A. D., Lippe, B. M., Chang, J., Pops, M. A., & Yager, J. (1981). Anorexia nervosa. *Annals of Internal Medicine, 91,* 371–381.

Theander, S. (1985). Outcome and prognosis in anorexia nervosa and bulimia: Some results of previous investigations, compared with those of a Swedish long-term study. *Journal of Psychiatric Research, 19,* 493–508.

Thibault, L., & Roberge, A. (1987). Nutritional status of subjects with anorexia. *International Journal of Vitamin and Nutrition Research, 57,* 447–452.

Winocur, J. (1990). Nutritional therapy. In N. Piran & A. S. Kaplan (Eds.), *A day hospital group therapy program for anorexia and bulimia nervosa.* New York: Brunner/Mazel.

Woell, C., Fichter, M. M., & Pirke, K. M. (1989). Eating behaviour of patients with bulimia nervosa. *International Journal of Eating Disorders, 8,* 557–568.

Woodside, D. B., Walfish, P., Kaplan, A. S., & Kennedy, S. H. (1991). Grave's disease in a woman with thyroid hormone abuse, bulimia nervosa, and a history of anorexia nervosa. *International Journal of Eating Disorders, 10,* 111–115.

Yates, A., Shisslak, C., Allender, J. R., & Wolman, W. (1988). Plastic surgery and bulimic patients. *International Journal of Eating Disorders, 7,* 557–560.

## 2

# Medical Illnesses Associated with Weight Loss and Binge Eating

Allan S. Kaplan
M.SC., M.D., FRCP(C)
Mark Katz, M.D.

The interface between medical illness and eating disorders may exist at a number of levels. Acute or chronic medical illness may precipitate episodes of anorexia or bulimia in a vulnerable individual via a number of mechanisms (see Chapter 9), including rapid weight changes, assault on body image, and stress on psychological functions such as one's sense of self-esteem and of control of the body. In addition, medical treatment— for example, insulin, chemotherapy, and steroids—may affect weight, body habitus, and body image. In patients with preexisting eating disorders, these same factors may perpetuate or intensify their eating pathology.

At another level, certain medical conditions may actually cause weight loss or a disturbance in caloric intake directly, and consequently need to be considered in the differential diagnosis of any patient who presents with a change in eating behavior or weight. Differentiating such somatic conditions from functional disorders associated with weight loss or disturbed eating is not difficult with a careful history and physical examination and appropriate investigation. In addition to anorexia and bulimia nervosa, the common psychiatric disorders associated with weight loss or disturbed eating are depression, schizophrenia, anorectic substance abuse, and conversion disorder. The clinical features that differentiate these disorders have been described in detail elsewhere (Garfinkel, Garner, Kaplan, Rodin, & Kennedy, 1983) and are summarized in Table 2.1.

This chapter will focus on the differentiation of anorexia and bulimia nervosa from somatic causes of weight loss or a change in caloric intake. Noteworthy is the fact that medical conditions that cause these symptoms normally lack the psychopathologic features found in anorexia and bulimia nervosa. Especially important here are the drive for thinness and fear of fatness that override all other concerns, and the excessive regulation of self-esteem by concerns with body weight and shape. There are no other conditions in which patients intentionally starve themselves in pursuit of a thinner shape and then binge eat, or intentionally vomit or take laxatives, diuretics, or diet pills in an attempt to rid themselves of unwanted calories. It is the presence of these behaviors associated with characteristic disturbed attitudes and beliefs about weight and shape that so clearly differentiates eating disorders from all other conditions.

It is with this background in mind that we will first review the physiological variables involved in the regulation of eating, although a comprehensive discussion of this complex topic is beyond the scope of this chapter (see Morley, Levine, & Krahn, 1988). We will then describe the medical conditions that often present with weight loss and review the somatic conditions that can present with increased or binge eating as prominent features.

## PHYSIOLOGICAL REGULATION OF EATING BEHAVIOR

Biological variables that influence eating behavior include various central nervous system structures, central and peripheral neurotransmitters, neuropeptides and neurohormones, olfactory and gustatory receptors, and metabolic variables including dietary macromolecular composition, weight status, and metabolic rate (Rosenthal & Heffernan, 1986).

In terms of central regulation of eating behavior, the hypothalamus has long been recognized as a key mediator of the appetitive drives, that is, hunger and satiety (Kirschbaum, 1951; Leibowitz, 1985). Although the concept of autonomous feeding and satiety centers within the hypothalamus is now recognized as an oversimplification (Rolls, 1981), there is evidence from both animal and human studies that the ventrolateral hypothalamus is particularly involved in stimulating feeding, while

TABLE 2.1.

Clinical Features of Anorexia Nervosa, Conversion Disorder, Schizophrenia, Depression, and Anorexic Substance Abuse

| Feature | Anorexia Nervosa | Conversion Disorder | Schizophrenia | Depression | Anorexic Substance Abuse |
|---|---|---|---|---|---|
| Intense drive for thinness | Marked | None | None | None | None |
| Self-imposed starvation | Marked (due to fear of increased body size) | None | Marked (due to delusions about food) | None | None |
| Disturbance in body image | Present (lack of awareness of change in body size and lack of satisfaction or pleasure in the body) | None | None | None | None |
| Appetite | Maintained (but with fear of giving in to impulse) | Variable | Maintained | True anorexia | True anorexia |
| Satiety | Usually bloating, nausea, early satiety | Variable | Variable | Variable | Variable |
| Avoidance of specific foods | Present (for carbohydrates or foods presumed to be high in "calories") | None | Present (of foods that are thought to be poisoned) | Loss of interest in all foods | All foods avoided |
| Bulimia | Present in 30% to 50% | May occur | Rare | Rare | Rare |
| Vomiting | Present (to prevent weight gain) | Present (expresses some symbolic meaning) | Rare (to prevent undesirable effects on the body) | None | Rare (related to nausea with drug) |
| Laxative abuse | Present (to prevent weight gain) | Infrequently present (express some symbolic meaning) | None | None | None |
| Activity level | Increased | Reduced or no change | No change | Reduced | Increased |
| Amenorrhea | Present | Present | Present | Present | Present |

the ventromedial hypothalamus is important in modulating satiety (Reeves & Plum, 1969; Quaade, Vaernet, & Larsson, 1974).

Other brain structures with intimate connections to the hypothalamus may also be important in regulating hunger and satiety, including limbic structures such as the amygdalae of the medial temporal lobes, the orbitofrontal cortex, and various brain stem nuclei (Terzian & Ore, 1955; Erb, Gwirtsman, Fuster, & Richeimer, 1989; Stricker, 1978).

The mechanisms whereby these brain structures regulate food intake involve feeding stimulatory and feeding inhibitory neurotransmitters of both central and peripheral origin. Feeding stimulatory neurotransmitters include norepinephrine acting on alpha$_2$-receptors, the endogenous opioids, dopamine at physiological doses, and the pancreatic polypeptides (neuropeptide Y and peptide YY), recently discovered potent stimulants of eating behavior (Leibowitz, 1985; Kaye, 1992; Morley & Levine, 1983; Clark, Kalra, Crawley, & Kalra, 1984). Feeding inhibitory neurotransmitters include serotonin, norepinephrine, and epinephrine acting on beta-receptors; dopamine in higher concentrations; and certain peripheral peptides and hormones such as cholecystokinin, somatostatin, and glucagon (Blundell, 1984; Kaye, 1992; Leibowitz, 1985).

In addition, peripheral factors such as insulin and adrenal corticosteroids are important modulators of neurotransmitter control of feeding behavior; for example, insulin plays a role in facilitating brain uptake of tryptophan, a precursor of the satiety-inducing monoamine serotonin (Rosenthal & Heffernan, 1986). Processes or medications that interfere with these brain structures or neurotransmitter systems consequently may produce abnormal eating behaviors, including reduced or excessive intake.

## SOMATIC CAUSES OF WEIGHT LOSS OR
## REDUCED CALORIC INTAKE

The mechanisms of weight loss caused by organic disease include reduced caloric intake (usually because of decreased appetite), an accelerated metabolism, and loss of calories in stool or urine. No attempt will be made to review all the diseases associated with weight loss. Only those conditions that are relatively common and often present as diagnostic dilemmas because of initial nonspecific weight loss or those conditions where there is clearly reduced caloric intake associated with central nervous system dysfunction will be discussed.

**Gastrointestinal Disorders**

The most important and common gastrointestinal illness causing weight loss in the age group vulnerable to an eating disorder is inflammatory bowel disease. Crohn's disease may present with diverse and nonspecific symptoms, which in addition to weight loss may include anorexia, fatigue, and fever. Crohn's disease has been described as the great imitator of disease (Mekhjian, Switz, Melnyk, Rankin, & Brooks, 1979). There are a number of case reports where Crohn's disease has been mistakenly diagnosed as anorexia nervosa (Jenkins, Treasure, & Thompson, 1988; Metcalfe-Gibson, 1978; Scully, Mark, & McNeely, 1985). However, the presence of characteristic laboratory evidence of both inflammation (i.e., elevated erythrocyte sedimentation rate [ESR]) and malabsorption (i.e., hypoalbuminemia) helps distinguish Crohn's biochemically from anorexia nervosa, as does the absence of the characteristic psychopathology described above. The mechanisms by which Crohn's disease may occur with an eating disorder will be discussed in Chapter 9.

Malabsorption syndrome such as occurs in coeliac disease (De Toni, Casamassima, & Gastald, 1986) is often associated with weight loss as a prominent feature. Abnormal fecal fat loss, or steatorrhea (greater than 6 g per 24 hours on a 100 g fat diet), is the common denominator in conditions causing malabsorption. This contrasts markedly with anorexia nervosa, where fecal fat loss is negligible in the face of restricted intake of fat. Loss of protein and resulting hypoalbuminemia are also common in malabsorption but uncommon in patients with eating disorders. Normal serum albumin levels are usually observed in anorexic patients, but these can decline with rehydration (Casper, Kirschner, Sandstead, Jacob, & Davis, 1980).

Less common gastrointestinal causes of weight loss that can be misdiagnosed as anorexia nervosa include peptic ulcer disease complicated by gastric outlet obstruction (Lee, Wing, Chow, Chung, & Yung, 1989), achalasia (Kenny, 1984), superior mesenteric artery syndrome (Froese, Szmuilowicz, & Bailey, 1978), chronic pancreatitis (Schoettle, 1979), gastric rugal hyperplasia (Cockett, 1987), and visceral myopathy (Francois et al., 1990). All these conditions are relatively rare but clearly distinguishable from anorexia nervosa with appropriate examination and investigation.

**Endocrine Disorders**

The three endocrine conditions most commonly associated with weight loss are hyperthyroidism, diabetes mellitus, and Addison's disease. In hyperthyroidism there is clearly a hypermetabolic state present, as manifested by elevated pulse rate, respiration rate, and blood pressure, accompanied by sweaty warm extremities. This picture is in marked contrast to the hypometabolic state typically found in anorexia nervosa. As described previously (Chapter 1), patients with anorexia nervosa will often have thyroid indices in the low or normal range (low normal $T_4$, low $T_3$, elevated reverse $T_3$, normal thyroid-stimulating hormone [TSH]). This is a thyroid conservation response to starvation and is in no way indicative of a primary thyroid abnormality. Treatment of this "euthyroid sick syndrome" with thyroxine is contraindicated. As discussed previously (Chapter 1), thyroid hormone abuse does occur in patients with anorexia and bulimia nervosa as a means of facilitating weight loss. There are even reports of patients with both Grave's disease and an eating disorder who refused appropriate treatment because of their fear of weight gain if they become euthyroid (Woodside, Walfish, Kaplan, & Kennedy, 1991; Kuboki, Suematsu, Ogata, Yamamoto, & Shizume, 1987; Rolla, Ghada, & Goldstein, 1985).

Diabetes mellitus typically presents with polydipsia, polyuria, and weight loss in an adolescent or young adult. Patients with anorexia or bulimia nervosa may drink excessive amounts of water in an attempt to counteract intense feelings of hunger by filling themselves with fluids or to facilitate vomiting. This is not, however, in response to increased thirst, nor is it usually accompanied by increased urine output. Patients with eating disorders can also suffer from diabetes mellitus; the complex issues that arise from this comorbid state are discussed at length in Chapter 9.

Addison's disease is a condition that is associated with some of the symptoms seen in anorexia nervosa including weight loss and vomiting, reduced caloric intake, hypoglycemia, and hypotension. However, patients with Addison's disease experience extreme weakness, easy fatigability, and have true anorexia, symptoms that occur only in the end stages of anorexia nervosa. Diagnosis is easily confirmed by tests of adrenocortical function.

Finally, there is anterior pituitary insufficiency, or Simmond's disease, which was for a period of time earlier in this century confused with anorexia nervosa (Sheehan & Summers, 1949). In actual fact, serious weight loss is rare in Simmond's disease, where there is striking loss of secondary sexual characteristics. Amenorrhea and low metabolic rate are the only symptoms that the two disorders have in common.

## Central Nervous System Disorders

A variety of central nervous system lesions can present with weight loss. There are case reports of patients being misdiagnosed as having anorexia nervosa when in fact they suffer from a variety of central nervous system lesions, including spinal cord meningioma (Reiser & Swigar, 1984) and a variety of hypothalamic tumors (Heron & Johnston, 1976; White, Kelly, & Dorman, 1977; Lewin, Mattingly, & Millis, 1972). The association of abnormal eating behavior and lesions in the hypothalamus is not surprising considering the role the hypothalamus plays in the regulation of eating behavior. When abnormal eating does accompany a hypothalamic tumor, it is usually associated with other symptoms suggestive of an intracranial lesion, such as headache, excessive thirst, spontaneous vomiting, diplopia, and coarse or diminished hair rather than lanugo hair.

## Malignancy

Occult malignancy is probably the most common cause of weight loss in the absence of other specific signs and symptoms. The examination should include specific emphasis on the gastrointestinal tract, pancreas, and liver, as these organs are the most common sites for an occult malignancy (Marton, 1981). Lymphoma and leukemia need to be seriously considered in the differential diagnosis of unexplained serious weight loss in a previously healthy adult. The exact mechanisms responsible for weight loss in malignant conditions are unclear but probably include all of those described above; that is, decreased intake, increased loss of calories, and increased metabolism. Decreased caloric intake as a result of an occult neoplasm is almost always accompanied by true anorexia. Patients with anorexia nervosa typically remain voraciously hungry until the end stages of the disorder. The term, in essence, is a misnomer.

## Infection

Unexplained weight loss can be the prominent feature of hidden infection. Tuberculosis, fungal diseases, amebic abscess, subacute bacterial endocarditis, and acquired immunodeficiency syndrome are all high on the list of suspects for such a presentation. The mechanism of weight loss in infection involves both anorexia and a catabolic state secondary to inflammation-induced acceleration of cellular metabolic requirements (Foster, 1983). The presence of signs of inflammation (fever, increased ESR) makes the differentiation of these conditions from anorexia nervosa usually straightforward.

**Medication**

There are a variety of medications, too numerous to review here, that can pharmacologically induce anorexia (eg. amphetamine-like substances; Carruba et al., 1986) or can increase metabolism (eg. thyroid) and directly contribute to weight loss.

## SOMATIC CAUSES OF BINGE EATING

An association between binge eating and medical illness dates back to the first century when "bulimy" was described in the Babylonian Talmud as part of an epileptic attack (Kaplan & Garfinkel, 1985). Parry-Jones and Parry-Jones (1991) described four historical cases from the 17th to 19th centuries involving profound hyperphagia that improved after evacuation of parasitic worms, and two other cases including a prodromal fever, and epileptic fits respectively associated with hyperphagia. In more recent times, the late 19th century, there were a number of reports of binge eating associated with a variety of central nervous system lesions, that is, tumors, and with trauma (Shearman, 1856; Paget, 1897). These, along with similar reports of anorexia occurring with brain lesions, stimulated a search for organic causes of bulimia, which was at that time subsumed under the broader mantle of anorexia nervosa. Kirschbaum (1951), in an extensive review of cerebral causes of excessive hunger, asserted that "over indulgence in food, though much less frequently observed, is a more significant and outstanding symptom for neuropathologic investigation than the opposite, rather common appearance of anorexia" (p. 95).

Currently, the literature on medical causes of binge eating is complicated by varying terminology (bulimia, binge eating, compulsive eating, hyperphagia, polyphagia, and hyperorexia) and by varying degrees of clarity and detail in the descriptions of the eating behavior. For the purpose of this chapter the term "hyperphagia" will be used to describe excessive, abnormal consumption of food seen in medical conditions as this is most consistent with the medical literature that provides much of the information discussed here.

## Central Nervous System Lesions

A variety of central nervous system (CNS) lesions may present with symptoms of increased appetite and hyperphagia.

### Tumors

Kirschbaum (1951), in a review of the literature, found seven cases of "axial" tumors causing hyperphagia, via either direct invasion of the hypothalamus or extrinsic compression and displacement of hypothalamic structures by suprasellar masses or third ventricle lesions. More recent reports have confirmed the association between hypothalamic tumors and hyperphagia (Reeves & Plum, 1969; Celesia, Archer, & Hyung, 1981; Coffey, 1989; Beal, Kleinman, Ojemann, & Hochberg, 1981). In most cases, other neurological symptoms (i.e., amnesia, dementia, or focal symptoms) or endocrine/autonomic features (obesity, hypersomnilence, polydipsia) were evident, although hyperphagia may be an early symptom. These cases have occurred with a variety of tumors, including primary malignant tumors such as gliomas, astrocytomas, and gleoblastoma multiformae; primary benign tumors including craniopharyngiomas, germinomas, gangliocytomas, hamartomas, and pinealomas; and metasatic tumors (leukemic infiltration).

Frontal lobe tumors may also present with hyperphagia (Kirschbaum, 1951; Hecaen, 1964). These include both primary tumors (e.g., glioma and meningioma) and metasatic tumors (rectal carcinoma). Kirschbaum (1951), citing five cases, described hyperphagia associated with periodic disorientation, emotional lability, memory impairment, and progressive dementia, and hypothesized a loss of cortical control over diencephalic systems. (The orbital cortex, which is phylogenetically similar to subcortical—that is, limbic—structures and has extensive connections to limbic and hypothalamic structures known to regulate eating behavior, may be particularly important in this regard.)

### Raised Intracranial Pressure

Raised intracranial pressure from either tumors or other conditions may present with hyperphagia. Krahn and Mitchell (1984) described a 29-year-old woman with a history of body image disturbance, purging behavior, and frequent binge episodes that often preceded severe headaches. She was found to have a bilateral papilloedema on fundoscopic exam, and a computed tomography (CT) scan of the head revealed dilated lateral and third ventricles secondary to congenital acqueductal stenosis. Following a ventricular peritoneal shunt, which alleviated her raised intracranial pressure, her bingeing and urges to binge disappeared.

### CNS Trauma/Surgery

Traumatic brain injuries may produce a striking although often transient hyperphagia, especially frontal lobe injuries and temporal lobe damage bilaterally (Paget, 1897; Kirschbaum, 1951; Morris & Hope, 1990; Lilly, Cummings, Benson, & Frankel, 1983). Neurosurgical procedures— for example, frontal or temporal lobectomies or frontal leukotomies—may also induce hyperphagia. Freeman and Watts (1942) noted transient hyperphagia in 70 of 74 patients with frontal lobotomies. With bilateral temporal lobe damage, especially to medial temporal lobe structures as the amygdaloid nuclei, one often sees hyperphagia as part of a complex behavioral syndrome, the Kluver-Bucy syndrome.

### The Kluver-Bucy Syndrome

First described by Kluver and Bucy (1939) following bilateral temporal lobectomy in Rhesus monkeys, this syndrome was reported in humans by Terzian and Ore (1955) in a young man following bilateral temporal lobectomy for intractable seizures. The syndrome consists of six features including placidity, hypersexuality, visual agnosias, hypermetamorphosis (the tendency to react to aspects of the external environment via tactile exploration), hyperorality (the excessive placing of food and nonfood items in the mouth), and hyperphagia that may include the consumption of nonfood items.

In humans, the syndrome has been described in both partial and complete forms, in association with a number of conditions affecting the medial temporal lobes bilaterally, including following head trauma, in postherpes encephalitis, and in association with degenerative CNS conditions such as Pick's and Alzheimer's diseases (Lilly, Cummings, Benson, & Frankel, 1983; Marlowe et al., 1975). It is regularly associated in humans with cognitive impairment, most commonly, severe disorders of memory and language. Hyperphagia may be an early feature, but, importantly, the other core features of bulimia nervosa including weight and body image preoccupation and dieting/purging behaviors are not seen with this syndrome.

*Degenerative Disorders*

Degenerative CNS conditions may also present with excessive eating often accompanied by bizarre eating behavior (Hope, Fairburn, & Goodwin, 1989). Pick's disease, a dementing illness characterized by frontal and temporal atrophy, may feature hyperphagia as a relatively early symptom; the excess eating may imply damage to either frontal or temporal lobes, the latter often presenting with other features of the Kluver-Bucy syndrome described above (Cummings & Duchen, 1981).

In Alzheimer's disease one may also see abnormal eating behavior including hyperphagia. Its occurrence is variable but is usually late in the course of the illness. Some investigators believe the temporal onset of hyperphagia and other features of the Kluver-Bucy syndrome may help to differentiate between Alzheimer's and Pick's diseases (Cummings & Duchen, 1981). Sourander and Sjögren (1970) reported that 47 of 60 patients with Alzheimer's showed hyperphagia; more recently Burns, Jacoby, and Levy (1990) described 10% of 178 patients with Alzheimer's engaged in binge-eating episodes. Pathological changes in both hypothalamus and amygdalae have been well documented in Alzheimer's, as have reductions in serotonin and serotonin receptors (Whitford, 1986; Herzog & Kemper, 1980).

Both Huntington's chorea (Whittier, 1976) and Parkinson's disease (Rosenberg, Herishanu, & Beilin, 1977) have also been associated with hyperphagia, as have cases with multiinfarct dementia (Erb et al., 1989; Drake, 1987).

*CNS Infections*

Infections of the CNS may also produce hyperphagia; encephalitis, particularly herpes simplex encephalitis, which carries a predilection for the temporal lobes, may produce hyperphagia, often as part of the Kluver-Bucy syndrome (Hierons, Janota, & Corsellis, 1978). Both neurosyphilis and encephalitis epidemica have also been reported to cause hyperphagia according to older reports in the literature (Kirschbaum, 1951).

*Seizure Disorders*

Seizure disorders, particularly complex partial seizures involving the temporal lobes, may cause hyperphagia either as ictal or postictal phenomena (Remick, Jones, & Campus, 1980). Kirschbaum (1951) described a number of patients who, during complex partial seizures, would become combative, and eat voraciously anything in sight, including nonfood items such as soap and curtains. Since then, a number of investigators, most notably Rau and Green (1975), have postulated that a subtype of bulimic patients may have subcortical epileptiform dysrhythmias as a primary or neurogenic cause for their binge eating.

Correlation has been made between binge eating and abnormal electroencephalograph (EEG) tracings, most commonly, 14 plus 6 per second, positive spike patterns. Rau and Green (1984) found 65% of 59 patients studies had abnormal EEGs (mostly with this pattern) and claimed positive results with the anticonvulsant Dilantin in treating their binge eating. This remains however, a controversial area. Mitchell, Hosfield, and Pyle (1983), using EEG tracings of sleep-deprived patients with nasopharyngeal leads and wake/sleep recordings, studied 25 patients with bulimia nervosa and found a vast majority (84%) had normal EEGs, a finding confirmed by Kaplan (1987). Many other investigators consider the 14 plus 6 spike pattern, which is common in normal adolescents and less common in normal adults, to be of little or no significance, perhaps related to maturational factors (Struve & Ramsey, 1977; Maulsby, 1979); and controlled trials of anticonvulsants in bulimia nervosa have failed to show robust treatment effects (Wermuth, Davis, Hollister, & Stunkard, 1977; Kaplan et al., 1983).

Nevertheless, it is possible that a subset of patients presenting with binge eating may have a seizure focus. Those most likely to be considered include patients who describe episodes that begin suddenly without psychological precipitants and with auralike phenomena, dissociative or amnestive periods, or episodes that are associated with other features of episodic dyscontrol or soft neurological signs (Rau & Green, 1984). Interestingly, it is recognized that eating may serve as a trigger for seizures in known epileptic individuals (eating epilepsy) (Koul, Koul, & Razdan, 1989).

### The Klein-Levine Syndrome

The Klein-Levine syndrome, which is associated with abnormal EEG tracings, is a rare disorder of unknown etiology affecting predominantly adolescent males, although young females may be affected as well. It is characterized by recurrent episodes of hypersomnia, compulsive and excessive eating when awake, and psychiatric disturbances that include sexual disinhibition and agitation, inappropriate speech, neglect of self-care, bizarre behaviors, mood changes, hallucinations, and delusions. In addition, cognitive impairment including confusion and memory loss may be evident. Attacks, which characteristically remit spontaneously after days to weeks, are often followed by impaired recall for symptomatic periods. The course is thought to be relatively benign with episodes eventually ceasing altogether in most cases (Orlosky, 1982).

### Congenital Abnormalities/Mental Retardation

The Prader-Willi syndrome is a congenital disorder of unknown etiology, although abnormalities of chromosome 15 have been reported in 50% to 70% of cases. The syndrome is characterized by obesity, short stature, neonatal hypotonia, hypogonadism, dysmorphic facies, and varying degrees of mental retardation, in addition to self-mutilation and striking abnormalities in feeding behavior (Holm, 1981). Hyperphagia that often leads to massive obesity is typically described as voracious bingeing in association with food searching, the stealing of food, and the consumption of nonfood items (Dech & Budow, 1991).

Mental retardation from other causes may be associated with a variety of abnormal eating behaviors including hyperphagia, food-searching behaviors, carbohydrate craving, and consumption of nonfood pica. A recent study by O'Brien and Whitehouse (1990) revealed that 14 of 48 mentally retarded adults showed hyperphagia; this was often seen in patients with coexisting depression in their sample.

## Other Disorders

### Diabetes Mellitus.

In the past decade many reports have documented the co-occurrence of bulimia and diabetes mellitus (for a review, see Marcus & Wing, 1990), with at least one systematic study documenting a higher than normal prevalence of eating disorders among insulin-dependent diabetics (Rodin, Daneman, Johnson, Kenshole, & Garfinkel, 1985). The mechanisms whereby diabetes mellitus may serve as a risk factor for eating disorders are discussed elsewhere (see Chapter 9). There is some evidence, however, that diabetes mellitus may facilitate binge eating more directly by causing increased appetite and excessive consumption of food. Rollo (1797) described two cases of diabetes associated with voracious appetite; this association was further discussed by Soltmann (1894). These early cases, arising before the advent of insulin therapy and the current societal focus on thin shape, highlight the potentially direct effects of diabetes on appetite and hyperphagia. Interestingly, this is not considered as a possibility in most recent publications addressing eating disorders and diabetes, although diabetic hyperphagia is in fact a well-recognized phenomenon in studies with diabetic animals (Carpenter & Grossman, 1983). The mechanism for hyperphagia is not clear but may involve impairment in serotonin-mediated satiety as a consequence of insulin deficiency; insulin is known to stimulate serotonin synthesis in the brain by increasing the tryptophan/large neutral amino acid ratio in the plasma, thereby facilitating transfer of tryptophan into the CNS where it is converted into serotonin (Stricker, 1978).

### Hyperthyroidism.

Hyperthyroidism may cause hyperphagia and at times weight gain via appetite stimulation. Fonseca, Wakeling, and Havard (1990) described two cases of eating disorders associated with hyperthyroidism. In one case, a patient with anorexia nervosa in remission began binge eating as a result of a hyperthyroid state; in the other, hyperthyroidism caused hyperphagia and weight gain, which led to excessive dieting and a subsequent clinical diagnosis of anorexia nervosa.

### Premenstrual syndrome.

Several investigators have documented a correlation between increased caloric intake, hyperphagia, and premenstrual syndrome (or late luteal phase dysphoric disorder as it is known in the revised third edition of the *Diagnostic and Statistical Manual of Mental Disorders* (DSM-III-R) (Giannini et al., 1985; Gladis & Walsh, 1987). Affected women note an increased appetite, carbohydrate craving, and increased intake premenstrually often associated with a dysphoric picture similar to "atypical" depression (Both-Orman, Rubinow, Hobane, Malley, & Grever, 1988).

### Gastrointestinal Disorders

Gastrointestinal problems such as coeliac sprue, short bowel syndrome, or problems following small bowel surgery, may lead to malabsorption with "adaptive" hyperphagia (Cosnes et al., 1990). In such cases, patients experience increased appetite and caloric intake secondary to the weight loss caused by malabsorption. In these patients, there is usually a history of significant diarrhea (which must be differentiated from laxative abuse in the bulimia nervosa patient) and other abdominal complaints. In addition, these patients are likely to be distressed, rather than pleased, by the weight loss that accompanies the malabsorption.

*Medication*

Medications may cause increased appetite and craving of carbohydrates, which might then manifest as binge-eating episodes. Examples include tricyclic antidepressants, particularly tertiary amines such as amitriptyline and clomipramine (Stolar, 1988). Monoamine oxidase inhibitors, particularly phenelzine, may also stimulate appetitive drives (Christenson, 1983). The relationship between antidepressants and binge eating, however, is complex; amitriptyline, for example, has been shown to both stimulate binge eating and reduce binges (Paykel, Mueller, & Dela Vergne, 1973; Mitchell & Groat, 1984).

Neuroleptics, including phenothiazines, thioxanthines, and butyrophenones, may also stimulate appetite and carbohydrate craving (Amdisen, 1964). Chlorpromazine may be the most common offender. Various mechanisms have been suggested that may account for the increased appetite seen with antidepressants and antipsychotics, including inhibition of serotonin and histamine receptors, catecholamine stimulation, and increasing insulin-induced hypoglycemia (Paykel et al., 1973; Stolar, 1988; Bernstein, 1988).

Lithium carbonate may stimulate appetite either by inducing thirst via renally mediated polydipsia, or via an inhibitory effect on serotonin turnover (Garland, Remick, & Zis, 1988). In addition, potent serotonergic antagonists such as cyproheptadine, pizotyline, and methysergide may exert a stimulatory effect on appetite via impairment of serotonergic activity (Stolar, 1988). Insulin may stimulate excessive hunger and carbohydrate craving via its hypoglycemic effects (Stolar, 1988). Cannabis (THC) has been shown to cause rapid stimulation of feeding behavior in both animal and human studies (Vaupel & Morton, 1982; Hollister et al., 1981). Opiates are well known to cause appetite enhancement, an effect that is blocked by naloxone, an opiate antagonist (Hollister et al., 1981).

Medications that stimulate weight gain by mechanisms other than appetite enhancement may lead to dieting behavior, which is a well-recognized risk factor for binge eating. Mechanisms of weight gain with these medications include fluid retention (corticosteroids, oral contraceptives, lithium), increased anabolic activity (androgenic and anabolic hormones), and increased fluid intake secondary to dry mouth (anticholinergic medication) (Mackinnon & Parker, 1983).

## IMPLICATIONS FOR CLINICAL ASSESSMENT

There are features in the history and physical exam that should raise one's level of suspicion about an underlying organic cause for weight loss or bulimic behavior. Some of these have already been described and include occurrence in males, onset in middle age or in the elderly, rapid onset of symptoms without previous dieting behavior, lack of weight and shape concerns, lack of awareness of behavior as inappropriate or distressing, true anorexia, absence of purging or dieting behavior, and the presence of bizarre eating behavior such as pica or hyperorality. In addition, positive symptoms suggestive of medical illness, especially neurological illness, include cognitive impairment, raised intracranial pressure or seizures, and symptoms of endocrine or hypothalamic dysfunction (in addition to those attributable to starvation alone). Evidence of inflammation, infection, or malabsorption points to an organic cause for weight loss. A careful enquiry as to drug use, both prescribed and illicit, should clarify the possible effect such drugs may have on eating behavior and weight.

Investigations should not be undertaken indiscriminantly but should be guided by findings on history, physical examination, and mental status examination. For example, the presence of possible neurological dysfunction would necessitate an EEG and/or CT scan of the brain to rule out seizure disorder or structural brain illness. Misdiagnosis or iatrogenesis can be avoided if clinicians are aware of the psychiatric and medical conditions that can be present with a disturbance in eating behavior or a change in weight.

## REFERENCES

Amdisen, A. (1964). Drug induced obesity: Experience with chlorpromazine, perphenazine and clopenthixol. *Danish Medical Bulletin, 11,* 182–189.

American Psychiatric Association. (1987). *Diagnostic and statistical manual of mental disorders* (3rd ed.—rev.) Washington, DC: Author.

Beal, M. F., Kleinman, G. M., Ojemann, R. G., & Hochberg, F. H. (1981). Gangliocytoma of third ventricle: Hyperphagia, somnolence and dementia. *Neurology, 31,* 1224–1228.

Bernstein, J. G. (1988). Medication effects on appetite and weight. *Handbook of drug therapy in psychiatry* (2nd ed.). Littleton, MA: PSG Publishing.

Blundell, J. E. (1984). Serotonin and appetite. *Neuropharmacology, 23,* 1537–1551.

Both-Orman, B., Rubinow, D. R., Hobane, M. C., Malley, M., & Grever, G. N. (1988). Menstrual cycle phase-related changes in appetite in patients with premenstrual syndrome and in control subjects. *American Journal of Psychiatry, 145*, 628–631.

Burns, A., Jacoby, R., & Levy, R. (1990). Psychiatric phenomena in Alzheimer's disease. IV: Disorders of behaviour. *British Journal of Psychiatry, 157*, 86–94.

Carpenter, R. G., & Grossman, S. P. (1983). Early streptozotocin diabetes and hunger. *Physiology and Behaviour, 31*, 175–178.

Carruba, M. O., Coen, E., Pizzi, M., Memo, M., et al. (1986). Mechanism of action of anorectic drugs: An overview. In M. O. Carruba & J. E. Blundell (Eds.), *Pharmacology of eating disorders: Theoretical and clinical developments*. New York: Raven Press.

Casper, R. C., Kirschner, B., Sandstead, H. H., Jacob, R. A., & Davis, J. M. (1980). An evaluation of trace metals, vitamins and taste function in anorexia nervosa. *American Journal of Clinical Nutrition, 33*, 1801–1808.

Celesia, G. G., Archer, C. R., & Hyung, D. C. (1981). Hyperphagia and obesity. *Journal of the American Medical Association, 246*, 151–153.

Christenson, R. (1983). MAOI's, anorgasmia and weight gain. *American Journal of Psychiatry, 140*, 1260.

Clark, J. J., Kalra, P. S., Crawley, W. R., & Kalra, S. P. (1984). Neuropeptide Y and human pancreatic polypeptide stimulate feeding behaviour in rats. *Endocrinology, 115*, 427–429.

Cockett, A. D. (1987). Anorexia nervosa and gastric rugal hyperplasia. *British Journal of Psychiatry, 150*, 697–699.

Coffey, R. J. (1989). Hypothalamic and basal forebrain germinoma presenting with amnesia and hyperphagia. *Surgical Neurology, 31*, 228–233.

Cosnes, J., Lamy, P., Beaugerie, L., Le Quintrec, M., Gendre, J. P., & Le Quintrec, Y. (1990). Adaptive hyperphagia in patients with post surgical malabsorption. *Gastroenterology, 99*, 1814–1819.

Cummings, J. L., & Duchen, L. W. (1981). Kluver-Bucy syndrome in Pick's disease: Clinical and pathologic correlations. *Neurology, 31*, 1415–1422.

De Toni, T., Casamassima, M. S., & Gastald, R. (1986). Celiac disease and anorexia nervosa. *Minerva Pediatric, 38*, 409–412.

Dech, B., & Budow, L. (1991). The use of fluoxetine on an adolescent with Prader Willi syndrome. *Journal of the American Academy of Child and Adolescent Psychiatry, 30*, 298–302.

Drake, M. E. (1987). Kleine Levin Syndrome after multiple cerebral infarctions. *Psychosomatics, 28*, 329–330.

Erb, J. L., Gwirtsman, H. E., Fuster, J. M., & Richeimer, S. H. (1989). Bulimia associated with frontal lobe lesions. *International Journal of Eating Disorders, 8,* 117–121.

Fonseca, V., Wakeling, A., & Havard, C. W. H. (1990). Hyperthyroidism and eating disorders. *British Journal of Psychiatry, 301,* 322–323.

Foster, D. W. (1983). Gain and loss in weight. In B. G. Petersdorf, R. D. Adams, & E. Braunwald (Eds.), *Harrison's principles of internal medicine.* New York: McGraw Hill.

Francois, Y., Descos, L., Berger, F., Beurlet, J., Cenni, J. C., Mallet-Guy, Y., & Gignal, J. (1990). Rare type of visceral myopathy mimicking anorexia nervosa. *Journal of the Royal Society of Medicine, 83,* 748–749.

Freeman, W., & Watts, J. W. (1942). *Psychosurgery.* Springfield and Baltimore: Charles C. Thomas.

Froese, A. P., Szmuilowicz, J., & Bailey, J. D. (1978). The superior mesenteric artery syndrome: Cause, or complication of anorexia nervosa. *Canadian Psychiatric Association Journal, 23,* 325–327.

Garfinkel, P. E., Garner, D. M., Kaplan, A. S., Rodin, G., & Kennedy, S. (1983). Differential diagnosis of emotional disorders that cause weight loss. *Canadian Medical Association Journal, 139,* 939–945.

Garfinkel, P. E., Garner, D. M., & Rodin, G. (1988). Eating disorders. In J. M. Kinney, K. N. Jeejeebhoy, & G. L. Hill (Eds.), *Nutrition and metabolism in patient care.* Philadelphia: W. B. Saunders.

Garland, E. J., Remick, R. A., & Zis, A. P. (1988). Weight gain with antidepressants and lithium. *Journal of Clinical Psychopharmacology, 8,* 323–330.

Giannini, A. J., Price, W. A., Loiselle, R. H., et al. (1985). Hyperphagia in premenstrual tension syndrome. *Journal of Clinical Psychiatry, 46,* 436–438.

Gladis, M. M., & Walsh, B. T. (1987). Premenstrual exacerbation of binge eating in bulimia. *American Journal of Psychiatry, 144,* 1592–1595.

Hecaen, H. (1964). Mental symptoms associated with tumours of the frontal lobe. In J. M. Warren & K. Averts (Eds.), *The frontal granular cortex and behaviour.* New York: McGraw Hill.

Heron, G. B., & Johnston, D. A. (1976). Hypothalamic tumor presenting as anorexia nervosa. *American Journal of Psychiatry, 133,* 580–582.

Herzog, A. G., & Kemper, T. L. (1980). Amygdaloid changes in aging and dementia. *Archives of Neurology, 37,* 625–629.

Hierons, R., Janota, I., & Corsellis, J. A. N. (1978). The late effects of necrotizing encephalitis of the temporal lobes and limbic areas: A clinical-pathological study of 10 cases. *Psychological Medicine, 8,* 21–42.

Hollister, L. E., Johnson, K., Bookhabzer, D., et al. (1981). Adverse effects of naloxone in subjects not dependent on opiates. *Drug and Alcohol Dependence, 8,* 37–41.

Holm, V. A. (1981). The diagnosis of Prader Willi Syndrome. In V. A. Holm, S. J. Sulzbecher, & P. Pipes (Eds.), *Prader Willi Syndrome*. Baltimore: University Press.

Hope, R. A., Fairburn, C. G., & Goodwin, G. M. (1989). Increased eating in dementia. *International Journal of Eating Disorders, 8,* 111–115.

Jenkins, A. P., Treasure, J., & Thompson, R. P. H. (1988). Crohn's disease presenting as anorexia nervosa. *British Medical Journal, 296,* 699–700.

Kaplan, A. S. (1987). Anticonvulsant treatment of eating disorders. In P. E. Garfinkel & D. M. Garner (Eds.), *The role of psychotropic drug use in treating eating disorders*. New York: Brunner/Mazel.

Kaplan, A. S., & Garfinkel, P. E. (1985). Bulimia in the Talmud [Letter]. *American Journal of Psychiatry, 14,* 721–123.

Kaplan, A. S., Garfinkel, P. E., Darby, P. L., & Garner, D. M. (1983). Carbamezapine in the treatment of bulimia. *American Journal of Psychiatry, 140,* 1225–1227.

Kaye, W. H. (1992). Neurotransmitter abnormalities in anorexia nervosa and bulimia nervosa. In G. H. Andersen & S. H. Kennedy (Eds.), *The biology of feast and famine: Relevance to eating disorders*. New York: Academic Press.

Kenny, R. D. (1984). Achalasia in an adolescent with behavioural features compatible with anorexia nervosa. *Journal of Adolescent Health Care, 5,* 283–285.

Kirschbaum, W. R. (1951). Excessive hunger as a symptom of cerebral origin. *Journal of Nervous and Mental Disease, 113,* 95–114.

Kluver, H., & Bucy, P. C. (1939). Preliminary analysis of functions of the temporal lobes in monkeys. *Archives of Neurology and Psychiatry, 42,* 979–1000.

Koul, R., Koul, S., & Razdan, S. (1989). Eating epilepsy. *Acta Neurologica Scandinavia, 80,* 78–80.

Krahn, D. D., & Mitchell, J. E. (1984). Case report of bulimia associated with increased intracranial pressure. *American Journal of Psychiatry, 141,* 1099–1100.

Kuboki, T., Suematsu, H., Ogata, E., Yamamoto, M., & Shizume, K. (1987). Two cases of anorexia nervosa associated with Grave's disease. *Endocrinologica Japonica, 34,* 9–12.

Lee, S. L., Wing, Y. K., Chow, C. C., Chung, S., & Yung, C. (1989). Gastric outlet obstruction masquerading as anorexia nervosa. *Journal of Clinical Psychiatry, 50,* 184–185.

Leibowitz, S. F. (1985). Brain neurotransmitters and appetite regulation. *Psychopharmacology Bulletin, 21,* 412–418.

Lewin, K., Mattingly, D., & Millis, R. R. (1972). Anorexia nervosa associated with hypothalamic tumor. *British Medical Journal, 2,* 629–630.

Lilly, R., Cummings, J. L., Benson, F., & Frankel, M. (1983). The human Kluver-Bucy syndrome. *Neurology, 33,* 1141–1145.

Mackinnon, G. L., & Parker, W. A. (1983, July). Current concepts in obesity. *Canadian Pharmaceutical Journal, 293*–302.

Marcus, M. D., & Wing, R. R. (1990). Eating disorders and diabetes. In D. S. Holmes (Ed.), *Neuropsychological and behavioural aspects of diabetes*. New York: Springer-Verlag.

Marlowe, W. B., Mancall, E. L., & Thomas, T. J. (1975). Complete Kluver Bucy syndrome in man. *Cortex, 11*, 53–59.

Marton, K. I. (1981). Involuntary weight loss: Diagnostic and prognostic significance. *Annals of Internal Medicine, 95*, 568.

Maulsby, R. L. (1979). EEG patterns of uncertain diagnostic significance. In D. W. Klass & D. D. Daly (Eds.), *Current practice of clinical electroencephalography*. New York: Raven Press.

Mekhjian, H. S., Switz, D. M., Melnyk, C. S., Rankin, G. B., & Brooks, R. K. (1979). Clinical features and natural history of Crohn's disease. *Gastroenterology, 77*, 898–906.

Metcalfe-Gibson, C. (1978). Anorexia nervosa and Crohn's disease. *British Journal of Surgery, 65*, 231–233.

Mitchell, J. E., & Groat, R. (1984). A placebo controlled double blind trial of amitriptyline in bulimia. *Journal of Clinical Psychopharmacology, 4*, 186–193.

Mitchell, J. E., Hosfield, W., & Pyle, R. L. (1983). EEG findings in patients with the bulimia syndrome. *International Journal of Eating Disorders, 2*(3), 17–21.

Morley, J. E., & Levine, A. S. (1983). The central control of appetite. *Lancet, i*, 398–401.

Morley, J. E., Levine, A. S., & Krahn, D. D. (1988). Neurotransmitter regulation of appetite and eating. In B. J. Blinder, B. F. Chaiton, & R. S. Goldstein (Eds.), *The eating disorders*. New York: PMA Publishing.

Morris, C. H., & Hope, R. A. (1990). Alteration in eating behaviour following head injury: A case report. *International Journal of Eating Disorders, 9*, 463–467.

O'Brien, G., & Whitehouse, A. M. (1990). A psychiatric study of deviant eating behaviour among mentally handicapped adults. *British Journal of Psychiatry, 157*, 281–284.

Orlosky, M. J. (1982). The Kleine-Levin syndrome: A review. *Psychosomatics, 23*, 609–618.

Paget, S. (1897). On cases of voracious hunger and thirst from injury or disease of the brain. *Transactions of the Annual Society of London, 30*, 113–119.

Parry-Jones, B., & Parry-Jones, W. L. (1991). Bulimia: Symptom and syndrome— its history in psychosomatic medicine. *International Journal of Eating Disorders, 10*, 129–143.

Paykel, E. S., Mueller, P. S., & Dela Vergne, P. M. (1973). Amitriptyline, weight gain and carbohydrate craving: A side effect. *British Journal of Psychiatry, 123,* 501–507.

Quaade, F., Vaernet, K., & Larsson, S. (1974). Stereotoxic stimulation and electrocoagulation of the lateral hypothalamus in obese humans. *Acta Neurochirurgica Stereotoxic (Wein), 30* 111–117.

Rau, J. H., & Green, R. S. (1975). Compulsive eating: A neuropsychologic approach to certain eating disorders. *Comprehensive Psychiatry, 16,* 223–231.

Rau, J. H., & Green, R. S. (1984). Binge purge syndrome. Neurological factors affecting binge eating: Body over mind. In R. G. Haukins, W. J. Fremouw, & P. F. Clements (Eds.), *Diagnosis, treatment and research.* New York: Springer.

Reeves, A. G., & Plum, F. (1969). Hyperphagia, rage and dementia accompanying a ventromedial hypothalamic neoplasm. *Archives of Neurology, 20,* 616–624.

Reiser, L. W., & Swigar, M. (1984). Anorexia nervosa masking the diagnosis of spinal meningioma: A case report. *General Hospital Psychiatry, 6,* 289–293.

Remick, R. A., Jones, M. W., & Campus, P. E. (1980). Postictal bulimia [Letter]. *Journal of Clinical Psychiatry, 41,* 256.

Rodin, G. M., Daneman, D., Johnson, L. E., Kenshole, A., & Garfinkel, P. E. (1985). Anorexia nervosa and bulimia in female adolescents with insulin dependent diabetes mellitus: A systematic study. *Journal of Psychiatric Research, 19,* 381–384.

Rolla, A. R., Ghada, A. E., & Goldstein, H. H. (1985). Untreated thyrotoxicosis as a manifestation of anorexia nervosa. *American Journal of Medicine, 81,* 163–165.

Rollo, J. (1797). *An account of two cases of the diabetes mellitus with remarks as they arose during the progress of the cure.* London: C. Dilly.

Rolls, E. T. (1981). Central nervous mechanisms related to feeding and appetite. *British Medical Bulletin, 37,* 131–134.

Rosenberg, P., Herishanu, Y., & Beilin, B. (1977). Increased appetite (bulimia) in Parkinson's disease. *American Geriatric Society, 25,* 277–278.

Rosenthal, N. E., & Heffernan, M. M. (1986). Bulimia, carbohydrate craving and depression: A central connection? In R. Wurtman & J. Wurtman (Eds.), *Nutrition and the brain.* New York: Raven Press.

Schoettle, V. C. (1979). Pancreatitis: A complication, a concomitant, or a cause of an anorexia nervosa-like syndrome. *Journal of the American Academy of Child Psychiatry, 18,* 384–390.

Scully, R., Mark, E. J., & McNeely, B. V. (1985). Case presentation: Crohn's disease and an eating disorder. *New England Journal of Medicine, 312,* 1175–1183.

Shearman, C. J. (1856). On neurosis of the vague, an idiopathic disease. *Medical Times and Gazette, 2,* 281–284.

Sheehan, H. L., & Summers, V. K. (1949). The syndrome of hypopituitarism. *Quarterly Journal of Medicine, 18*, 319–378.

Soltmann, D. (1894). Anorexia cerebralis und centrale nutritionsneurosin. *Jahrbook fur Kinderheilk-unde and Physische Erziehung, 353*, 1–13.

Sourander, P., & Sjögren, H. (1970). The concept of Alzheimer's disease and its clinical implications. In G. E. W. Wolstenholme & M. O'Connor (Eds.), *Alzheimer's disease and related conditions*. London: J&A Churchill.

Stolar, M. H. (1988). The effects of psychopharmacological agents on appetite and eating. In B. J. Blinder, B. F. Chaitlin, & R. Goldstein (Eds.), *The eating disorders*. New York: PMA Publishing.

Stricker, E. M. (1978). Physiology in medicine: Hyperphagia. *New England Journal of Medicine, 298*, 1010–1013.

Struve, F. A., & Ramsey, P. O. (1977). Concerning the 14-and-6-per-second positive spike cases in post traumatic medical-legal EEG's reported by Gibbs & Gibbs: A statistical commentary. *Clinical Electroencephalography, 8*, 203–205.

Terzian, H., & Ore, G. (1955). Syndrome of Kluver and Bucy reproduced in man by bilateral removal of the temporal lobes. *Neurology, 15*, 373–380.

Vaupel, D. B., & Morton, E. C. (1982). Anorexia and hyperphagia produced by five pharmacologic classes of hallucinogens. *Pharmacology, Biochemistry and Behaviour, 17*, 539–545.

Wermuth, B. M., Davis, K. L., Hollister, L. E., & Stunkard, A. J. (1977). Phenytoin treatment of the binge eating syndrome. *American Journal of Psychiatry, 134*, 1249–1253.

White, J. H., Kelly, P., & Dorman, K. (1977). Clinical picture of anorexia nervosa associated with hypothalamic tumor. *American Journal of Psychiatry, 134*, 323–325.

Whitford, G. M. (1986). Alzheimer's disease and serotonin: A review. *Pharmacopsychiatry, 15*, 133–142.

Whittier, J. R. (1976). Asphyxiation, bulimia and insulin levels in Huntington disease (chorea). *Journal of the American Medical Association, 235*, 1423–1424.

Woodside, D. B., Walfish, P., Kaplan, A. S., & Kennedy, S. H. (1991). Grave's disease in a woman with thyroid hormone abuse, bulimia nervosa and a history of anorexia nervosa. *International Journal of Eating Disorders, 10*, 111–115.

# 3

# *Binge Eating in Obese Patients*

## G. Terence Wilson, PH.D.

In 1959, Stunkard described what has come to be called binge eating in the obese patient, namely, the consumption of large amounts of food in a relatively brief time, followed by discomfort, distress, and self-recrimination. But the problem of binge eating in obese patients was largely overlooked until recently. The reasons are probably twofold: First, views on the nature of obesity have changed over the past three decades. It is now seen as a chronic physical disorder under strong genetic control with identifiable biological causes (e.g., Kern, Ong, Saffari, & Carty, 1990; Stunkard, Harris, Pedersen, & McClearn, 1990). The rapid ascendancy of this genetic-biological perspective led to a relative decline in research on psychological or behavioral analysis of obesity that would have focused more attention on the behavior of binge eating. Second, the third edition of the *Diagnostic and Statistical Manual of Mental Disorders* (DSM-III; American Psychiatric Association, 1980) included bulimia as an eating disorder, a syndrome in which binge eating was the core feature. This resulted in attention being directed primarily toward *normal weight* patients who both binged and purged (what DSM-III-R termed "bulimia nervosa" [APA, 1987]), even though the prevalence of bulimia nervosa seems to be much lower than that of binge eating in the obese.

This chapter was prepared while the author was a fellow at the Center for Advanced Study in the Behavioral Sciences, Stanford, California. The author is grateful for financial support provided by the John D. and Catherine T. MacArthur Foundation. Thanks are also due Chris Fairburn, M.D., for his careful reading of an earlier draft of this chapter.

Estimates of binge eating among obese individuals seeking treatment range from 2% to 46% (Kuldau & Rand, 1986; Marcus, Wing, & Hopkins, 1988). In a study of 70 obese subjects not in treatment, 33% met modified DSM-III criteria for bulimia, suggesting that binge eating is prevalent beyond the clinic (Hudson et al., 1988). A limitation of all clinical studies, aside from their selective sampling, has been the use of varying definitions of "binge eating" and questionable methods of assessing it (Fairburn & Beglin, 1990).

## DIAGNOSIS AND ASSESSMENT

Interpretation and comparison of existing studies of the "obese binge eater" or "obese bulimic" are clouded by the use of varying definitions of a "binge," questionable methods for assessing binge eating, and different diagnostic criteria for selecting clinical samples of obese bulimics.

In their series of studies, Marcus and colleagues (1988, 1990a,b) defined binge eating in the obese according to a cut-off on the Binge Eating Scale (BES) (Gormally, Black, Daston, & Rardin, 1982). Marcus and her colleagues reported that 98% of subjects identified in this way met the DSM-III criteria for bulimia as determined by a clinical interview. Nonetheless, exclusive reliance on the BES for characterizing obese binge eaters is problematic—it does not provide specific frequencies of binge eating, nor does it generate DSM-III-R criteria for any of the eating disorders.

Agras and his colleagues have used different criteria and assessment methods in their studies of the nature and treatment of binge eating in the obese (McCann & Agras, 1990; Telch, Agras, Rossiter, Wilfley, & Kenardy, 1990). They have adopted modified DSM-III-R criteria for bulimia nervosa: "(1) recurrent episodes of binge eating in which the subject perceived herself to consume a large amount of food[1] in a short time period, (2) a feeling of lack of control or inability to stop eating during the eating binges, (3) an average of 2 or more binge episodes a week for the past six months, and (4) persistent concern with body shape and weight" (Telch et al., 1990, p. 630). In contrast to Marcus et al. (1990a,b) and others, they exclude patients with any past or present history of purging. Nevertheless, most if not all of these patients would have met DSM-III-R criteria for bulimia nervosa, since extreme dieting is a compensatory behavior designed to influence weight and shape as required by DSM-III-R. The Stanford group have shown that their patients restrict their food intake between binges, presumably to compensate for the caloric consequences of binge-eating (Rossiter, Agras, Telch, & Bruce, 1990). The provisional criteria for DSM-IV subtype bulimia nervosa into purgers and nonpurgers. Within this framework the Telch et al. (1990) subjects would be diagnosed with bulimia nervosa, nonpurging subtype.

Only a small minority of obese binge eaters engage in self-induced vomiting or laxative abuse, and few would meet provisional DSM-IV criteria for the purging subtype of bulimia nervosa. Mitchell, Pyle, Eckert, Hatsukami, and Soll (1990) reported that of 591 cases of bulimia nervosa (using DSM-III-R diagnostic criteria) seen at the University of Minnesota Eating Disorders Clinic, the obese patients (only 4.2% of the sample) had lower rates of binge eating and vomiting than normal weight patients with bulimia nervosa, but they were more likely to abuse laxatives. Hudson et al. (1988) similarly found that only 9% of a sample of obese bulimics (DSM-III criteria) engaged in vomiting, compared with 83% of a sample of normal weight bulimics. The difference in rates of laxative abuse was not statistically significant.

Williamson, Prather, McKenzie, and Blouin, (1990) differentiate among normal weight patients with bulimia nervosa, obese binge eaters, and obese nonbingers. They refer to obese binge eaters as "compulsive overeaters," a term that is widely used in the clinical literature even though DSM-III-R explicitly excludes eating as a form of obsessive-compulsive disorder. The criteria for compulsive overeating are similar to DSM-III criteria for bulimia. An important exclusionary criterion is the use of any form of purging. Compulsive overeaters meeting these criteria do not differ in terms of weight from obese nonbingers, and are significantly more overweight than patients with bulimia nervosa (Williamson et al., 1990).

Williamson et al. (1990) present data showing that their compulsive overeaters differ significantly from patients with bulimia nervosa, but not from obese nonbingers, in terms of body image. The Stanford group include abnormal attitudes about weight and shape as a diagnostic criterion for nonpurging bulimia nervosa in obese patients, and Marcus et al. (1988) emphasized that their patients are similar to patients with bulimia nervosa in this respect, although neither group specified how attitudinal disturbance was assessed. Thus it would appear that the compulsive overeaters of Williamson et al. (1990) may differ from the patients in the Marcus et al. (1988) and the Telch et al. (1990) studies. Alternatively, the apparent discrepancy over abnormal attitudes about body weight and shape might be a product of the different assessment methods used by these two groups of investigators.

Most recently, Spitzer and his colleagues have proposed a new diagnosis of binge eating disorder (BED) (Spitzer et al., 1992). The criteria of BED include recurrent binge eating (consumption of a larger amount of food than most people would eat under the circumstances, plus perceived loss of control over eating),[2] associated features such as eating rapidly or until uncomfortably full, and marked distress regarding binge eating. Spitzer et al. (1992) state that BED is not diagnosed if patients meet criteria for bulimia nervosa. Initial data from a multisite field trial of 1,984 subjects indicate that BED is common (30%) among patients in weight control treatment programs. Although BED can be identified across the weight spectrum, it is significantly more common among the obese. Patients with BED who were in treatment for obesity weighed 16.4 pounds more than patients without BED at their highest adult weight (Spitzer et al., 1992). It seems likely, however, that many (if not most) patients with BED would meet the proposed DSM-IV diagnosis of bulimia nervosa, nonpurging subtype. Another limitation of the BED diagnosis is that it fails to address the significance of attitudes toward body weight and shape.

It is clear from the foregoing summary that there is diagnostic variability and inconsistency in the identification of the obese bulimic or binge eater. The common denominator across the different diagnostic schemes is the phenomenon of binge eating. But even here there is inconsistency in how a binge is defined, and questions about the validity of its assessment. A small minority of obese binge eaters vomit or abuse laxatives. Most (but perhaps not all) diet to compensate for their binge eating, but few engage in exercise as a compensatory behavior. The significance of attitudes about body weight and shape is unclear. This element has been inadequately assessed at best, deemphasized or neglected at worst. Clinical experience and Spitzer and colleagues' (1992) field trial indicate that although obese binge eaters are predominantly women, the proportion of men with this problem is greater than in normal weight bulimia nervosa. Finally, obese binge eaters are significantly more likely than obese nonbingers to report a history of weight cycling, namely, fluctuations of at least 20 lb (Spitzer et al., 1992).

Improved clinical assessment requires specific and valid measures of bulimic episodes, dietary restricting, methods for compensating for weight gain, and attitudes about weight and shape. A combination of self-monitoring and the EDE interview, a valid and comprehensive assessment of specific eating disorder psychopathology, is recommended (Rosen & Srebnik, 1990).

## ASSOCIATED PSYCHOPATHOLOGY

Studies have consistently shown significantly greater levels of psychopathology in obese binge eaters than in obese nonbingers. Marcus et al. (1990a) found that 60% of obese binge eaters (defined by a score of 29 or higher on the BES) had a history of at least one psychiatric disorder, as opposed to 28% of nonbingers. Among obese patients seeking treatment, Kolotkin, Revis, Kirkley, and Janick (1987) found that the greater the severity of binge eating, the greater the psychological disturbance as measured by the Minnesota Multiphasic Personality Inventory (MMPI). The greater psychopathology of the binge eater was evident across a range of psychiatric symptoms, including anxiety, depression, and sexual dysfunction. But the difference was most pronounced in terms of affective disorder—32% of obese bingers reported a history of affective disorder as opposed to only 8% of obese nonbingers. Hudson et al. (1988) reported that a remarkable 91% of obese subjects they recruited who met DSM-III criteria for bulimia had a lifetime prevalence rate of affective disorder, compared to 45% in nonbulimic patients.

The discrepancy in results between the two studies might be explained in part by different subject selection criteria, as Marcus et al. (1990a) point out. The nonbulimic subjects in the study of Hudson et al. (1988) might have included individuals who engaged in binge eating, even though they did not meet DSM-III criteria for bulimia. This would have the effect of increasing the prevalence of psychiatric disorder in the nonbulimic group. It is also likely that the subjects in these two investigations differed in other ways. A majority of the subjects in the Hudson et al. (1988) study were recruited because they snacked on carbohydrates or a combination of protein and carbohydrates. These subjects might well experience higher rates of depression than other obese subjects, bingers and nonbingers alike.

A high rate of psychiatric comorbidity was also found in Schwalberg's (1990) study of 22 obese binge eaters (defined by a BES score of 25 or greater, and a frequency of at least three binges a week for 2 months). He found a 60% lifetime prevalence rate of affective disorder; 25% of the sample were currently diagnosable with depression. Of possibly greater significance was the lifetime prevalence rate of 70% for anxiety disorders, especially generalized anxiety disorder (GAD). Hudson et al. (1988) reported a relatively low level of anxiety disorders (17%) in their sample. Nor did Marcus et al. (1990a) find a significant difference between their groups with respect to anxiety disorders. They did, however, find that more obese bingers experienced somatic symptoms of anxiety than did nonbingers. Moreover, they did not assess for GAD, which was the major anxiety disorder in Schwalberg's (1990) subjects. Methodological differences among the studies should also be noted. Schwalberg (1990) used the most comprehensive and valid assessment procedure for anxiety disorders—the ADIS-R (Dinardo & Barlow, 1988) structured interview—of all the studies on obese binge eaters.

Comparisons of obese binge eaters with normal weight patients with bulimia nervosa have yielded conflicting findings. Hudson et al. (1988) found no difference between patients with normal weight bulimia nervosa and obese bulimics in terms of affective disorders. But the patients with normal weight bulimia nervosa had significantly higher lifetime prevalence rates of anxiety disorders and substance abuse disorders than the obese bulimics. Similarly, W. S. Agras (personal communication, 1991) found that patients with bulimia nervosa showed a significantly greater rate of personality disorders than obese binge eaters, who in turn had higher rates than normals. In contrast, Schwalberg (1990) found no differences in depression, anxiety disorders, substance abuse, or borderline personality between normal weight patients with bulimia nervosa and obese binge eaters. A fourth study by Mitchell and colleagues (1990), found that their sample of 25 overweight patients with bulimia nervosa reported significantly more self-injurious behavior and suicide attempts than their normal weight counterparts. Finally, Williamson (1990) compared the MMPI profiles of what they call compulsive overeaters with those of patients with anorexia nervosa, bulimia nervosa, and (nonbingeing) obesity. The greatest psychopathology was evident in the patients with anorexia nervosa and bulimia nervosa. The differences between the compulsive overeaters (obese binge eaters) and obese nonbingers were not pronounced.

One of the difficulties in interpreting these results is that the studies employed different criteria in selecting samples of obese binge eaters. For example, virtually all of Mitchell and colleagues' (1990), some of Hudson and colleagues' (1988), and none of W. S. Agras's (personal communication, 1990) or Schwalberg's (1990) subjects purged. Nonetheless, we can conclude that binge eating in the obese, whether or not accompanied by purging, is significantly associated with other forms of psychopathology. It is unclear whether or not this psychiatric comorbidity is the cause, concomitant, or consequence of the eating disorder.

Patients with normal weight bulimia nervosa typically show high rates of associated psychopathology, particularly depression and anxiety disorders (Laessle, Tuschl, Waadt, & Pirke, 1989). However, as discussed below, retrospective studies indicate that depression usually develops after the onset of bulimia nervosa and decreases following successful treatment of bulimia nervosa (Levy, Dixon, & Stern, 1989). Given the important treatment implications of this finding, it is important to ask whether a similar pattern holds true for obese binge eaters. Schwalberg (1990) questioned his subjects about the onset of their different disorders. Consistent with previous studies of bulimia nervosa, he found that depression followed the onset of both normal weight bulimia nervosa and obese binge eating. However, the majority of obese binge eaters (and normal weight bulimics) reported that the onset of their anxiety disorders preceded their disordered eating.

Lowe and Caputo (in press) assessed the relative contributions of psychopathology, on the one hand, and specific psychological aspects of eating and weight, on the other, in predicting binge eating in obese patients. Psychopathology was measured using subscales of the Eating Disorders Inventory (EDI) (Garner, Olmsted, & Polivy, 1983), namely, the Ineffectiveness, Perfectionism, Interpersonal Distrust, Interoceptive Awareness, and Maturity Fears subscales. The psychological aspects of eating were the Drive for Thinness and Body Dissatisfaction subscales of the EDI, and the three factors of Stunkard and Messick's (1985) Three-Factor Eating Questionnaire (TEQ). Five variables reliably predicted binge eating in a double cross-validation procedure, four of which assessed specific eating and weight characteristics. The authors prudently caution that their results do not necessarily indicate that psychopathology is relatively unimportant in predicting binge-eating in the obese. The EDI subscales they used to define psychopathology provide too limited an assessment of the psychopathology that has been reported in obese binge eaters.

## MODELS OF BINGE EATING IN THE OBESE

Three different theoretical models of binge eating in the obese can be identified: the addiction model, the affective disorders model, and the biopsychosocial model.

### The Addiction Model

This model views an eating disorder as a disease. It assumes that certain people have a biological vulnerability (probably genetically determined) to certain foods (e.g., sugar, defined as a toxic chemical), which can cause dependence. It holds that the disorder is a progressive illness that can never be eliminated but only managed as a lifelong problem and that treatment must begin by interrupting (detoxifying) the abuse of food. Since the etiologies of chemical dependence and bulimic eating disorders are similar, treatment for bulimic disorders should not differ fundamentally from that of alcohol or drug dependence. It follows logically from these premises that the recommended treatment is a 12-step program—Overeaters Anonymous (OA)—that is modeled after Alcoholics Anonymous (AA) (Yeary, 1987). Bemis (1985, 1989) has referred to this addiction as disease (AAD) model as the abstinence model of eating disorders. A critical analysis of this AAD model of eating disorders shows that it simply fails to account for the core characteristics of eating disorders (Wilson, 1991).

Nor is it accurate to view eating disorders as addictions within the cognitive-behavioral model of addictive behaviors. People with eating disorders, on the one hand, and substance abuse disorder, on the other, confront the challenge of exerting self-control over their consummatory behavior. The cognitive-behavioral model of addictive behaviors provides a state-of-the-art analysis of the psychological processes and procedures that are responsible for successful or unsuccessful self-regulation of behavior. As such, as Wardle (1987) points out, the model is useful in suggesting specific therapeutic strategies for eating disorders that were developed in the treatment of substance abuse disorders. But the problem even with this cognitive-behavioral model of addiction is that although it differs fundamentally from the disease model, the emphasis is nonetheless on curbing or controlling consumption. The biopsychosocial model of bulimia nervosa that is presented here has a different focus. It underscores the need for patients to reduce dietary restraint, to develop a regular pattern of more frequent eating of larger amounts and more varied types of food. The goal is different from the intent behind controlled drinking programs for alcohol abusers, for instance. To quote Wardle (1987), "The final goals of treatment are almost exactly opposite. From the patient's point of view, the adoption of an addiction model, with its implicit connotations of consuming something harmful, could only delay the process of returning to normal eating" (p. 54).

## The Affective Disorders Model

One of the most carefully studied models of bulimia nervosa holds that the eating disorder is secondary to an underlying affective illness (Pope &

Hudson, 1988). The same line of thinking has been extended to obese binge eaters who do not purge (Hudson et al., 1988). Several key predictions of this model have been tested and found wanting. The available evidence fails to support the view that bulimia nervosa or binge eating in the obese is caused by an underlying affective illness (Kaye et al., 1990; Levy et al., 1989; Strober & Katz, 1987). Depression typically follows the onset of bulimia nervosa and binge eating in the obese, and is reduced or eliminated with the successful treatment of the primary eating disorder (Garner et al., 1990). Although eating disorders are not a variant of affective disorder, some investigators interpret the often observed association between the two disorders as an indication of a shared biological or psychological vulnerability (Hsu, 1990).

**The Biopsychosocial Model**

The biopsychosocial model of bulimia nervosa[3] (Fairburn, 1985; Hsu, 1990) can be readily extended to account for binge eating in the obese (Wardle, 1987). In summary, it is assumed the current cultural norms of beauty pressure women, in particular, to pursue thinness. To achieve this goal, they diet, often in an extreme and unhealthy manner. Dieting is closely linked to the onset of binge eating in eating disorders (Patton, 1988), although whether this relationship is causal or not has yet to be established (Blundell, 1990). We do know that dieting can have a number of biological and psychological effects that would predispose to eating problems and binge eating (Tuschl, 1990). The majority of young women diet and do not develop an eating disorder. It is therefore further assumed that dieting interacts with some preexisting vulnerability in the person to produce an eating disorder. The nature of this vulnerability is unknown, but it is probably heterogeneous.

We know even less about putative vulnerability factors in obese binge eaters than in normal weight patients with bulimia nervosa. However, clinical experience suggests that as with bulimia nervosa, dieting is a proximal antecedent of binge eating in the obese, but systematic study of this relationship is required.

An unresolved issue is whether binge eating precedes or follows the development of obesity. One hypothesis is that obese binge eaters are predominantly obese individuals, whose weight is genetically and biologically determined. Because of stringent dieting driven by cultural ideals of body weight and shape, they have developed a secondary eating disorder that complicates or worsens their weight problem. From this viewpoint, successful treatment of the binge eating would have only a modest effect on weight in the long run. An alternative view is that binge eating occurs first, and is responsible, at least in part, for the development of obesity. It is argued that because most obese binge eaters do not vomit to compensate for their binges (for whatever reasons—we do not know), they gain weight, whereas those who binge and purge develop normal weight bulimia nervosa (e.g., Hudson et al., 1988).

In the ultimate analysis, only prospective risk factor studies will be able to sort out the relationship between dieting, binge eating, and obesity. There are, however, reasons for questioning whether binge eating without purging causes obesity. First, a small minority of obese binge eaters purge (Mitchell et al., 1990). Why are they obese if vomiting compensates for excess caloric intake? Second, obese binge eaters appear to have significantly more obese relatives than do normal weight patients with bulimia nervosa (Alger, Schwalberg, Bigaouette, Howard, & Reid, 1990; Hudson et al., 1988; Viesselman & Roig, 1985). This finding, if replicated in better controlled studies, would be consistent with the view that unlike normal weight patients with bulimia nervosa, obese binge eaters are predisposed to be overweight. They diet to avoid this outcome, and some develop binge eating.

## TREATMENT

Obese binge eaters commonly seek help from OA. Spitzer et al. (1992) reported a higher prevalence of BED in their OA sample than in other obesity treatment samples—a frequency of 71.2%. The abstinence model that informs OA prescribes increased and endless dietary restraint, featuring absolute avoidance of particular foods (e.g., sugar), highly structured eating patterns (Yeary, 1987), and as Bemis (1989) points out, a sense of powerlessness and reinforcement of a dichotomous thinking pattern. There has been no controlled evaluation of the 12-step OA program, and few informal reports of its effectiveness (Malenbaum, Herzog, Eisenthal, & Wyshak, 1988). We do not know the outcome of OA, an unfortunate state of affairs given its apparent popularity as a treatment among obese binge eaters.

The absence of any controlled analysis of the OA approach is troubling on other accounts. It derives from an addiction model that is seriously flawed as a conceptual framework for bulimic eating disorders (Wilson, 1991). The therapeutic objectives of the addiction model are virtually the opposite of those of the cognitive-behavioral model described above. It is difficult to reconcile such sharply contrasting models. The well-documented effectiveness of cognitive-behavioral treatment raises several problems for the assumptions and goals of the OA approach. And whereas OA does not rule out psychological therapy, it does not encourage it other than to address other related personal issues (Malenbaum et al., 1988). Yeary and Heck (1989) bluntly state that "it is as fruitless to attempt psychotherapy with a still-symptomatic bulimic as it is with an intoxicated alcoholic" (p. 244). This extreme statement is simply wrong. The most convincing refutation of such premature dismissal of the effectiveness of psychological treatment comes not from the repeatedly documented success of cognitive-behavioral therapy (CBT), but from interpersonal psychotherapy (IPT). In IPT there is no focus on the patient's eating habits—only on the past and present interpersonal issues in the person's life. Yet IPT has been shown to be as effective as CBT in reducing binge eating and altering disturbed attitudes to body weight and shape (Fairburn et al., 1991).[4]

Only two forms of treatment for obese binge eaters have been evaluated in controlled clinical trials—cognitive-behavioral therapy (CBT) and pharmacological treatment.

## Cognitive-Behavioral Therapy

The now standard behavioral treatment for obesity (Brownell & Wadden, in press) has been applied somewhat indiscriminately to clinical samples of obese patients that have included binge eaters. Very few studies have tried to assess the differential outcome of binge eaters and non–binge eaters in these studies. Judging from the sketchy data of studies that have made this comparison, obese binge eaters are more likely to drop out of treatment, lose less weight if they remain in treatment, and relapse (regain weight) sooner following treatment (Keefe, Wyshogrod, Winberger, & Agras, 1984; Marcus et al., 1988). Outcome in these studies focused on weight loss, with no independent assessment of binge eating itself. Treatment aimed directly at binge eating is a recent development.

According to the biopsychosocial model of the maintenance and treatment of bulimia nervosa as summarized above, unhealthy dieting appears to be closely—some would say causally—linked to binge eating (Hsu, 1990; Polivy & Herman, 1985). It follows from this conceptual model that among other therapeutic goals, a primary focus of treatment would be the direct modification of faulty eating behavior and abnormal attitudes toward food and body weight. Patients would need to reduce dietary restraint, and "normalize" their eating patterns (e.g., three meals a day with flexible food choices, including previously "forbidden" foods).[5]

Both patients with normal weight bulimia nervosa and obese binge eaters initially resist this treatment approach (Wilson, 1989). They either fear gaining more weight or, especially in the case of obese binge eaters, wish to lose weight. Although the evidence shows that successful treatment of bulimia nervosa does not involve weight gain in the majority of patients (Fairburn, Kirk, O'Connor, & Cooper, 1986; Fairburn et al., 1991), patients are apprehensive about reducing dietary restraint. This reluctance, based on their being overweight, complicates treating the obese patient with bulimia nervosa or binge eating with CBT. Addressing this issue, Hsu (1990) has observed that "clinicians must first decide whether to treat the obesity or the binge-eating. Weight reduction and cessation of bulimia are not identical or interchangeable goals. It is possible that in some individuals the two goals may actually be incompatible" (p. 181). In terms of the biopsychosocial model of eating disorders described here, however, the binge eating must be overcome before weight reduction becomes the goal of treatment.

Once binge eating is eliminated and more regular patterns of eating are reestablished, the primary focus of treatment can shift to addressing weight control. The establishing of regular, healthy eating patterns is likely to result in an increase in metabolic rate, a decrease in level of insulin secretion, a reduction in preferential deposition of calories as body fat, and the relearning of conditioned satiety signals that help govern amount of food intake (Wardle, 1987). As initial results suggest, the prognosis for weight reduction should be worse for obese patients who binge than those who do not (Marcus et al., 1988). This outcome is consistent with the finding that compared with nonbingers, obese binge eaters are more likely to report a history of weight cycling (Spitzer et al., 1992). Among the effects of weight cycling are increased metabolic efficiency, an increased preference for dietary fat, and altered body composition favoring greater deposition of fat (Brownell & Wadden, 1991).

*Effectiveness of CBT*

Several well-controlled outcome studies have documented the effectiveness of CBT treatment for bulimia nervosa in normal weight patients (Fairburn et al., 1991). Reduction of bulimic episodes and purging averages 80% or more, with roughly 60% or better for total remission at posttreatment in several well-controlled studies. Abnormal attitudes regarding body weight and shape are significantly improved, and associated forms of general psychopathology, such as depression, substantially decreased.

Two controlled evaluations of CBT treatment of binge eating in the obese have been reported. In the first study, group CBT produced a 94% reduction in binge eating and a 79% abstinence rate compared with only a 9% reduction and 0% abstinence in a waiting list control group (Telch et al., 1990). In marked contrast to studies of the treatment of bulimia nervosa, no significant differences were found in attitudes toward food and weight that are considered to be a core problem in bulimia nervosa (Fairburn, 1985). Depression decreased in both groups. Subsequent treatment of the waiting list control group produced very similar results. Given the failure to effect changes in the core attitudes about body weight and eating, it is not surprising that the relapse rate during the 10 weeks following treatment was high. At follow-up there was a 69% reduction in mean binge frequency and a 46% abstinence rate. The discrepancy between these findings and those obtained with bulimia nervosa could indicate a difference between the two disorders. Alternatively, it could be attributable to the treatment used by Telch et al. (1990). Therapy consisted of only 10 sessions, as compared with the more customary 16 or more treatment sessions for normal weight bulimia nervosa. It is also possible that the group format may be less effective than individual treatment, although adequately designed studies have yet to address this important issue (Garner, Fairburn, & Davis, 1987).

Significantly, there were no changes in patients' weight at posttreatment or follow-up, showing no effect of virtual elimination of binge eating on body weight. Nevertheless, several benefits can be anticipated from the elimination of binge eating in obese patients using CBT. First, it should make it easier for them to participate and remain in standard behavioral treatment programs for obesity. Second, by reducing rapid alternating of weight loss and gain (weight cycling), it should have positive effects on body composition and cardiovascular health. Third, it should increase patients' sense of personal control, which has a variety of positive psychological sequelae, including improved adherence to behavior change strategies. And fourth, it should improve mood and reduce associated psychopathology such as anxiety and depression.

The second study compared a standard behavioral treatment program for weight loss with a modified treatment designed specifically for the obese binge eater (Krug, Houston, Smith, Kaminsky, & Fisher, 1990). The modified behavioral treatment "included normalization of eating habits, assertiveness and problem skills training, and cognitive behavioral techniques for reducing dysfunctional attitudes related to depression, eating and weight control. To reduce binge eaters' rigid focus on dieting and calories, the program emphasized healthy, low-fat eating, but instructed participants not to count calories" (Krug et al., 1990, p. 1). Obese patients were matched on binge-eating severity (low, moderate, or high on the BES) and percentage overweight. Subjects in each triad were randomly assigned to either the standard or the modified treatment program.

The preliminary report of this study describes an overall average reduction in binge severity from baseline to posttreatment and a 6-month follow-up, with no difference between the two treatments. Moreover, neither treatment had a significant effect on dietary restraint, which was measured with the Herman and Polivy Restraint Scale. In terms of weight loss, however, significant interactions at posttreatment and follow-up showed the differential effectiveness of the two treatments according to level of binge-eating severity. The standard treatment was more effective with binge eaters of low to moderate severity, whereas the modified treatment was more effective with binge eaters with high severity. Both treatments resulted in significant reductions in depression at posttreatment.

The results of Krug and colleagues (1990) raise more questions than they provide answers. Specific changes in binge eating need to be detailed. The BES cannot provide the necessary data. Direct self-monitoring of binge eating or a precise and valid measure such as the EDE is required. It is unclear whether the absence of a differential treatment effect on binge eating was due to the relative ineffectiveness of the modified treatment, or the effectiveness of the standard behavioral treatment.

## Pharmacological Therapy

Antidepressant drugs produce significant short-term reductions in binge eating and purging in normal weight patients with bulimia nervosa, although the outcome is inferior to CBT (Wilson, in press). Pharmacotherapy has been criticized because it appears to achieve its effects by reducing hunger and increasing dietary restraint. To the extent that the cognitive-behavioral model of the maintenance of binge eating is valid, then effective treatment requires that dietary restraint be reduced and regular, healthy eating patterns established. Once the drug is discontinued, relapse occurs rapidly and predictably (Walsh, Hadigan, Devlin, Gladis, & Roose, 1990). We should expect the same findings with binge eating in obese patients.

Antidepressant drugs would be expected to have specific effects on psychopathology, such as affective and anxiety disorders, and related negative affective states that are often the proximal antecedents of binge eating. To the extent that binge eating is causally related to some form of affective or anxiety disorder, as some have claimed, then an indirect effect on binge eating could be predicted. But, as noted earlier in this chapter, there is no evidence to support this view. Bulimia nervosa is not a product of an underlying affective disorder. There is no reason to think otherwise about binge eating in the obese. Schwalberg (1990) did find that anxiety disorders do frequently cooccur with bulimic disorders (Laessle et al., 1989), but there is no direct evidence suggesting that binge eating is a function of a co-occurring anxiety disorder.

### Effectiveness of Antidepressant Medication

Marcus et al. (1990b) randomly assigned obese bingers and nonbingers to one of two treatments—standard behavioral treatment for obesity plus fluoxetine, or behavioral treatment plus a placebo. Contrary to the authors' predictions, adding fluoxetine to behavioral treatment had no differential effect on binge eating. It produced neither greater weight loss in obese binge eaters nor a greater reduction in binge eating. An overall improvement on the Bulimia subscale of the EDI, which the authors interpret as an index of binge eating (a questionable view), could be attributed only to participation in treatment. Although fluoxetine produced a greater weight loss overall, relapse promptly and predictably followed its discontinuation.

McCann and Agras (1990) found that desipramine reduced binge eating in obese patients by 66%, and produced a 45% abstinence rate, after 12 weeks of treatment. The comparable figures for placebo treatment were an increase of 14% and a 17% abstinence rate. Dietary restraint was significantly increased, and hunger suppressed. Hunger recovered, and binge eating increased markedly, within 4 weeks after the drug was discontinued. The parallel between these findings and those obtained with desipramine treatment of normal weight bulimia nervosa is striking. Although additional studies are needed, currently available information points to the same conclusion as with the pharmacological treatment of normal weight bulimia nervosa. Antidepressant medication cannot be recommended as the treatment of choice for binge eating in obese patients, even though it might be useful in treating the associated general psychopathology.

**Other Obesity Treatments**

The analysis of binge eating presented here suggests that any treatment that focuses exclusively on weight loss via caloric restriction will be counterproductive. Very-low-calorie diets (VLCDs) are one example. VLCD programs alone cannot be recommended for obese patients in general, let alone for obese binge eaters. VLCDs should be used only as part of a multifaceted treatment program that addresses changes in eating life-style and behavior, exercise, and general nutrition (Wadden, Van Itallie, & Blackburn, 1990). Unfortunately, there are no good data on the effects of combined VLCD and behavior change programs on obese binge eaters.

Gastric surgery is another form of treatment that may be contraindicated for obese binge eaters. There are clinical reports that surgery may worsen the problem, which then complicates the course of postoperative recovery.

## CONCLUDING COMMENTS

We still know little about the obese binge eater. Progress will depend on improved definition of basic concepts and phenomena (e.g., binge eating), and valid measures of the specific psychopathology of the eating disorder.

The connection between obesity and binge eating is unclear. The presence of binge eating tends to undermine the effectiveness of weight loss treatments for the obese. Being overweight might well be shown to complicate the effective and lasting treatment of binge eating.

CBT is an effective treatment for normal weight bulimia nervosa. It shows promise as a method for treating obese binge eaters. Pharmacological treatment has modest short-term effects on bulimia nervosa, but as with obesity, rapid relapse results when the medication is withdrawn. There is little reason to expect that antidepressant drugs will be any more successful with obese binge eaters.

## ENDNOTES

1. Both DSM-III-R and proposed DSM-IV criteria define a binge as the uncontrolled consumption of a large amount of food. In contrast, the Stanford group count even small eating episodes as a

"binge" provided that the patient feels she or he has eaten a large amount (Rossiter et al., 1990). At present we do not know the diagnostic or therapeutic significance of these different definitions of a binge.

2. This definition of binge-eating is taken from the Eating Disorder Examination (EDE) (Cooper & Fairburn, 1987).
3. The model summarized here is often referred to as the cognitive, or cognitive-behavioral, model because of the emphasis on cognitive-behavioral influences in the maintenance and modification of the disorder.
4. Agras and his colleagues at Stanford Medical School have also found that a group adaptation of interpersonal psychotherapy that does not address eating or weight directly can be effective in reducing binge eating in nonpurging, obese bulimics (W. S. Agras, personal communication, 1991).
5. An extreme version of this concept of reducing dietary restraint is represented by Hirschmann and Munter's (1988) approach to the treatment of compulsive overeating. They reject dieting, and recommend demand feeding of the most desired foods at any time, and in unlimited amount, on the assumption that more normal patterns of eating will emerge.

**REFERENCES**

Alger, S. A., Schwalberg, M. J., Bigaouette, J. M., Howard, L. J., & Reid, L. D. (1990). Using drugs to manage binge-eating among obese and normal weight patients. In L. D. Reid (Ed.), *Opioids, bulimia, and alcohol abuse and alcoholism*. New York: Springer-Verlag.

American Psychiatric Association Task Force on Nomenclature and Statistics. (1980). *Diagnostic and statistical manual of mental disorders*. Washington, DC: American Psychiatric Association.

Bemis, K. M. (1985). Abstinence and nonabstinence models for the treatment of bulimia. *International Journal of Eating Disorders, 4*, 407–437.

Bemis, K. M. (1989). Phobia, obsession, or addiction: What underlies the eating disorders? Paper presented at the National Conference on the Eating Disorders, Columbus, Ohio, October.

Blundell, J. (1990). How culture undermines the biopsychosocial system of appetite control. *Appetite, 14*, 113–115.

Brownell, K. D., & Wadden, T. (1991). The heterogeneity of obesity: Fitting treatments to individuals. *Behavior Therapy, 22*, 153–177.

Cooper, Z., & Fairburn, C. G. (1987). The Eating Disorder Examination: A semistructured interview for the assessment of the specific psychopathology of eating disorders. *International Journal of Eating Disorders, 6*, 1–8.

Dinardo, P. A., & Barlow, D. H. (1988). *Anxiety disorders schedule—revised.* Albany: Department of Psychology, State University of New York at Albany.

Fairburn, C. G. (1985). Cognitive-behavioral treatment for bulimia. In D. M. Garner & P. E. Garfinkel (Eds.), *Handbook for psychotherapy for anorexia nervosa and bulimia.* New York: Guilford Press.

Fairburn, C. G., & Beglin, S. J. (1990). Studies of the epidemiology of bulimia nervosa. *American Journal of Psychiatry, 147*, 401–408.

Fairburn, C. G., Jones, R., Peveler, R. C., Carr, S. J., Solomon, R. A., O'Connor, M. E., Burton, J., & Hope, R. A. (1991). Three psychological treatments for bulimia nervosa: A comparative trial. *Archives of General Psychiatry, 48*, 463–469.

Fairburn, C. G., Kirk, J., O'Connor, M., & Cooper, P. J. (1986). A comparison of two psychological treatments for bulimia nervosa. *Behaviour Research and Therapy, 24*, 629–643.

Garner, D. M., Fairburn, C. G., & Davis, R. (1987). Cognitive-behavioral treatment of bulimia nervosa: A critical appraisal. *Behavior Modification, 11*, 398–431.

Garner, D. M., Olmsted, M. P., Davis, R., Rockert, W., Goldbloom, D., & Eagle, M. (1990). The association between bulimic symptoms and reported psychopathology. *International Journal of Eating Disorders, 9*, 1–15.

Garner, D. M., Olmsted, M. P., & Polivy, J. (1983). Development and validation of a multidimensional eating disorder inventory for anorexia nervosa and bulimia. *International Journal of Eating Disorders, 2*, 15–34.

Gormally, J., Black, S., Daston, S., & Rardin, D. (1982). The assessment of binge-eating severity among obese persons. *Addictive Behaviours, 7*, 47–55.

Hirchmann, J. R., & Munter, C. H. (1988). *Overcoming overeating.* New York: Fawcett Columbine.

Hsu, L. K. G. (1990). *Eating disorders.* New York: Guilford Press.

Hudson, J. I., Pope, H. G., Wurtman, J., Yurgelun-Todd, D., Mark, S., & Rosenthal, N. E. (1988). Bulimia in obese individuals: Relationship to normal-weight bulimia. *Journal of Nervous and Mental Disease, 176*, 144–152.

Kaye, W. H., Ballenger, J. C., Lydiard, R. B., Stuart, G. W., Laraia, M. T., O'Neill, P., Fossey, M. D., Stevens, V., Lesser, S., & Hsu, G. (1990). Monoamine levels in normal-weight bulimia: Evidence for abnormal noradrenergic activity. *American Journal of Psychiatry, 147*, 225–229.

Keefe, P. H., Wyshogrod, D., Winberger, E., & Agras, W. S. (1984). Binge eating and outcome of behavioral treatment of obesity: A preliminary report. *Behaviour Research and Therapy, 22,* 319–321.

Kern, P. A., Ong, J. M., Saffari, B., & Carty, J. (1990). The effects of weight loss on the activity and expression of adipose-tissue lipoprotein lipase in very obese humans. *New England Journal of Medicine, 322,* 1053–1059.

Kolotkin, R. L., Revis, E. S., Kirkley, B. G., & Janick, L. (1987). Binge eating in obesity: Associated MMPI characteristics. *Journal of Consulting Clinical Psychology, 55,* 872–876.

Krug, L. M., Houston, C., Smith, M., Kaminsky, K., & Fisher, E. (1990). Standard vs. modified behavioral weight control treatment for obese binge eaters: Preliminary findings. Paper presented at the Annual Convention of the Association for Advancement of Behavior Therapy, San Francisco, November 2.

Kuldau, J. W., & Rand, C. S. W. (1986). The night eating syndrome and bulimia in the morbidly obese. *International Journal of Eating Disorders, 5,* 143–148.

Laessle, R. G., Tuschl, R. J., Waadt, S., & Pirke, K. M. (1989). The specific psychopathology of bulimia nervosa: A comparison with restrained and unrestrained (normal) eaters. *Journal of Consulting Clinical Psychology, 57,* 772–775.

Levy, A. B., Dixon, K. N., & Stern, S. L. (1989). How are depression and bulimia related? *American Journal of Psychiatry, 146,* 162–169.

Lowe, M. R., & Caputo, C. (1991). Binge eating in obesity: Toward the specification of predictors. *International Journal of Eating Disorders, 10,* 49–55.

Malenbaum, R., Herzog, D., Eisenthal, S., & Wyshak, G. (1988). Overeaters Anonymous: Impact on bulimia. *International Journal of Eating Disorders, 7,* 139–143.

Marcus, M. D., Wing, R. R., & Hopkins, J. (1988). Obese binge-eaters: Affect, cognitions and response to behavioral weight control. *Journal of Consulting Clinical Psychology, 56,* 433–439.

Marcus, M. D., Wing, R. R., Ewing, L., Kern, E., Gooding, W., & McDermott, M. (1990a). Psychiatric disorders among obese binge eaters. *International Journal of Eating Disorders, 9,* 69–77.

Marcus, M. D., Wing, R. R., Ewing, L., Kern, E., McDermott, M., & Gooding, W. (1990b). A double-blind, placebo-controlled trial of fluoxetine plus behavior modification in the treatment of obese binge-eaters and non-binge-eaters. *American Journal of Psychiatry, 147,* 876–881.

McCann, U. D., & Agras, W. S. (1990). Successful treatment of nonpurging bulimia nervosa with desipramine: A double-blind, placebo-controlled study. *American Journal of Psychiatry, 147,* 1509–1513.

Mitchell, J. E., Pyle, R. L., Eckert, E. D., Hatsukami, D., & Soll, E. (1990). Bulimia nervosa in overweight individuals. *Journal of Nervous and Mental Disease, 178,* 324–327.

Patton, G. C. (1988). The spectrum of eating disorder in adolescence. *Journal of Psychosomatic Research, 32,* 579–584.

Polivy, J., & Herman, C. P. (1985). Dieting and bingeing: A causal analysis. *American Psychologist, 40,* 193–201.

Pope, H. G., & Hudson, J. I. (1988). Is bulimia nervosa a heterogeneous disorder? Lessons from the history of medicine. *International Journal of Eating Disorders, 7,* 155–166.

Prather, R. C., & Williamson, D. A. (1988). Psychopathology associated with bulimia, binge eating, and obesity. *International Journal of Eating Disorders, 7,* 177–184.

Rosen, J. D., & Srebnik, D. (1990). Assessment of eating disorders. In P. McReynolds, J. C. Rosen, & G. Chelune (Eds.), *Advances in psychological assessment* (Vol. 7). New York: Plenum.

Rossiter, E. M., Agras, W. S., Telch, C. F., & Bruce, B. (1990). A descriptive investigation of the eating patterns of nonpurging bulimic subjects. Paper presented at the Annual Convention of the Association for Advancement of Behavior Therapy, San Francisco, November 2.

Schwalberg, M. D. (1990). A comparison of bulimics, obese binge eaters, social phobics, and individuals with panic disorder on anxiety, depression, chemical abuse, and borderline personality disorder. Unpublished doctoral dissertation, State University of New York at Albany.

Spitzer, R. L., Devlin, M., Walsh, B. T., Hasin, D., Wing, R., Marcus, M., Stunkard, A. J., Wadden, T., Yanovski, S., Agras, W. S., Mitchell, J., & Nonas, C. (1992). Binge eating disorder: A multisite field trial of the diagnostic criteria. *International Journal of Eating Disorders, 11,* 191–204.

Strober, M., & Katz, J. L. (1987). Do eating disorders and affective disorders share a common etiology? A dissenting opinion. *International Journal of Eating Disorders, 6,* 171–180.

Stunkard, A. J. (1959). Eating patterns and obesity. *Psychiatric Quarterly, 33,* 284–295.

Stunkard, A. J., Harris, J. R., Pedersen, N. L., & McClearn, G. E. (1990). The body-mass index of twins who have been reared apart. *New England Journal of Medicine, 322,* 1483–1487.

Stunkard, A. J., & Messick, S. (1985). The Three Factor Eating Questionnaire to measure dietary restraint, disinhibition and hunger. *Journal of Psychosomatic Research, 29,* 71–83.

Telch, C. F., Agras, W. S., Rossiter, E., Wilfley, D., & Kenardy, J. (1990). Group cognitive-behavioral treatment for the non-purging bulimic: An initial evaluation. *Journal of Consulting & Clinical Psychology, 58,* 629–635.

Tuschl, R. J. (1990). From dietary restraint to binge eating: Some theoretical considerations. *Appetite, 14,* 105–109.

Viesselman, J. O., & Roig, M. (1985). Depression and suicidality in eating disorders. *Journal of Clinical Psychiatry, 46,* 118–124.

Wadden, T. A., Van Itallie, T. B., & Blackburn, G. L. (1990). Responsible and irresponsible use of very-low-calorie-diets in the treatment of obesity. *Journal of the American Medical Association, 263,* 83–85.

Walsh, B. T., Hadigan, C., Devlin, M., Gladis, M., & Roose, S. (1991). Long-term outcome of antidepressant treatment for bulimia nervosa. *Archives of General Psychiatry, 148,* 1206–1212.

Wardle, J. (1987). Compulsive eating and dietary restraint. *British Journal of Clinical Psychology, 26,* 47–55.

Williamson, D. A. (1990). *Assessment of eating disorders.* New York: Pergamon Press.

Williamson, D. A., Prather, R. C., McKenzie, S. J., & Blouin, D. C. (1990). Behavioral assessment procedures can differentiate bulimia nervosa, compulsive overeater, obese, and normal subjects. *Behavioral Assessment, 12,* 239–252.

Wilson, G. T. (1989). Bulimia nervosa: A cognitive-social learning analysis. In A. J. Stunkard & A. Baum (Eds.), *Recent advances in behavioral medicine.* New York: Erlbaum.

Wilson, G. T. (1991). The addiction model of eating disorders: A critical analysis. *Advances in Behaviour Research and Therapy, 13,* 27–72.

Wilson, G. T. (in press). Cognitive-behavioral versus pharmacological treatment of bulimia nervosa. *Verhaltenstherapie.*

# 4

# Medical Complications of Anorexia Nervosa and Bulimia Nervosa

Martina de Zwaan, M.D.
James E. Mitchell, M.D.

Anorexia nervosa and bulimia nervosa may be associated with serious medical complications (Pomeroy & Mitchell, 1989). The restoration of metabolic and physiological homeostasis is the first step in the treatment of a patient with an eating disorder. Until this is accomplished, the patient cannot benefit from nutritional and psychological interventions. In anorexia nervosa, medical consequences are primarily related to the effects of voluntary starvation. Immediate danger may derive from hypophosphatemia, bone marrow failure, cardiac decompensation, and shock. Patients with bulimia nervosa more often experience severe fluid and electrolyte abnormalities due to purging behavior, and emergency situations may include severe hypovolemia, depletion of total body potassium, and cardiac arrhythmias (Comerci, 1990). Fortunately, most of the medical disturbances are not severe, and most resolve quickly after symptom remission. Table 4.1 summarizes the causes of the major medical complications in eating disorders.

**Starvation**

Metabolic and endocrine adaptation to starvation is the most important variable in the management of patients with anorexia nervosa, but is also

60

TABLE 4.1.

Development of Medical Complications in Anorexia Nervosa and Bulimia Nervosa

| Abnormal Eating and Weight Regulating Behaviors | Consequences |
| --- | --- |
| Binge eating | Mechanical irritation and dilatation of the stomach "Overnutrition" |
| Starvation, chaotic eating pattern | Excessive weight loss→metabolic and endocrine adaptation<br>Malnutrition→nutritional deficits |
| Self-induced vomiting | Mechanical irritation→injuries of the upper GI tract, injuries of the mediastinum<br>Fluid and electrolyte abnormalities—organ system dysfunctions |
| Laxative abuse | Mechanical irritation→injuries of the lower GI tract<br>Fluid and electrolyte abnormalities→organ system dysfunctions<br>Addiction |
| Diuretic abuse | Fluid and electrolyte abnormalities—organ system dysfunctions<br>Addiction |
| Diet pills | Addiction |
| Ipecac syrup | Vomiting, toxicity |

present in many normal weight bulimic patients as a result of their intermittent dieting behavior. This represents an adaptation to inadequate intake through reducing catabolism to conserve energy. Most of the physical abnormalities that have been demonstrated in people with eating disorders have also been described in starved individuals who do not have an eating disorder (Keys, Brozek, Henschel, Mickelsen, & Taylor, 1950; Fichter, Pirke, Poellinger, Wolfram, & Brunner, 1986).

**Purging Behavior**

The prevalence and methods of mitigating the fattening effects of food are summarized in Table 4.2. These associated behaviors often prove to be the most physically damaging and can cause life-endangering medical complications.

TABLE 4.2.
Prevalence of Bulimia-Related Behavior in Female
Outpatients with Bulimia Nervosa (Mitchell et al., 1985).

| Behavior | Frequency % Bulimic Patients | |
|---|---|---|
| | Ever | Daily or more |
| Binge Eating | 100 | 82.2 |
| Self-induced vomiting | 88.1 | 71.8 |
| Chewing and spitting out food | 64.5 | — |
| Laxatives | 60.6 | 19.7 |
| Diet pills | 50.2 | 25.1 |
| Diuretics | 33.9 | 10.2 |
| Saunas | 12.1 | 3.4 |

**Self-Induced Vomiting**

Self-induced vomiting is the method most commonly employed by bulimic individuals and is performed as soon as possible after eating in order to minimize the absorption of food. Early in the course of the illness, many individuals insert their fingers into their throat to induce the gag reflex. However, vomiting becomes progressively easier over time and many eventually require only drinking a quantity of water toward the end of the episode or bending over the toilet and applying some pressure to the abdomen. Some abuse the over-the-counter drug ipecac syrup, which contains the alkaloid emetine, as a way of promoting vomiting, a particularly dangerous procedure. Emetine causes gastrointestinal, cardiovascular, and neuromuscular toxicity. Unfortunately, there is a tolerance effect to vomiting and patients must ingest increasing doses. Since the half-life of ipecac is 56 hours, multiple regular doses are accumulative and with time may become toxic (Tolstoi, 1990).

**Laxatives**

Abuse of laxatives is another method to counteract the effects of ingested food. Some individuals take laxatives only after episodes of overeating; others take them as a routine weight control method. Laxative abuse is a relatively ineffective method of avoiding calorie absorption, as such drugs primarily affect the large intestine, whereas most nutrients are absorbed in the small intestine. One study showed that laxatives produce a decrease in energy absorption of only 12% of intake (Bo-Linn, Santa Ana, Morowski, & Fordtran, 1983). However, fluid absorption takes place in the large intestine. Consequently, laxatives that act directly on the colon produce a temporary fluid loss caused by watery diarrhea that gives patients a sense of weight loss. Reflex fluid retention and weight gain leads to further usage, and over time tolerance to the laxatives develops and the dosage has to be increased. Individuals often ingest up to 60 or more tablets daily instead of a customary dose of one or two tablets only. Laxative preparations are readily available without prescription and are probably the type of drug most commonly abused by bulimic patients. Patients misuse primarily stimulant-type laxatives containing phenolphthalein, examples being Ex-Lax and Correctol (Mitchell & Boutacoff, 1986).

## Diuretics

Another rather ineffective method to prevent weight gain is diuretic abuse. As with laxatives, with diuretics individuals may develop a sense of having lost weight, owing to the resultant dehydration. Reflex fluid retention again causes weight gain and sustains diuretic use. Most but not all bulimic patients who misuse or abuse diuretics use over-the-counter preparations, which usually contain ammonium chloride, pamabron, or caffeine. The three groups of prescription drugs most often abused by patients with eating disorders are the thiazides, loop diuretics, and potassium-sparing diuretics. Thiazides and loop diuretics such as furosemide can produce marked potassium and sodium depletion. Elevated urine potassium levels in the presence of significant hypokalemia may indicate diuretic abuse. The aldosterone-antagonist diuretics such as spironolactone actually may be helpful for the patient with secondary hyperaldosteronism and associated hypokalemia. Their abuse may even cause hyperkalemia with associated hypotension, and myocardial conduction abnormalities may complicate their use. Diuretics are often questionably prescribed for the control of idiopathic edema or premenstrual edema among women. Chronic diuretic use in young women should signal to the clinician the possibility of an unrecognized eating problem.

## Diet Pills

Some patients take appetite suppressants. Most of the diet pills used by patients with bulimia nervosa are obtained over the counter. These usually contain phenylpropanolamine and are occasionally taken in amounts that exceed therapeutic recommendations. Only rarely do patients with eating disorders use amphetamines or thyroid preparations. Many patients with bulimia nervosa experiment with diet pills, but most do not take them on an ongoing basis because they find them relatively ineffective as a weight control technique. Side effects of daily use include rebound fatigue and hyperphagia, insomnia, mood changes, irritability, and, in extremely large doses, psychosis.

## Other Purging Behavior

Excessive exercise and hyperactivity often occur in eating disorders. It is our clinical impression that such exercising tends not to be as rigorous in patients with bulimia nervosa as it is in patients with anorexia nervosa.

Patients with diabetes mellitus may utilize an effective, and very dangerous, way of achieving weight loss by neglecting their insulin requirements. They intentionally underdose as a way to purge calories by means of glucosuria. They correctly reason that increased insulin would lead to increased use of glucose and subsequent weight gain (Hudson, Hudson, & Wentworth, 1983a). However, the consequences of this for their diabetes can be severe.

Women with bulimia nervosa who have young babies may continue breast feeding for inordinate lengths of time in order to perpetuate energy loss through lactation. Other abnormal eating-related behaviors in bulimia nervosa are excessive use of enemas (7%), chewing and spitting out food without swallowing it (64.5%), the occurrence of rumination (the regurgitation, chewing, and reswallowing of food; 35%), and the misuse of saunas as a weight loss technique (Mitchell, Hatsukami, Eckert, & Pyle, 1985).

## Comorbidity

Eating disorders are frequently associated with alcohol and/or drug abuse, which can cause medical complications of their own.

## SIGNS AND SYMPTOMS

### Symptoms

Complaints are frequently nonspecific and may include fatigue, lethargy, weakness, impaired concentration, nonfocal abdominal pain, dizziness, faintness, sore muscles, chills, "cold sweat," frequent sore throats, diarrhea, and constipation. While the signs and symptoms of anorexia nervosa are usually obvious, patients with bulimia nervosa may appear physically healthy upon initial examination. Since bulimic patients often fail to report their abnormal eating pattern, the evaluating physician may not be able to uncover the etiology of the complaints or abnormal laboratory results.

### Signs

#### Bulimia Nervosa

There are signs observable on examination that should alert the clinician to the possible diagnosis of bulimia nervosa:

1. Lesions on the skin over the dorsum of the dominant hand, resulting from the use of the hand to stimulate the gag reflex (Russell's sign; Russell, 1979). This change may be more common early in the course of the illness, since as the illness progresses patients often no longer require mechanical stimulation to induce vomiting.
2. Hypertrophy of the salivary glands, particularly the parotid glands, is common, and usually bilateral and painless. This is sometimes referred to as "puffy cheeks" by patients. The exact prevalence is unknown, as is the pathophysiology. It may be caused by binge eating, vomiting, and perhaps excessive gum chewing (Hsu, 1990). Interestingly, the problem may persist for several months beyond normalization of eating patterns. Biopsy results range from normal tissue (Levine, Falko, Dixon, Gallup, & Saunders, 1980) to inflammatory enlargement (Walsh, Croft, & Katz, 1981). In one series of 108 bulimic patients (Mitchell, Pyle, Eckert, Hatsukami, & Lentz, 1983a), 27.8% had elevated serum amylase levels, apparently primarily salivary in origin. The amylase elevations are usually modest and infrequently reach double the normal level. In some patients the pancreatic isoenzyme contributes to the total serum amylase elevation (Gwirtsman et al., 1986). Since there are case reports of pan-

creatic abnormalities on computed tomography (CT) scanning in patients with bulimia nervosa, it is necessary to fractionate serum amylase in order to rule out pancreatic isoenzyme elevation and pancreatitis (Kaplan, 1987a; Gavish et al., 1987).

3. Dental complications are frequent in these patients and are caused by the highly acid gastric contents leading to erosion of the enamel and secondarily to decalcification. The erosion is often particularly marked on the lingual surface of the upper teeth. The presence of erosion is related to the duration and frequency of vomiting, and vomiting at least three times a week for 4 years causes dental problems in a majority of bulimic patients (Altshuler, Dechow, Waller, & Hardy, 1990; Simmons, Grayden, & Mitchell, 1986). Other types of dental changes include increased temperature sensitivity and a possible increased rate of caries development. The rapidly developing caries is presumably related to the intake of pure sugar and foods of high carbohydrate content. For a full description of dental complications see Chapter 5.

4. If examined soon after a binge-and-vomit episode, the bulimic patient may appear flushed, and petechial hemorrhages may be seen on the cornea, soft palate, or face.

5. Other signs may include muscle weakness, and peripheral edema.

### Anorexia Nervosa
Signs of anorexia nervosa are usually more obvious.

1. The emaciated appearance of patients with anorexia nervosa should immediately suggest the diagnosis.

2. The skin is usually dry, sometimes shows a yellowish discoloration, possibly related to increased carotene deposition, and appears "dirty." In up to 29% of anorectics, trunk, face, and extremities are covered by fine body hair (lanugo) (Gupta, Gupta, & Haberman, 1987). Brittle hair and nails as well as scalp and pubic hair loss are common.

3. Orthostatic changes and hypotension (often below 80/50 mmHg) are very common, and the periphery is usually cold and cyanotic.

4. Body temperature (rectal temperature below 96.6F) and pulse rate (usually below 60 bpm) may be reduced. Patients with anorexia nervosa often fail to respond to cold with characteristic shivering or piloerection (Palla & Litt, 1988).

5. Other signs on physical examination may include edema (20%

prevalence in this population) of lower extremities (e.g., pretibial), petechiae, and in rare cases pathological fractures.

## SPECIFIC MEDICAL COMPLICATIONS OF EATING DISORDERS

### Fluid and Electrolyte Abnormalities

Nearly 50% of bulimic patients demonstrate fluid or electrolyte abnormalities due to vomiting or laxative or diuretic abuse as well as low salt intake and the resulting dehydration. In anorexia nervosa, electrolyte abnormalities are less common and are usually due to malnutrition or, in rare cases, to purging behavior. In many cases, the frequency of electrolyte abnormalities does not seem to correlate with either the type of behaviors (starvation, vomiting, diuretics abuse, laxative abuse, enemas) or the reported frequency of these behaviors (Mitchell et al., 1983a). Many patients with electrolyte abnormalities are asymptomatic, and it is impossible to predict when complications might occur. On the other hand, physicians should keep in mind that patients with bulimia nervosa often underreport the frequency of their abnormal eating behavior, and consequently electrolyte abnormalities may be present. It must be noted that there is a high probability for multiple electrolyte disturbances to coexist if a single abnormal electrolyte determination is found (Hall et al., 1988). The electrolyte abnormalities represent one complication of eating disorders that may require emergency treatment and/or periodic monitoring.

### Dehydration

Dehydration results in volume depletion. Patients may feel dizzy, lightheaded, and weak. In extreme cases syncopy and confusional episodes may occur. They may experience hypotension and tachycardia. Hemoconcentration develops, causing alterations of serum osmolarity and hematocrit values. Volume depletion leads to a secondary hyperaldosteronism (pseudo Bartter's syndrome), and reflex peripheral edema (Mitchell, Pomeroy, Seppala, & Huber, 1988). This fluid retention can be quite dramatic, particularly after withdrawal of laxatives or diuretics.

There is evidence that serum aldosterone levels may provide a biological marker of purging behavior that can be used to detect self-induced vomiting, laxative or diuretic abuse, or severe restriction of food and water intake among patients with eating disorders (Jonas & Mickely,

1990). This might help to detect purging in patients denying such behavior.

## Hyponatremia

Hyponatremia occurs in about 5% of patients with bulimia nervosa (Mitchell et al., 1983a). Acute hyponatremia may cause CNS dysfunction, manifested by lethargy and weakness and progressing to seizures, coma, or death when the serum sodium falls below 120 mEq/L. These complications are extremely rare.

## Hypokalemia

Hypokalemia occurs in about 14% of patients with bulimia nervosa (Mitchell et al., 1983a), and the clinical manifestations of hypokalemia are quite common. Hypokalemia causes weakness in skeletal and smooth muscle, including decreased gastrointestinal motility that contributes to the hypoperistalsis sometimes observed in these patients. Cardiac conduction defects and a variety of arrhythmias have been observed. There is evidence that severe hypokalemia may directly cause a type of myocardial necrosis called hypokalemic cardiomyopathy. Tetany may result from hypokalemic alkalosis. Hypokalemia may contribute to the development of rhabdomyolysis and glucose intolerance. Low potassium can also affect renal function. Kaliopenic nephropathy is a tubular dysfunction resulting in diminished concentrating ability. In most cases supplemental oral potassium will be sufficient. However, in extreme cases of hypokalemia, intravenous potassium supplementation may be necessary, since diuretic abuse and vomiting may result in a severe contraction alkalosis, which makes correction of potassium levels difficult. Hydrogen ion shifts into the extracellular fluid to compensate, and potassium shifts into the cells (Mitchell et al., 1988). Furthermore, renal excretion of potassium is increased because of the secondary hyperaldosteronism resulting from the hypovolemia. Sodium is reabsorbed instead of potassium in order to retain water, since the body's highest priority is the maintenance of an adequate blood volume.

## Hypochloremia

A lack of chloride, as seen in 24% of the patients in the study of Mitchell and associates (1983a), limits the kidney's ability to excrete bicarbonate when volume depletion is present at the same time. Bicarbonate is the only anion other than chloride that can directly accompany sodium reabsorption to any significant degree. Since volume contraction leads to increased sodium reabsorption, bicarbonate must also be reabsorbed, which worsens the alkalosis. Consequently, hypochloremia is usually seen in combination with elevated serum bicarbonate (Mitchell et al., 1983a).

## Metabolic Alkalosis

High serum bicarbonate is the most usual abnormality in patients with bulimia nervosa (27% in Mitchell et al., 1983a), and was positively correlated with subjects who frequently (at least once a day) engaged in vomiting. Vomiting tends to generate metabolic alkalosis through loss of gastric hydrochloric acid (HCL) and volume contraction. Again it must be emphasized that metabolic alkalosis may augment hypokalemia and must be corrected prior to potassium supplementation. This usually requires the cessation of vomiting.

## Metabolic Acidosis

Metabolic acidosis is less common (8% in Mitchell et al., 1983a) than metabolic alkalosis. Low serum bicarbonate may be present in patients who have recently abused laxatives, resulting from the loss of alkaline fluid from the bowel secondary to laxative-induced diarrhea. This develops in some patients despite frequent vomiting. Acidosis is strongly suggestive of laxative abuse, whereas negative results do not rule out this problem, since it is likely that acidosis is transient (Mitchell, Hatsukami, Pyle, Eckert, & Boutacoff, 1987a). Metabolic acidosis may mask a major deficiency in total body potassium, since hydrogen ion shifts into the cells and potassium into the extracellular fluid, thereby producing spuriously normal serum potassium levels.

## Hypomagnesemia

Hall and associates (1988) emphasize that hypomagnesemia is an important and often overlooked electrolyte abnormality in eating disorder patients. Symptoms related to magnesium depletion include diminished concentration, muscular weakness, muscular cramps (carpopedal spasm), cardiac arrhythmias, anxiety, restlessness, irritability, and confusion.

Comparable to potassium, magnesium is distributed primarily as an intracellular ion, and even slight reductions of serum levels might indicate profound total body hypomagnesemia. Low magnesium is frequently associated with hypokalemia, since the kidneys are unable to adequately reabsorb potassium when magnesium levels are low. Clinically refractory hypokalemia should suggest to the clinician the coexistence of a magnesium deficiency. Correction of this may be necessary before potassium can be adequately replaced.

## Hypophosphatemia

Dietary deficiency alone rarely causes significant hypophosphatemia, since phosphorus is ubiquitous in food and since the kidney is able to adapt to a low phosphate intake. Furthermore, fat metabolism, which is not phosphorus dependent, predominates during starvation. Glucose, however, inhibits fat metabolism and requires phosphate for glycolysis. Consequently, severe hypophosphatemia may occur in patients with anorexia nervosa during parenteral refeeding with a large carbohydrate load and without sufficient amounts of phosphate (Weinsier, Krumdieck, & Krumdieck, 1981). Hypophosphatemic symptoms are due to reduced cellular energy stores and tissue hypoxia leading to cell breakdown and neuromuscular changes. Clinical consequences are muscular weakness, fatigue, gastrointestinal complaints such as nausea and vomiting, anorexia, and osteomalacia due to increased resorption of bone phosphorus as an attempt to correct the low serum level (Waldholtz & Andersen, 1988). Severe effects may be hematologic (hemolytic anemia), muscular (rhabdomyolysis, congestive cardiomyopathy, respiratory failure), or CNS dysfunction similar to a metabolic encephalopathy, causing symptoms such as irritability, paresthesias, confusion, seizures, and coma. Care should be taken to avoid the administration of a large glucose load to a severely malnourished patient.

## Gastrointestinal Complications

Gastrointestinal complications are a major source of morbidity for patients with eating disorders (Ceuller & VanThiel, 1986).

### Larynx and Esophagus

Impaired taste perception in bulimia nervosa has been reported; this may relate to vomiting behavior (Rodin, Bartoshuk, Peterson, & Shank,

1990). Elevated taste detection and recognition thresholds have also been observed in anorectic patients (Casper, Kirschner, Sandstead, Jacob, & Davis, 1980; Katz et al., 1987). Although zinc levels have been shown to influence taste perception, low zinc levels in patients with anorexia nervosa did not correlate with abnormalities in taste function. Loss of the gag reflex from frequent mechanical stimulation also may result, as well as lower esophageal relaxation and subsequent reflex regurgitation (Palla & Litt, 1988). Rare but very serious side effects are esophagitis, esophageal tears (Mallory-Weiss syndrome) with bleeding, or perforation (Boerhaave syndrome) due to repeated vomiting, which requires immediate surgical intervention (Larsen, Jensen, & Axelsen, 1983).

### Stomach and Duodenum

Some patients with anorexia nervosa exhibit delayed gastric emptying, especially when they are low in weight (Dubois, Gross, Ebert, & Castell, 1979; Robinson, Clarke, & Barrett, 1988). Although gastrointestinal symptoms such as vomiting, a feeling of "fullness," bloating, early satiety, and postprandial discomfort are common, they have not been shown to positively correlate with delayed gastric emptying (Hutson & Wald, 1990). Recent data suggest that gastric emptying improves quite rapidly as refeeding commences and is therefore secondary to restriction in food intake (Szmukler, Young, Lichtenstein, & Andrews, 1990). In bulimia nervosa gastric emptying time is similar to that of sex-matched controls and is delayed only in a few patients.

More serious side effects include gastric and duodenal ulcer, bleeding, gastric dilatation (Mitchell, Pyle, & Miner, 1987b), necrosis (Abdu, Garritano, & Culver, 1987), and perforation (Saul, Dekker, & Watson, 1981) due to the ingestion of large amounts of food during an eating binge, or due to overly aggressive refeeding of patients with anorexia nervosa. In anorexia nervosa severe weight loss may lead to the loss of the fat cushion surrounding the superior mesenteric neurovascular bundle. Consequently compression of the third portion of the duodenum may occur (superior mesenteric artery syndrome; Sours & Vorhaus, 1981). Surgical intervention may be required. It must be stressed that this condition may follow severe weight loss not associated with anorexia nervosa and that the syndrome itself may cause severe weight loss. It has also been suggested that chronic vomiting may cause the development of hiatal hernia (Gross, 1983).

*Small Intestine*

Other medical complications of bulimic behavior have been described, including malabsorption syndromes, the development of steatorrhea and protein-losing gastroenteropathy (Mitchell & Boutacoff, 1986), osteomalacia, and pseudofractures.

*Large Intestine*

Constipation is extremely common among patients with anorexia nervosa as well as among patients with bulimia nervosa as a result of chronic starvation and/or laxative abuse. The treatment of choice is the transient use of bulk-type laxatives, roughage, regular exercise, and hydration. Stimulant types of laxatives taken for long periods of time may result in gastrointestinal bleeding and may cause permanent impairment of colonic functioning due to degeneration of the ganglion cells of Auerbach's plexi (carthartic colon), and may necessitate colonic resection.

*Pancreas*

Pancreatitis, with severe abdominal pain, abdominal distension, fever, and increased heart rate, may result from abrupt pancreatic stimulation during frequent binge eating (Gavish et al., 1987), may occur during refeeding (Gryboski, Hillemeier, Kocoshis, Anyan, & Seashore, 1980), or may be due to chronic diuretic abuse.

*Liver*

Elevations of liver enzymes have been described in patients with anorexia nervosa. These abnormalities may be present during weight loss (nutritional hepatitis) and may worsen during weight gain during treatment, suggesting mild fatty degeneration secondary to refeeding (Halmi & Falk, 1981). Patients abusing ipecac often show elevated liver enzyme levels, since the liver has the highest emetine concentration (Tolstoi, 1990).

## Mediastinal and Pulmonary Complications

Bradypnea as respiratory compensation for alkalosis is possible. Aspiration pneumonia may occur as a result of aspiration of vomitus. Pneumomediastinum, pneumothorax, subcutaneous emphysema, and rib fractures have been described as complications that are due to vigorous vomiting or retching especially in patients with anorexia nervosa who have concomitant osteoporosis and who engage in purging behavior

(Mitchell, Seim, Colon, & Pomeroy, 1987c; McAnarney, Greydanus, Campanella, & Hoekelman, 1983). Free mediastinal air is suggestive of either primary pseudomediastinum due to alveolar rupture, or to esophageal perforation (Boerhaave syndrome), a potentially life-threatening but rare event in eating disorders (Overby & Litt, 1988).

## Cardiovascular Complications

In a series of 65 preadolescent and adolescent anorectics and bulimics, gross electrocardiogram (EKG) changes were seen in about 80% of the patients on admission (Palla & Litt, 1988). Sinus bradycardia ("quiet" heart), hypotension, and orthostatic blood pressure changes are common in patients with eating disorders and reflect the adaptive metabolic effects of starvation. Heart rates lower than 40 beats per minute are not unusual in patients with anorexia nervosa, and bradycardias as low as 25 beats per minute have been reported in strict dieters (Palla & Litt, 1988; Brotman, Rigotti, & Herzog, 1985). The loss of muscle mass can cause decreases in left ventricular wall thickness, cardiac chamber size, and myocardial oxygen uptake in anorexics. This causes such EKG changes as decreased QRS amplitude, nonspecific ST segment and T wave changes, and various arrhythmias. Prolonged QT intervals may predispose to life-threatening arrhythmias and might be responsible for cases of sudden death (Isner, Roberts, Heymsfield, & Yager, 1985). It is important to note that cardiac arrhythmias are most commonly seen in patients with hypokalemia ("U" wave) but that they can also occur in the absence of electrolyte abnormalities (Schocken, Holloway, & Powers, 1989). Serious cardiac illnesses have been described in patients with both anorexia and bulimia nervosa (Harris, 1983; Russell, 1979). Patients who engage in both purging behavior and severe food restriction may develop life-threatening complications such as impending or frank shock. Peripheral edema can develop from rebound fluid retention after purging, and hypoproteinemia due to severe food restriction. The alkaloid emetine, which is contained in ipecac syrup, is apparently responsible for the serious myopathy that can develop, including fatal cardiomyopathy (Palmer & Guay, 1986). Refeeding cardiomyopathy is a possible consequence of overly aggressive refeeding in anorexia nervosa. In addition, an association between mitral valve prolapse and both anorexia nervosa and bulimia nervosa has been reported (Meyers, Starke, Pearson, & Wilken, 1986; Johnson, Humphries, Shirley, Mazzoleni, & Noonan, 1986). Single cases of pericardial effusion (Palla & Litt, 1988) have been discovered on echocardiograms in asymptomatic patients.

## Metabolic Consequences

### Glucose

Patients with diabetes mellitus and an eating disorder may have very unstable blood glucose levels. These fluctuations may cause serious long-term consequences. Purging places such patients at risk for hypoglycemia because of a relative excess amount of insulin. With binge eating, patients are at risk of hyperglycemia, sometimes to the point of diabetic ketoacidosis, particularly when they do not adjust their insulin dose to respond to caloric intake. Poor glycemic control may be a clue to an underlying eating disorder (Hudson, Pope, & Jonas, 1983a; Hillard, Lobo, & Keeling, 1983; Szmukler, 1984; Rosmark et al., 1986).

In euglycemic subjects both starvation and carbohydrate deprivation may lead to reduced fasting serum glucose levels and abnormalities in glucose tolerance testing. Some authors have previously demonstrated fasting hypoglycemia in patients with anorexia nervosa as well as diabetic glucose tolerance curves in a subgroup of patients (Casper, Davis, & Pandey, 1977). Despite their normal weight, patients with bulimia nervosa also tend to have lower serum glucose levels, suggesting dietary deficiencies (Pirke, Pahl, & Schweiger, 1985). Recently, Goldbloom, Zinman, & Hicks (1989) reported low C-peptide levels in combination with normal insulin levels in patients with bulimia nervosa, suggesting both decreased insulin secretion and delayed insulin clearance. The authors hypothesize that this might reflect an adaptive mechanism to binge eating (delayed insulin clearance) and intermittent fasting (low secretion).

### Fat

After the glycogen stores have been emptied, glucose is produced from amino acids, and free fatty acids are mobilized from body fat stores and partially converted to ketone bodies, which can be utilized by brain tissue. Anorectic and normal weight bulimic patients show about the same frequency of elevated levels of B-hydroxybutyric acid. Surprisingly, elevated serum cholesterol levels have been reported frequently in patients with anorexia nervosa (Mira, Stewart, Vizzard, & Abraham, 1987). Both diminished bile acid excretion and diminished cholesterol turnover have been suggested as causative factors (Nestel, 1973).

*Protein*

In rare cases hypoproteinemia due to starvation may lead to the massive edema most frequently observed in severely anorectic patients.

*Trace Elements and Vitamins*

Elevated serum carotene levels are found in up to 72% of patients with anorexia nervosa. This may be associated with carotenodermia (Gupta, Gupta, & Haberman, 1987) and elevated B-carotene levels (Curran-Celentano, Erdman, Nelson, & Grater, 1985). Trace element, mineral, and vitamin deficiencies are surprisingly rare. The clinical picture of zinc deficiency is similar to some symptoms of anorexia nervosa, including poor skin healing and hair loss, decreased appetite and weight loss, fatigue, mood disturbance, growth retardation, delayed sexual development, and menstrual disturbance (Casper et al., 1980; Katz et al., 1987). Several authors have recommended that the diet of anorectic patients be routinely supplemented with zinc, but the effectiveness of this treatment has not been demonstrated.

*Bones*

Patients with anorexia nervosa (either restricting or bulimic) and former anorectics with current bulimia nervosa show significantly lower bone mineral density than do normal weight bulimics and controls (Andersen & LaFrance, 1990; Davis et al., 1990). These abnormalities result in an increased propensity for pathological fractures (Biller et al., 1989). An increased risk of up to seven-fold has been described (Rigotti, Neer, Skates, Herzog, & Nussbaum, 1991). Extreme low weight, prolonged amenorrhea with reduced endogenous estrogen exposure, early onset of the eating disorder, hypercortisolism, and reduced mechanical strain or relative inactivity strongly correlate with bone demineralization in anorectic patients (Davis et al., 1990; Salisbury & Mitchell, 1991). Malnutrition (calcium, protein) and alterations in parathyroid hormone, vitamin D, and growth hormone levels also might be involved. The relationship of low levels of estrogen and calcium to osteoporosis has been well documented in the menopausal female and in female athletes, confirming the role of low estrogen exposure as a cause of the low bone mineral density in patients with past or current anorexia nervosa. Two recent studies (Rigotti et al., 1991; Bachrach, Katzman, Litt, Guido, & Marcus, 1991) address prospectively the longitudinal course of bone density in patients with anorexia nervosa. Rigotti and colleagues (1991) did not find a significant change in annual bone density for the group as a whole, and there was no difference between patients with weight recovery and patients who did not attain at least 80% of their ideal body weight. Furthermore, the change of bone mineral density did not differ between women who regained their menses, took calcium or estrogen supplementation, or engaged in regular physical activity and women without any of these factors. Bachrach and colleagues (1991) found a significant positive correlation between changes in weight and changes in bone density in adolescents with anorexia nervosa, but bone density remained significantly below that of healthy girls after 1 year.

These results suggest that osteoporosis in patients with anorexia nervosa is a serious problem that is not rapidly reversed by weight regain. It is still not known after what period of time, and in what percentage of patients, bone density will completely normalize after recovery. Furthermore, the efficacy of estrogen and/or calcium supplementation in maintaining or restoring bone mineral density in these patients still needs to be established in controlled studies.

*Muscles*

Electrolyte abnormalities can cause muscle weakness or cramps. The alkaloid emetine, which is contained in ipecac, is responsible for causing muscular toxicity. Patients who abuse ipecac may show proximal muscle weakness and a waddling gait. Their muscle biopsy and electromyography may be abnormal. They may show abnormal EKGs and echocardiograms because of cardiomyopathy. Their muscle enzyme levels may be increased (serum creatine kinase) (Tolstoi, 1990).

**Renal Complications**

Renal abnormalities have been reported in up to 70% of patients with anorexia nervosa (Brotman, Stern, & Brotman, 1986). Discontinuation of diuretics may result in reflex edema formation. The use of a mild sodium restriction during the first few days following discontinuation of diuretics may be useful. Starvation may lead to low blood urea nitrogen. Dehydration, on the other hand, produces elevated blood urea nitrogen, decreased glomerular filtration rate, and decreased urinary concentrating ability, which may explain the polyuria experienced by some patients (Boag, Weerakoon, Ginsburg, Havard, & Dandona, 1985). Erratic fluctuations in plasma levels of the antidiuretic hormone arginine vasopressin (Gold, Kaye, Robertson, & Ebert, 1983) may contribute to the defect in urinary concentration in patients with anorexia nervosa. Chronic dehydration and low serum potassium may cause long-term renal damage (kaliopenic nephropathy). Renal calculi may occur (Silber & Kass, 1984; Brotman et al., 1986). Many patients show mild pyuria and hematuria, usually normalizing with hydration and refeeding (Palla & Litt, 1988).

## Endocrine Complications

Neuroendocrine symptoms and signs are common in patients with eating disorders, and have been extensively reviewed (Newman & Halmi, 1988; see Chapter 6 this volume). It has been speculated that they may reflect an underlying hypothalamic dysfunction. However, since most of the endocrine abnormalities remit with recovery, it is more likely that they result from starvation and weight loss ("nutritional hypothesis") (Fichter et al., 1988). Healthy subjects under starvation conditions develop similar neuroendocrine disturbances. The clinical manifestations of these disturbances are reviewed here; their underlying pathophysiology will be reviewed in Chapter 6.

### Hypothalamic-Pituitary-Ovarian Axis

Menstrual irregularities are among the most prominent symptoms of eating disorders in women (Pirke, Fichter, Chloud, & Doerr, 1987; Pirke, 1990). While amenorrhea is an infrequent symptom in bulimia nervosa as compared to anorexia nervosa, irregular menses is quite common. It is well established that women with anorexia nervosa and sometimes women with bulimia nervosa secrete less gonadotrophin-releasing hormone (LHRH) (Weiner, 1985), and have low plasma levels of luteinizing hormone (LH) and follicle-stimulating hormone (FSH) and the ovarian hormones estrogen and progesterone (Newman & Halmi, 1988). An immature response of LH and FSH to gonadotrophin-releasing hormones is seen in many anorectic patients, and blunted LH responses to estradiol have been found in both bulimic and anorectic subjects (Devlin et al., 1989). It is noteworthy that studies in healthy normal women show that after only 2 to 3 weeks of a 1,000 kcal diet and a weight loss of 2 to 3 kg the first effects on menstrual function can be observed (Pirke et al., 1986). Furthermore, anorectic patients metabolize estradiol, the main ovarian estrogen, differently from normal women, producing a biologically less active metabolite (Fishman & Bradlow, 1977).

In some patients with anorexia nervosa, amenorrhea precedes the onset of weight loss, and the resumption of menses does not always correlate with weight restoration.

Furthermore, many individuals with normal weight bulimia nervosa demonstrate gonadotrophin patterns similar to those of patients with anorexia nervosa. Thus, it is not clear whether menstrual irregularities are solely attributable to starvation and weight loss. The influence of psychological factors such as depression and weight phobia (Hsu, 1990), as well as nutritional deficiencies (Pirke, Sweiger, Laessle, Dickhaut, & Waechter, 1986) and the excessive exercise pattern, have been discussed as contributing factors. Chronic low estrogen secretion is associated with an increased risk of osteoporosis and fractures that might be crippling in later age. Delayed onset of puberty as well as growth retardation may be consequences of early-onset anorexia nervosa and primary amenorrhea. Reduced progesterone secretion possibly increases the risk of hormone-sensitive tumors. Oral contraceptives might be warranted for treatment-refractory patients. Furthermore, gonadal disturbance impairs fertility (Schweiger, Laessle, Fichter, & Pirke, 1988); this issue is discussed further in Chapter 8. Cystic ovarian changes can occur in anorexia nervosa and also can occur in some bulimic patients (Treasure, 1988).

## Hypothalamic-Pituitary-Thyroid Axis

Starvation results in a depression of the conversion of thyroxine ($T_4$) into triiodthyronine ($T_3$), with increased conversion to reverse $T_3$ ($rT_3$) which is the less active form of the hormone (Casper, 1986). However, thyroid-stimulating hormone (TSH) levels in anorexia nervosa are normal, and the response to an infusion of thyrotropin-releasing hormone (TRH) is also normal, although the peak response may be significantly delayed. Bulimic patients, in general, have normal $T_4$ and $T_3$ levels. With the exception of one study (Gwirtsman, Yager, Gillard, & Lerner, 1983), a blunted TSH response to TRH has not been more commonly found in subjects with bulimia nervosa than in normal controls (Kaplan, 1987b).

The metabolic changes in anorexia nervosa may contribute considerably to many of the psychovegetative complaints of these patients. Such patients exhibit several features characteristic of a hypometabolic state, including cold intolerance, bradycardia, constipation, dry skin and hair, slow relaxing reflexes, fatigue, and low basal metabolic rate. Reduced metabolic rate, which is only slowly normalized after remission, leads to weight gain even with normal caloric intake and thus reinforces the restrained eating pattern (Devlin et al., 1990). Since these changes are thought to be an adaptation to malnutrition and to respond to caloric replenishment, hormonal replacement is not indicated.

### Hypothalamic-Pituitary-Adrenal Axis

In contrast to the diminished activity of the hypothalamic-pituitary-ovarian (HPO) axis, the activity of the hypothalamic-pituitary-adrenal (HPA) axis is elevated in anorexia nervosa. Sustained hypercortisolism is one of the best characterized neuroendocrine abnormalities in anorexia nervosa (Gold et al., 1986; Gwirtsman et al., 1989). This is caused both by increased production of cortisol relative to the patient's body size, and by slowed metabolism (Hudson et al., 1983a). Furthermore, the normal diurnal variation in cortisol level is lost, and there is dexamethasone nonsuppression as well as decreased cortisol response to insulin-induced hypoglycemia. The HPA system has been less extensively evaluated in patients with bulimia nervosa. Some studies have found that 24-hour cortisol secretion and adrenocorticotrophic hormone (ACTH) levels in bulimics were similar to those in controls (Gold et al., 1986; Walsh et al., 1987b; Gwirtsman et al., 1989), while more recent studies found elevated plasma cortisol and ACTH levels with a blunted response to corticotropin-releasing hormone (CRH) in normal weight bulimic women (Mortola, Rasmussen, & Yen, 1989; Kennedy, Garfinkel, & Parienti, 1989). Cortisol nonsuppression after dexamethasone administration has also been observed in approximately 50% of patients with bulimia nervosa. This is significantly above the normal rate in studies reporting controls (Mitchell et al., 1987c). Although the significance of this finding is unclear, it may result from malabsorption of the dexamethasone (Walsh et al., 1987a).

### Growth Hormone

Fasting growth hormone levels are often elevated in patients with anorexia nervosa at low weight, probably because of a reduction of the negative feedback by somatomedin. In some studies growth hormone responses to provocative tests—such as the use of glucose loading, clonidine, or TRH—have been reported to be pathologically increased in both eating disorders (see Mitchell, 1990), whereas others have found normal challenge test results (Kaplan, Garfinkel, Warsh, & Brown, 1989). However, this is probably of little clinical consequence.

### Prolactin

Prolactin levels are usually normal in patients with eating disorders (Pirke et al., 1987; Casper et al., 1977), but TRH administration may produce impaired prolactin response in anorexia nervosa and bulimia nervosa.

### Adrenal Function

Starvation induces a reduction of noradrenergic turnover, which might contribute considerably to many of the psychovegetative complaints of anorectic and bulimic patients. Postural changes such as systolic BP decreases of 20 mmHg or more and pulse increases of more than 35 beats per minute are common in patients with anorexia nervosa, and even more frequent (80%–90%) in patients who purge regularly (Palla & Litt, 1988).

### Gastrointestinal Hormones

An impaired cholecystokinin (CCK) response to eating has been found in a pilot study of 14 bulimics (Geracioti & Liddle, 1988). This returned to normal levels after an open trial of antidepressants in a subgroup of five patients. This abnormality may have pathophysiologic significance with regard to satiety regulation in bulimia nervosa.

## Hematologic Changes

Leukopenia, anemia, and thrombocytopenia may be a consequence of dietary deficiency and may require supplementation. The anemia is usually normocytic and normochromic, but iron deficiency anemia may occur if there is chronic laxative abuse that leads to rectal bleeding. Mild anemia can be expected in 30% of cases, while leukopenia may be present in up to 50% of cases (Brotman et al., 1985). Thrombocytopenia and a deficiency of vitamin K–dependent coagulation factors may increase the bleeding tendency. Bone marrow cell suppression and in rare cases necrosis (Smith & Spivac, 1985) can accompany severe inanition. Surprisingly, there is no evidence of an increased risk of bacterial infections (Bowers & Eckert, 1978). ESR is usually low and distinguishes anorexia nervosa from most of the other diseases that cause severe weight loss. These hematologic abnormalities usually are readily reversible with nutritional replenishment, and have only rarely been described in bulimia nervosa patients.

## Neurological Complications

Cerebral hypoperfusion and a reduced seizure threshold resulting from changes in serum pH and hyponatremia may lead to epileptic seizures in rare cases. Patients with anorexia nervosa, and less frequently, with bulimia nervosa, display enlarged external CSF spaces and ventricular dilatation on cranial computed tomography (CT) scans (Krieg, Backmund, & Pirke, 1987; Krieg, Pirke, Lauer, & Backmund, 1988; Krieg, Lauer, & Pirke, 1989; Dolan, Mitchell, & Wakeling, 1988; Kiriike et al., 1990) and magnetic resonance imaging (MRI) (Hoffman et al., 1989). These are reversible to a certain degree after weight gain ("pseudoatrophy"). Positron emission tomography (PET) scan examinations have revealed significant glucose hypermetabolism in the caudate region as well as significant cortical hypermetabolism in patients with anorexia nervosa (Herholz et al., 1987). Others found abnormal hemispheric lateralization (no normal right-greater-than-left asymmetry) in patients with bulimia nervosa (Wu et al., 1990). Krieg and associates (1989) found an inverse correlation between ventricular size and the plasma levels of $T_3$, a low concentration indicating a starvation effect. However, this association could not be replicated by others (Kiriike et al., 1990). Other neurological findings in patients with eating disorders such as abnormal electroencephalograph (EEG) and sleep EEG patterns as well as increased rapid eye movement (REM) sleep latency have not been consistently replicated (Mitchell, 1983b) and need further research.

## CONCLUSION

Anorexia nervosa and bulimia nervosa are unusual among psychiatric disorders in that they are often accompanied by a variety of physical abnormalities. Most of the abnormalities are logically explainable considering the behaviors in which these patients engage, particularly the restrictive eating that leads to emaciation in anorexia nervosa. What has become strikingly clear over the last few decades is that every major organ system can develop abnormalities in either of these disorders, and that the abnormalities can vary from minor changes of academic interest to severe changes that represent life-threatening aberrations. The challenge to mental health professionals is to be aware of the possibility of these changes to ensure that patients are properly evaluated for them. The challenge to the physicians who care for these patients, be they psychiatrists or nonpsychiatric physicians, is to use the traditional tools of medicine to diagnose and treat these abnormalities, including a careful medical history, a complete physical examination, and appropriate laboratory testing. The first

TABLE 4.3.
Medical Complications of Anorexia Nervosa

| Findings in Anorexia Nervosa | Possible Mechanism | Frequency[a] | Possible Consequences | Treatment |
|---|---|---|---|---|
| *Electrolytes* | | | | |
| Electrolytes usually normal but may show low potassium, sodium, chloride, calcium, magnesium, and high or low bicarbonate | Malnutrition, purging | Less frequent than BN | For details see Table 4.4 on bulimia nervosa | May need supplementation |
| Hypophosphatemia | Refeeding with large glucose load | Rare | Cell breakdown: anemia, rhabdomyolysis seizures | Careful refeeding, phosphate supplementation |
| *Gastrointestinal* | | | | |
| Impaired taste | Vomiting, zinc deficiency? | Unclear | May cause subjective distress | Improves with recovery |
| Delayed gastric emptying | Starvation | Rare | Specific clinical symptoms | Specific treatment needed |
| Gastric or duodenal ulcer | ? | Rare | Specific clinical symptoms | Specific treatment needed |
| Acute gastric dilatation, necrosis, rupture | Rapid refeeding | Rare | Severe abdominal pain→rigid abdomen, shock→may lead to death | Surgical emergency |
| Superior mesenteric artery syndrome | Severe weight loss, loss of fat cushion surrounding the neurovascular bundle | Rare | Subjective distress, further weight loss | May require surgical intervention |
| Constipation | Starvation, laxatives, low T$_3$ | Common | May increase or lead to laxative use | Hydration, bulk type laxatives, exercise |
| Pancreatic dysfunction, pancreatitis | Rapid feeding | Rare | Specific clinical symptoms | Specific treatment needed |
| Hepatitis, increased hepatic enzymes | Starvation (nutritional), mild fatty degeneration secondary to refeeding | Rare | May increase during weight gain in treatment | Regular monitoring, usually mild and reversible |

| Complication | Etiology | Frequency | Clinical symptoms | Comment |
|---|---|---|---|---|
| *Pulmonary* | | | | |
| Pneumomediastinum, pneumothorax | starvation + osteoporosis + vomiting | Rare | Specific clinical symptoms | Specific treatment needed |
| Subcutaneous emphysema, rib fractures | | | | |
| *Cardiovascular* | | | | |
| Bradycardia ("quiet heart") | Starvation, $T_3$ deficiency | Rare | Dizziness, fainting, weakness | Improves with recovery |
| Hypotension, orthostasis | Catecholamine reduction | Up to 87% | | |
| EKG changes (low voltage, ST, T, QT changes) | Starvation, electrolyte imbalance, refeeding, cardiomyopathy | Up to 85% | Chest pain, syncopy, arrhythmias, congestive heart failure | Specific treatment needed |
| Sudden cardiac death | Starvation, hypokalemia refeeding, cardiomyopathy | Rare | | |
| Peripheral edema | Hypoproteinemia, electrolyte imbalance, rapid refeeding | 20% | May increase or lead to laxative and/or diuretic use | Monitor renal and cardiac function |
| Cardiomyopathy | Rapid refeeding | Rare | Congestive heart failure | May need specific treatment, slow weight gain regimen |
| Pericardial effusion | Unclear | Rare | | Specific treatment needed |
| Mitral valve prolapse | Unclear | Up to 40% | | Weight gain often alleviates prolapse |

*(continued)*

TABLE 4.3. (*continued*)
Medical Complications of Anorexia Nervosa

| Findings in Anorexia Nervosa | Possible Mechanism | Frequency[a] | Possible Consequences | Treatment |
|---|---|---|---|---|
| *Metabolic* | | | | |
| Fasting hypoglycemia, abnormal glucose intolerance | Starvation, hypokalemia | Common | | Improves with recovery |
| High β-hydroxybutyric acid, high free fatty acids | Starvation, lipolysis | 100% | | Improves with recovery |
| Hypocholesterolemia | Malnutrition | Rare | | |
| Hypercholesterolemia | Dietary imbalance/decreased bile acis excretion/diminished cholesterol turnover | Common | | |
| Hypoproteinemia | Starvation | Rare | Edema, anasarca | Depends on degree |
| Hypozincemia | Malnutrition | Rare | Poor skin healing, hair loss, weight loss, fatigue, menstrual disturbances; impaired taste? | Zinc supplementation? |
| Vitamin deficiencies | Malnutrition | Rare | Pellagra, scurvy | Supplementation |
| Hypercarotenemia | Unclear, carrot and vegetable intake high | Common | Yellowish skin (carotenodermia) | |
| Abnormal temperature regulation | Starvation | 100% | Cold intolerance | Improves with recovery |
| *Bones* | | | | |
| Osteoporosis, osteopenia | Malnutrition, low estrogen, high cortisol | | Short stature, pathological fractures, growth retardation, reversibility still unknown | Calcium/estrogen supplementation if chronic symptoms |

| Finding | Frequency | Cause | Clinical features | Comments |
|---|---|---|---|---|
| **Renal** | | | | |
| Elevated blood urea nitrogen, changes in urinary concentration capacity, decreased glomerular filtration rate | 70% | Dehydration, unusual unless purging, fluctuations of arginine vasopressin | May be sign of renal failure, Polyuria, polydipsia | May need specific treatment |
| Proteinuria | ? | Excessive exercising, chronic hypokalemia | May be sign of renal damage | |
| Kaliopenic nephropathy (fibrosis) | Rare | Chronic hypokalemia, dehydration | | Specific treatment needed |
| Pyuria, hematuria (mild) | ? | Dehydration | Usually mild, without clinical relevance | Improves with recovery |
| Renal calculi, kidney stones | Rare | Dehydration | | |
| **Endocrine** | | | | |
| Amenorrhea, low plasma LHRH, low plasma LH and FSH, low plasma estrogen and progesterone, blunted LH and FSH response to LHRH | 100% | Secondary or primary; related to weight loss, but may precede weight loss (in 1/3); possible other factors: exercise, depression, weight phobia | Delayed onset of puberty, skin dryness, osteoporosis, small uterus and cervix, pink and dry vaginal mucosa, breast atrophy, infertility | Estrogen supplementation? usually reversible with weight gain, but often delayed |
| Polycystic ovaries | Rare | Unclear | Unclear | |
| Low $T_3$ | Common | Starvation, preferential $rT_3$ formation | Hypometabolic state: cold intolerance, dry skin and hair, bradycardia, constipation, fatigue, slowed reflexes | Reversible by even small amount of weight gain |

(continued)

**TABLE 4.3.** *(continued)*

Medical Complications of Anorexia Nervosa

| Findings in Anorexia Nervosa | Possible Mechanism | Frequency[a] | Possible Consequences | Treatment |
|---|---|---|---|---|
| High plasma cortisol, loss of normal cortisol diurnal variation, longer half-life of cortisol, dexamethasone nonsuppression, decreased cortisol response to insulin | Starvation | 100% | Osteoporosis | Reverses with weight gain |
| High fasting growth hormone levels | Starvation, low somatomedin C | ? | Arrest of linear bone growth, increased lipolysis | |
| Erratic fluctuations of arginine vasopressin | Starvation | ? | Changes in urinary concentration capacity, partial diabetes insipidus | Delayed normalization after weight restoration |
| Low peripheral catecholamines | Starvation | ? | (Postural) hypotension | |
| *Hematologic* | | | | |
| Anemia | Starvation, low iron folate intake, rehydration, bleeding | 15% | Usually mild, without clinical relevance | Improves with recovery, rarely needs supplementation |
| Leukopenia, relative lymphocytosis | | 50% | Usually mild, without clinical relevance | |
| Bone marrow hypocellularity | | 50% | In rare cases necrosis possible | |
| Thrombocytopenia | | 30% | In rare cases possibility of bleeding tendency | |
| Reduced levels of complement factors | Vitamin K deficiency | Rare | Prolonged prothrombine time, in rare cases possibility of bleeding tendency | |

| | | % | DD for other diseases causing weight loss | |
|---|---|---|---|---|
| Very low ESR | | | | |
| *Neurological* | | | | |
| Epileptic seizures | Hypoperfusion, hyponatremia, changes in plasma pH | Up to 10% | | May need specific treatment |
| CT scan changes, PET scan changes | Starvation? | ? | Unclear | Improves with recovery |
| EEG & sleep EEG changes (conflicting) | Possibly related to starvation | Up to 43% | Unclear | |
| *Musculocutaneous* | | | | |
| Muscle weakening, muscle cramps, tetany | Electrolyte imbalance, starvation | | | Improves with correction of electrolyte imbalance and malnutrition |
| Petechiae, purpura | Thrombocytopenia, vitamin K deficiency | ? | Hemorrhage | May need supplements |
| Hair loss, brittle hair and nails, lanugo hair | Starvation | 100% | Hair loss | Improves with recovery |
| Yellowing of skin | Hypercarotenemia? | | | |
| Dry skin, cold extremities | Low $T_3$, catecholamine red | 100% | | |

[a]Frequency data derive from the following papers: Jacobs and Schneider, 1985; Brotman et al., 1985; Simmon et al., 1986; Palla and Litt, 1988.

TABLE 4.4.

Medical Complications of Bulimia Nervosa

| Findings in Anorexia LNervosa | Possible Mechanism | Frequency[a] | Possible Consequences | Treatment |
|---|---|---|---|---|
| *Electrolytes* | | | | |
| Low potassium | Vomiting, laxative and diuretic abuse | 14% | Cardiac arrest and renal failure, may be a sign of renal failure, rhabdomyolysis | IV or oral supplementation, cessation of purging, regular monitoring |
| Low sodium | Low salt intake, purging | 5% | CNS dysfunctions (rare) | May need emergency treatment |
| Low chloride | Low salt intake, purging | 24% | Makes correction of alkalosis difficult | Probability for multiple electrolyte disturbances |
| Metabolic alkalosis | Vomiting | 27% | Makes correction of hypokalemia difficult | |
| Metabolic acidosis | Laxative abuse | 8% | May be marker for laxative use | |
| Dehydration, hypovolemia | Low fluid intake, purging | Common | Hypotension, tachycardia, dizziness secondary hyperaldosteronism→promotes K loss through kidneys, may be marker for purging behavior | Rehydration, cessation of purging |
| Hypophosphatemia | Purging behavior | Rare | Anemia, rhabdomyolysis, seizures | Supplementation |
| Hypomagnesemia | Purging behavior | 20% | Cardiac arrhythmias, muscle cramps, makes correction of hypokalemia difficult | Supplementation |

| | | | | |
|---|---|---|---|---|
| Hypocalcemia | | Rare | | |
| *Gastrointestinal* | | | | |
| Impaired taste | Vomiting, damage of taste receptors (palate)? | ? | | May need specific treatment |
| Gastric and duodenal ulcer | Binge eating and vomiting | Rare | | |
| Acute gastric dilatation, necrosis, rupture | Binge eating | Rare | Severe abdominal pain→rigid abdomen, shock→may lead to death | Surgical emergency |
| Steatorrhea, gastroenteropathy | Laxatives | Rare | | |
| Esophageal tearing, perforation | Vomiting | Rare | Severe chest, abdominal, or back pain | Specific treatment needed |
| Esophagitis | Vomiting | Rare | | Improves with recovery, delayed |
| Parotid swelling | Binge eating? Vomiting? | 8% | | Reverses with cessation of vomiting |
| Increased amylase | Binge eating + vomiting | 30–60% | DD pancreatitis | Specific treatment needed |
| Ileus | Hypokalemia | Rare | | |
| Constipation | Laxatives, starvation, hypokalemia, low T₃ | Common | May increase laxative use | Hydration, bulk type laxatives, exercise |
| Cathartic colon | Chronic laxative abuse | Rare | Irreversible | May need colon resection (rare) |
| Melanosis coli, rectal bleeding | Chronic laxative abuse | | Iron deficiency anemia | Specific treatment needed |
| Pancreatitis | Binge eating, diuretic abuse? | Rare | Specific clinical symptoms | Specific treatment |
| Hepatitis | Starvation, alcohol abuse | Rare | | |
| Abnormal liver enzymes | Ipecac abuse | Rare | | |

(continued)

**TABLE 4.4.** (*continued*)
Medical Complications of Anorexia Nervosa

| Findings in Anorexia Nervosa | Possible Mechanism | Frequency[a] | Possible Consequences | Treatment |
|---|---|---|---|---|
| *Pulmonary* | | | | |
| Bradypnea | Compensation of metabolic alkalosis | | | Improves with recovery |
| Aspiration pneumonia | Aspiration of vomitus | Rare | Specific clinical symptoms | Specific treatment needed |
| Pneumomediastinum | Vomiting | Rare | Specific clinical symptoms | Specific treatment needed |
| *Cardiovascular* | | | | |
| Bradycardia | Starvation, low $T_3$ | ? | Dizziness, weakness | Improves with recovery |
| Hypotension, orthostasis | Catecholamine reduction | | | |
| EKG changes ("U" wave, ST, T, QT changes) | Electrolyte disturbance, ipecac, cardiomyopathy, heart failure | Common | Serious arrhythmias, congestive heart failure | Specific treatment needed |
| Sudden cardiac death | Hypokalemia, ipecac use | Rare | | |
| Peripheral edema | Usually from rebound fluid retention after purging | Common | May increase laxative and/or diuretic abuse | Monitor cardiac and renal function |
| Cardiomyopathy, myocarditis | Ipecac abuse | Rare | May lead to death | Specific treatment needed |
| Mitral valve prolapse | Unclear | Rare | Unclear | |
| *Metabolic* | | | | |
| Fasting hypoglycemia | Starvation | ? | | Improves with recovery |
| High β-hydroxybutyric acid, high free fatty acids | Starvation, lipolysis | Common | | Improves with recovery |
| Hypercholesterolemia | High-cholesterol binge foods? | ? | Atherosclerosis? | |
| Hypoproteinemia | Starvation | Rare | Edema | |
| Hypercarotenemia | Unclear, carrot and vegetable intake high | Rare | Unclear | |
| Abnormal temperature regulation | Starvation | Rare | Cold intolerance | |

| | | | | |
|---|---|---|---|---|
| *Renal* | | | | |
| Low blood urea nitrogen | Starvation | | | Improves with recovery |
| High blood urea nitrogen, decreased glomerular filtration rate | Renal function impairment, usually result of chronic purging | | May be sign of renal failure, polyuria, polydipsia | Specific treatment |
| Proteinuria | Excessive exercising, chronic hypokalemia | Rare | | Specific treatment needed |
| Kaliopenic nephropathy (fibrosis) | Chronic hypokalemia | | | |
| Pyuria, hematuria | Dehydration | | Usually mild, no clinical relevance | Rehydration |
| *Endocrine* | | | | |
| Menstrual irregularities | Semistarvation, correlates with body weight | 25% | | Usually reversible with recovery |
| Low LH and FSH | | ? | | |
| Low estradiol and progesterone | | ? | | |
| Dexamethasone nonsuppression | Malabsorption? depression? | 50% | | |
| Blunted GH response to challenge tests | ? | Rare | Unclear | |
| Elevated fasting prolactin levels | ? | Rare | Unclear | |
| Low $T_3$ | Semistarvation, preferential $T_3$ formation | ? | Hypometabolic state | Rapidly reversible with recovery |
| Low CCK response to eating | Pathophysiology of BN? needs to be confirmed | ? | Disturbed satiety mechanism | |
| *Hematologic* | | | | |
| Anemia | Dietary deficiency, bleeding | Rare | | May need supplements |

*(continued)*

TABLE 4.4. *(continued)*
Medical Complications of Anorexia Nervosa

| Findings in Anorexia Nervosa | Possible Mechanism | Frequency[a] | Possible Consequences | Treatment |
|---|---|---|---|---|
| *Neurological* | | | | |
| Epileptic seizures | Malnutrition, electrolyte imbalance | Rare | | May need specific treatment |
| CT scan changes | Starvation? | ? | | Improves with recovery |
| PET scan changes | | | | |
| EEG changes (conflicting) | Unclear | Up to 60% | Unclear | |
| *Musculocutaneous* | | | | |
| Muscle weakening, rhabdomyolysis | Electrolyte imbalance, ipecac abuse | | | Correction of underlying problem |
| Calluses on dorsum of dominant hand (Russell's sign) | Induce gag reflex, repeated abrasion | Common | None | |
| *Dental* | | | | |
| Enamel erosions | Vomiting | 38% | | Alkaline rinses recommended |
| Caries | Carbohydrate rich binge food | | | |
| Periodontal disease | | | | |

[a]Frequency data derive from the following papers: Mitchell et al., 1983a, Jacobs and Schneider, 1985; Brotman et al., 1985; Simmon et al., 1986; Palla and Litt, 1988.

task in dealing with these patients is medical stabilization. This is requisite before our other assessments and treatments can be properly utilized.

## REFERENCES

Abdu, R. A., Garritano, D., & Culver, O. (1987). Acute gastric necrosis in anorexia nervosa and bulimia. *Archives of Surgery, 122,* 830–832.

Altshuler, B. D., Dechow, P. C., Waller, D. A., & Hardy, B. W. (1990). An investigation of the oral pathologies occurring in bulimia nervosa. *International Journal of Eating Disorders, 9,* 191–199.

Andersen, A. E., & La France, N. (1990). Persisting osteoporosis in bulimia nervosa patients with past anorexia nervosa [Abstract #191]. *Fourth International Conference on Eating Disorders.* New York, April 27–29.

Bachrach, L. K., Katzman, D. K., Litt, I. F., Guido, D., & Marcus, R. (1991). Recovery from osteopenia in adolescent girls with anorexia nervosa. *Journal of Clinical Endocrinology and Metabolism, 72,* 602–606.

Biller, B. M. K., Saxe, V., Herzog, D. B., Rosenthal, D. I., Holzman, S., & Klibanski, A. (1989). Mechanisms of osteoporosis in adult and adolescent women with anorexia nervosa. *Journal of Clinical Endocrinology and Metabolism, 68,* 548–554.

Boag, F., Weerakoon, J., Ginsburg, J., Havard, C. W. H., & Dandona, P. (1985). Diminished creatinine clearance in anorexia nervosa: Reversal with weight gain. *Journal of Clinical Pathology, 38,* 60–63.

Bo-Linn, G. W., Santa Ana, C. A., Morowski, S. G., & Fordtran, J. S. (1983). Purging and calorie absorption in bulimic patients and normal women. *Annals of Internal Medicine, 99,* 14–17.

Bowers, T. K., & Eckert, E. (1978). Leukopenia in anorexia nervosa. *Archives of Internal Medicine, 138,* 1520–1523.

Brotman, A. W., Stern, T. A., & Brotman, D. L. (1986). Renal disease and dysfunction in two patients with anorexia nervosa. *Journal of Clinical Psychiatry, 47,* 433–434.

Brotman, A. W., Rigotti, N., & Herzog, D. B. (1985). Medical complications of eating disorders: Outpatient evaluation and management. *Comprehensive Psychiatry, 26,* 258–272.

Casper, R. (1986). The pathophysiology of anorexia nervosa and bulimia nervosa. *Annual Review of Nutrition, 6,* 299–316.

Casper, R. C., Kirschner, B., Sandstead, H. H., Jacob, R. A., & Davis, J. M.

(1980). An evaluation of trace metals, vitamins, and taste function in anorexia nervosa. *American Journal of Clinical Nutrition, 33*, 1801–1808.

Casper, R. C., Davis, J. M., & Pandey, G. N. (1977). The effects of the nutritional status and weight changes on hypothalamic function tests in anorexia nervosa. In R. A. Vigersky (Ed.), *Anorexia nervosa* (pp. 137–147). New York: Raven Press.

Ceuller, R. E., & VanThiel, D. H. (1986). Gastrointestinal consequences of the eating disorders: Anorexia nervosa and bulimia. *American Journal of Gastroenterology, 81*, 1113–1124.

Comerci, G. D. (1990). Medical complications of anorexia nervosa and bulimia nervosa. *Medical Clinics of North America, 74*, 1293–1310.

Curran-Celentano, J., Erdman, J. W., Nelson, R. A., & Grater, S. J. E. (1985). Alterations in vitamin A and thyroid hormone status in anorexia nervosa and associated disorders. *American Journal of Clinical Nutrition, 42*, 1183–1191.

Davis, K. M., Pearson, P. H., Huseman, C. A., Greger, N. G., Kimmel, D. K., & Recker, R. R. (1990). Reduced bone mineral in patients with eating disorders. *Bone, 11*, 143–147.

Devlin, M. J., Walsh, B. T., Kral, J. G., Heysfield, S. B., Pi-Sunyer, F. X., & Dantzic, S. (1990). Metabolic abnormalities in bulimia nervosa. *Archives of General Psychiatry, 47*, 144–148.

Devlin, M. J., Walsh, B. T., Katz, J. L., Roose, S. P., Linkie, D. M., Wright, L., Van de Wiele, R., & Glassman, A. H. (1989). Hypothalamic-pituitary-gonadal function in anorexia nervosa and bulimia. *Psychiatry Research, 28*, 11–24.

Dolan, R. J., Mitchell, J., & Wakeling, A. (1988). Structural brain changes in patients with anorexia nervosa. *Psychological Medicine, 18*, 349–353.

Dubois, A., Gross, H. A., Ebert, M. H., & Castell, D. O. (1979). Altered gastric emptying and secretion in primary anorexia nervosa. *Gastroenterology, 77*, 319–323.

Fichter, M. M., Pirke, K. M., Poellinger, J., Wolfram, G., & Brunner, E. (1988). Restricted caloric intake causes neuroendocrine disturbances in bulimia. In K. M. Pirke, W. Vandereycken, & D. Ploog (Eds.), *The psychobiology of bulimia nervosa* (pp. 42–56). Berlin, Heidelberg: Springer-Verlag.

Fichter, M. M., Pirke, K. M., & Holsboer, F. (1986). Weight loss causes neuroendocrine disturbances: Experimental study in healthy starving subjects. *Psychiatry Research, 17*, 61–72.

Fishman, J., & Bradlow, H. L. (1977). Effect of malnutrition on the metabolism of sex hormones in man. *Clinical Pharmacology and Therapeutics, 22*, 721–728.

Gavish, D., Eisenberg, S., Berry, E. M., Kleinman, Y., Witztum, E., Norman, J., & Leitersdorf, E. (1987). Bulimia: An underlying behavioral disorder in hyperlipidemic pancreatitis: A prospective multidisciplinary approach. *Archives of Internal Medicine, 147*, 705–708.

Geracioti, T. D., & Liddle, R. A. (1988). Impaired cholecystokinin secretion in bulimia nervosa. *New England Journal of Medicine, 319*, 683–688.

Gold, P. W., Gwirtsman, H., Avgerinos, P. C., Nieman, L. K., Gallucci, W. T., Kaye, W., Jimerson, D., Ebert, M., Rittmaster, R., Loriaux, D. L., & Chrousos, G. P. (1986). Abnormal hypothalamic-pituitary-adrenal function in anorexia nervosa. *New England Journal of Medicine, 314*, 1335–1342.

Gold, P. W., Kaye, W., Robertson, G. L., & Ebert, M. (1983). Abnormalities in plasma and cerebrospinal-fluid arginine vasopressin in patients with anorexia nervosa. *New England Journal of Medicine, 308*, 1117–1123.

Goldbloom, D., Zinman, B., & Hicks, L. (1989). The baseline metabolic state in bulimia nervosa: Abnormality and adaptation. *Psychosomatic Medicine, 51*, 246.

Gross, M. (1983). Aspects of bulimia. *Cleveland Clinical Quarterly, 50*, 19–25.

Gryboski, J., Hillemeier, C., Kocoshis, S., Anyan, W., & Seashore, J. S. (1980). Refeeding pancreatitis in malnourished children. *Journal of Pediatrics, 97*, 441–4434.

Gupta, M. A., Gupta, A. K., & Haberman, H. F. (1987). Dermatologic signs in anorexia nervosa and bulimia nervosa. *Archives of Dermatology, 123*, 1386–1390.

Gwirtsman, H. E., Kaye, W. H., George, D. T., Jimerson, D. C., Ebert, M. H., & Gold, P. W. (1989). Central and peripheral ACTH and cortisol levels in anorexia and bulimia. *Archives of General Psychiatry, 46*, 61–69.

Gwirtsman, H. E., Roy-Byrne, P., Yager, J., & Gerner, R. H. (1983). Neuroendocrine abnormalities in bulimia. *American Journal of Psychiatry, 140*, 559–563.

Gwirtsman, H. E., Yager, J., Gillard, B. K., & Lerner, L. (1986). Serum amylase and its isoenzymes in normal weight bulimia. *International Journal of Eating Disorders, 5*, 255–361.

Hall, R. C. W., Hoffman, R. S., Beresford, T. P., Wooley, B., Tice, L., & Hall, A. K. (1988). Hypomagnesemia in patients with eating disorders. *Psychosomatics, 29*, 264–272.

Halmi, K. A., & Falk, J. R. (1981). Common physiological changes in anorexia nervosa. *International Journal of Eating Disorders, 1*, 16–27.

Harris, R. T. (1983). Bulimarexia and related serious eating disorders with medical complications. *Annals of Internal Medicine, 99*, 800–807.

Herholz, K., Krieg, J. C., Emrich, H. M., Pawlik, G., Beil, C., Pirke, K. M., Pahl, J. J., Wagner, R., Wienhard, K., Ploog, D., & Heiss, W. D. (1987). Regional cerebral glucose metabolism in anorexia nervosa measured by positron emission tomography. *Biological Psychiatry, 22*, 43–51.

Hillard, J. R., Lobo, M. C., & Keeling, R. P. (1983). Bulimia and diabetes: A potentially life-threatening combination. *Psychosomatics, 24*, 292–295.

Hoffman, G. W., Ellinwood, E. H., Rockwell, W. J. K., Herfkens, R. J., Nishita, J. K., & Guthrie, L. F. (1989). Cerebral atrophy in anorexia nervosa: A pilot study. *Biological Psychiatry, 26*, 321–324.

Hudson, J. I., Hudson, M. S., & Wentworth, S. M. (1983b). Self-induced glycosuria: A novel method of purging in bulimia. *Journal of the American Medical Association, 249*, 2501.

Hudson, J. I., Pope, H. G., & Jonas, J. M. (1983a). Hypothalamic-pituitary-adrenal axis hyperactivity in bulimia. *Psychiatry Research, 8*, 111–117.

Hutson, W. R., & Wald, A. (1990). Gastric emptying in patients with bulimia nervosa and anorexia nervosa. *American Journal of Gastroenterology, 85*, 41–46.

Hsu, L. K. S. (1990). *Eating Disorders*. New York: Guilford Press.

Isner, J. M., Roberts, W. C., Heymsfield, S. B., & Yager, J. (1985). Anorexia nervosa and sudden death. *Annals of Internal Medicine, 102*, 49–52.

Jacobs, M. B., & Schneider, J. A. (1985). Medical complications of bulimia: A prospective evaluation. *Quarterly Journal of Medicine, 214*, 177–182.

Johnson, G. L., Humphries, L. L., Shirley, P. B., Mazzoleni, A., & Noonan, J. A. (1986). Mitral valve prolapse in patients with anorexia nervosa and bulimia. *Archives of Internal Medicine, 146*, 1525–1529.

Jonas, J. M., & Mickely, D. (1990). Elevated serum aldosterone: A possible marker for purging behavior [Abstract #195]. *Fourth International Conference on Eating Disorders*. New York, April 27–29.

Kaplan, A. S., Garfinkel, P. E., Warsh, J. J., & Brown, G. M. (1989). Clonidine challenge test in bulimia nervosa. *International Journal of Eating Disorders, 8*, 425–435.

Kaplan, A. S. (1987a). Hyperamylasemia and bulimia: A clinical review. *International Journal of Eating Disorders, 6*, 537–543.

Kaplan, A. S. (1987b). Thyroid function in bulimia. In J. I. Hudson & H. G. Pope (Eds.), *The psychobiology of bulimia* (pp. 15–28). Washington, DC: American Psychiatric Press.

Katz, R. L., Keen, C. L., Litt, I. F., Hurley, L. S., Kellam-Harrison, K. M., & Glader, L. J. (1987). Zinc deficiency in anorexia nervosa. *Journal of Adolescent Health Care, 8*, 400–406.

Kennedy, S. H., Garfinkel, P. E., Parienti, V., Costa, D., & Brown, G. M. (1989). Changes in melatonin levels but not cortisol levels are associated with depression in patients with eating disorders. *Archives of General Psychiatry, 46*, 73–78.

Keys, A., Brozek, J., Henschel, A., Mickelsen, O., & Taylor, H. L. (1950). *The biology of human starvation*. Minneapolis: University of Minnesota Press.

Kiriike, N., Nishiwaki, S., Nagata, T., Inoue, Y., Inoue, K., & Kawakita, Y.

(1990). Ventricular enlargement in normal weight bulimia. *Acta Psychiatrica Scandinavica, 82,* 264–266.

Krieg, J. C., Lauer, C., & Pirke, K. M. (1989). Structural brain abnormalities in patients with bulimia nervosa. *Psychiatry Research, 27,* 39–48.

Krieg, J. C., Pirke, K. M., Lauer, C., & Backmund, H. (1988). Endocrine, metabolic, and cranial computed tomographic findings in anorexia nervosa. *Biological Psychiatry, 23,* 377–387.

Krieg, J. C., Backmund, H., & Pirke, K. M. (1987). Cranial computed tomography findings in bulimia. *Acta Psychiatrica Scandinavica, 75,* 144–149.

Larsen, K., Jensen, B. S., & Axelsen, F. (1983). Perforation and rupture of the esophagus. *Scandinavian Journal of Thoracic and Cardiovascular Surgery, 17,* 311–316.

Levine, P. A., Falko, J. M., Dixon, K., Gallup, E. M., & Saunders, W. (1980). Benign parotid enlargement in bulimia. *Annals of Internal Medicine, 93,* 827–829.

McAnarney, E. R., Greydanus, D. E., Campanella, V. A., & Hoekelman, R. A. (1983). Rib fractures and anorexia nervosa. *Journal of Adolescent Health Care, 4,* 40–43.

Meyers, D. G., Starke, H., Pearson, P. H., & Wilken, M. K. (1986). Mitral valve prolapse in patients with anorexia nervosa. *Annals of Internal Medicine, 105,* 384–385.

Mira, M., Stewart, P. M., Vizzard, J., & Abraham, S. (1987). Biochemical abnormalities in anorexia nervosa and bulimia. *Annals of Clinical Biochemistry, 24,* 29–35.

Mitchell, J. E. (1990). *Bulimia nervosa.* Minneapolis: University of Minnesota Press.

Mitchell, J. E., & Boutacoff, L. I. (1986). Laxative abuse complicating bulimia: Medical and treatment implications. *International Journal of Eating Disorders, 5,* 325–334.

Mitchell, J. E., Hatsukami, D., Eckert, E. D., & Pyle, R. L. (1985). Characteristics of 275 patients with bulimia. *American Journal of Psychiatry, 142,* 482–485.

Mitchell, J. E., Hatsukami, D., Pyle, R. L., Eckert, E. D., & Boutacoff, L. I. (1987a). Metabolic acidosis as a marker for laxative abuse in patients with bulimia. *International Journal of Eating Disorders, 6,* 557–560.

Mitchell, J. E., Hosfield, W., & Pyle, R. L. (1983b). EEG findings in patients with the bulimia syndrome. *International Journal of Eating Disorders, 2,* 17–23.

Mitchell, J. E., Pomeroy, C., Seppala, M., & Huber, M. (1988). Pseudo-Bartter's syndrome, diuretic abuse, idiopathic edema and eating disorders. *International Journal of Eating Disorders, 7,* 225–237.

Mitchell, J. E., Pyle, R. L., Eckert, E. D., Hatsukami, D., & Lentz, R. (1983a).

Electrolyte and other physiological abnormalities in patients with bulimia. *Psychological Medicine, 13,* 273–278.

Mitchell, J. E., Pyle, R. L., & Miner, R. A. (1987b). Gastric dilatation as a complication of bulimia. *Psychosomatics, 23,* 96–97.

Mitchell, J. E., Seim, H. C., Colon, E., & Pomeroy, C. (1987c). Medical complications medical management of bulimia. *Annals of Internal Medicine, 107,* 71–77.

Mortola, J. F., Rasmussen, D. D., & Yen, S. S. C. (1989). Alterations of the adrenocorticotropin-cortisol axis in normal weight bulimic women: Evidence for a central mechanism. *Journal of Clinical Endocrinology and Metabolism, 68,* 517–522.

Nestel, P. J. (1973). Cholesterol metabolism in anorexia nervosa and hypercholesterolemia. *Journal of Clinical Endocrinology and Metabolism, 38,* 325–328.

Newman, M. M., & Halmi, K. A. (1988). The endocrinology of anorexia nervosa and bulimia nervosa. *Endocrinology and Metabolism Clinics of North America, 17,* 195–212.

Overby, K. J., & Litt, I. F. (1988). Mediastinal emphysema in an adolescent with anorexia nervosa and self-induced emesis. *Pediatrics, 8,* 134–136.

Palla, B., & Litt, I. F. (1988). Medical complications of eating disorders in adolescents. *Pediatrics, 81,* 613–623.

Palmer, E. P., & Guay, A. T. (1986). Reversible myopathy secondary to abuse of ipecac in patients with major eating disorders. *New England Journal of Medicine, 313,* 457–459.

Pirke, K. M. (1990). Menstrual cycle and neuroendocrine disturbances of the gonadal axis in bulimia nervosa. In M. M. Fichter (Ed.), *Bulimia nervosa: Basic research, diagnosis & therapy* (pp. 258–269). Chichester, England: John Wiley.

Pirke, K. M., Fichter, M. M., Chloud, C., & Doerr, P. (1987). Disturbances of the menstrual cycle in bulimia nervosa. *Clinical Endocrinology, 27,* 245–251.

Pirke, K. M., Pahl, J., & Schweiger, U. (1985). Metabolic and endocrine indices of starvation in bulimia: A comparison with anorexia nervosa. *Psychiatry Research, 14,* 13–39.

Pirke, K. M., Schweiger, U., Laessle, R., Dickhaut, B., & Waechter, M. (1986). Dieting influences the menstrual cycle: Vegetarian versus nonvegetarian diet. *Fertility and Sterility, 46,* 1083–1088.

Pomeroy, C., & Mitchell, J. D. (1989). Medical complications and management of eating disorders. *Psychiatric Annals, 19,* 488–493.

Rigotti, N. A., Neer, R. M., Skates, S. J., Herzog, D. B., & Nussbaum, S. R. (1991). The clinical course of osteoporosis in anorexia nervosa. *Journal of the American Medical Association, 265,* 1133–1138.

Robinson, P. H., Clarke, M., & Barrett, J. (1988). Determinants of delayed gastric emptying in anorexia nervosa and bulimia nervosa. *Gut, 29,* 458–464.

Rodin, J., Bartoshuk, L., Peterson, C., & Schank, D. (1990). Bulimia and taste: Possible interactions. *Journal of Abnormal Psychology, 99,* 32–39.

Rosmark, B., Berne, C., Holmgren, S., Lago, C., Renholm, G., & Sohlberg, S. (1986). Eating disorders in patients with insulin-dependent diabetes mellitus. *Journal of Clinical Psychiatry, 47,* 547–550.

Russell, G. (1979). Bulimia nervosa: An ominous variant of anorexia nervosa. *Psychological Medicine, 9,* 429–448.

Salisbury, J. J., & Mitchell, J. E. (1991). Bone mineral density and anorexia nervosa in women. *American Journal of Psychiatry, 148,* 768–774.

Saul, S. H., Dekker, A., & Watson, C. G. (1981). Acute gastric dilatation with infarction and perforation. *Gut, 22,* 978–983.

Schocken, D. D., Holloway, J. D., & Powers, P. S. (1989). Weight loss and the heart. *Archives of Internal Medicine, 149,* 877.

Schweiger, U., Laessle, R. G., Fichter, M. M., & Pirke, K. M. (1988). Consequences of dieting at normal weight: Implications for the understanding and treatment of bulimia. In K. M. Pirke, W. Vandereycken, & D. Ploog (Eds.), *The psychobiology of bulimia nervosa* (pp. 74–82). Berlin, Heidelberg: Springer-Verlag.

Silber, T. J., & Kass, E. J. (1984). Anorexia nervosa and nephrolithiasis. *Journal of Adolescent Health Care, 5,* 50–52.

Simmons, M. S., Grayden, S. K., & Mitchell, J. E. (1986). The need for psychiatric-dental liaison in the treatment of bulimia. *American Journal of Psychiatry, 143,* 783–784.

Smith, R. R. L., & Spivac, J. L. (1985). Marrow cell necrosis in anorexia nervosa and involuntary starvation. *British Journal of Hematology, 60,* 525–530.

Sours, J., & Vorhaus, L. (1981). Superior mesenteric artery syndrome in anorexia nervosa: A case report. *American Journal of Psychiatry, 138,* 519–520.

Szmukler, G. I., Young, G. P., Lichtenstein, M., & Andrews, J. T. (1990). A serial study of gastric emptying in anorexia nervosa and bulimia. *Australian and New Zealand Journal of Medicine, 20,* 220–225.

Szmukler, G. I. (1984). Anorexia nervosa and bulimia in diabetics. *Journal of Psychosomatic Research, 28,* 365–369.

Tolstoi, L. G. (1990). Ipecac-induced toxicity in eating disorders. *International Journal of Eating Disorders, 9,* 371–375.

Treasure, J. L. (1988). The ultrasonographic features in anorexia nervosa and bulimia nervosa: A simplified method of monitoring hormonal states during weight gain. *Journal of Psychosomatic Research, 32,* 624–634.

Waldholtz, B. D., & Andersen, A. E. (1988). Hypophosphatemia during starvation in anorexia nervosa. *International Journal of Eating Disorders, 4,* 551–555.

Walsh, B. T., Lo, E. S., Cooper, T., Lindy, D. C., Roose, S. P., Gladis, M., & Glassman, A. H. (1987a). Dexamethasone suppression test and plasma dexamethasone levels in bulimia. *Archives of General Psychiatry, 44,* 797–800.

Walsh, B. T., Roose, S. P., Katz, J. L., Dysenfurth, I., Wright, L., Van de Wiele, R., & Glassman, A. H. (1987b). Hypothalamic-pituitary-adrenal-cortical activity in anorexia nervosa and bulimia. *Psychoneuroendocrinology, 12,* 131–140.

Walsh, B. T., Croft, C. B., & Katz, J. L. (1981). Anorexia nervosa and salivary gland enlargement. *International Journal of Psychiatry in Medicine, 11,* 255–261.

Weiner, H. (1985). The physiology of eating disorders. *International Journal of Eating Disorders, 4,* 347–388.

Weinsier, R. L., Krumdieck, P. H., & Krumdieck, C. L. (1981). Death resulting from overzealous total parenteral nutrition: The refeeding syndrome revisited. *American Journal of Clinical Nutrition, 34,* 393–399.

Wu, C. J., Hagman, J., Buchsbaum, M. S., Blinder, B., Derrfler, M., Tai, W. Y., Hazlett, E., & Sicotte, N. (1990). Greater left cerebral hemispheric metabolism in bulimia assessed by positron emission tomography. *American Journal of Psychiatry, 147,* 309–312.

# 5

# Dental Aspects of Anorexia Nervosa and Bulimia Nervosa

## R. John McComb
### B.D.S., M.SC., FRCD(C)

The presentation of anorexia nervosa or bulimia nervosa to the dentist as a result of referral from a psychiatrist, psychologist, or eating disorders clinic will circumvent the diagnostic problems associated with the condition. Under these circumstances, the dentist may assume a willingness, or at least a resignation, on the part of the patient about acknowledging the condition and the implications for the dentition. Dentists are increasingly aware, however, that patients may come to them for dental care because of pain related to excessive tooth erosion due to vomiting. Rather than acknowledge the cause, the bulimic patients may be inclined to obfuscate the history by means of elaborate excuses. Thus, confronted with a patient who is determined to thwart the objectives of taking a clinical history, the dentist must rely on signs and symptoms as the key to the diagnosis of anorexia or bulimia nervosa. There is no one diagnostic feature of the head or mouth that is pathognomonic for anorexia or bulimia nervosa but rather an array of evidence, which, taken in aggregate, may help the dentist to reach the probable diagnosis. Hopefully, the dentist can begin the task of encouraging the patient to seek additional help.

## SIGNS OF THE HEAD AND NECK

The dentist will normally take a medical and dental history during the process of a new patient examination, and record any abnormalities of the face, head, and neck before beginning a detailed examination of the mouth. It is during this process that the first signs of anorexia or bulimia nervosa may be observed.

The aphorism "that those who do not know history are doomed to repeat it" is particularly apt for practitioners interested in anorexia and bulimia. A historical account of the disease is provided (Garfinkel and Garner, 1982). This details how Gull's original description of apepsia hysterica in 1868 (later renamed anorexia nervosa) became confused with another disease, newly described by Simmonds in 1914. In the latter condition destruction of the adenohypophysis is the primary feature and is associated with cachexia. The subsequent misreporting of anorexia nervosa as Simmonds' disease during the 1920s and 1930s persisted until 1939, when Sheldon cited a paper by Kylin of Sweden as "a monograph on Simmonds' disease which will always be one of the more important papers on anorexia nervosa" (Sheldon, 1939, p. 739). He attributed the delayed appreciation of Gull's recognition of anorexia nervosa to German and Swedish workers being unaware of the English language description. In fact, Sheldon pointed out that the disease had been "rediscovered and renamed four or five times after 1930."

Garfinkel and Garner described the endocrine abnormalities in anorexia nervosa and helped explain the manifestations of the disease. Many of these may be observed by the dentist. Appreciation of the presentations of anorexia and bulimia nervosa should help avoid investigations for hormone irregularities intended to support a diagnosis of Simmonds' disease.

### Thyroid Function

In anorexic and anorexic bulimic patients, the adaptive response of the thyroid to starvation may resemble the euthyroid sick syndrome. There is a demonstrated decreased peripheral conversion of thyroxine to triiodothyronine (Moshang & Utiger, 1977). This is reversible upon cessation of starvation. The effects of the adaptive hypothyroidism can give rise to cold intolerance; dry, brittle, and fine hair; dry skin; bradycardia; and hypercarotenemia, all of which can be recognized by the observant dentist. (These changes are discussed in more detail in Chapters 4 and 6.)

## Hirsutism

The full constellation of endocrine irregularities encountered in ano-rexia nervosa is beyond the scope of the dentist, but increased facial hair or "peach fuzz" is a sign that the dentist should recognize (Brady, 1980). Although lanugo hair is a late manifestation in about 20% of cases and is thus not considered helpful as a criterion for diagnosis (Askevold, 1983), it should be remembered that many of the bulimic patients who seek help because of a dental problem do so at a late stage. It would be expected that this subgroup of bulimic patients would demonstrate facial hair more fre-quently. Sheldon (1939) also noted that the presence of increased hair growth separates Simmonds' disease from starvation and anorexia nervosa.

## Parotid Enlargement

Parotid swelling may occur in other disorders, such as diabetes and alco-holism, and in cases of starvation, as seen with soldiers in prison camps (Katsilambros, 1961). The swelling has been referred to as "nutritional mumps" (Batsakis & McWhirter, 1972). Benign parotid enlargement in anorexia nervosa is well described in the literature (Levin, Faldo, Dixon, Gallup, & Saunders, 1980; Walsh, Croft, & Katz, 1981–82) and in Chapter 4. It is worth noting, however, that the parotids are not affected exclusively and that the submandibular glands may also be involved (Kriens, Schmidt, Anders, & Horms, 1975). As with many of the orofacial signs of anorexia and bulimia nervosa, the differential diagnosis of bilaterally enlarged sali-vary glands should be considered. In the case of asymptomatic bilateral enlargement, this may include Sjögren's disease, lymphocytic infiltrates, sarcoidosis, or other granulomatous disorders. Although the swelling is usu-ally painless, it has also been reported to be painful and tender over many months (Hasler, 1982). This raises the question of whether biopsy is justi-fied to aid diagnosis. The histological changes that have been described by Batsakis and McWhirter (1972) are increased size of individual acinic cells with corresponding increase in secretory granules, fatty deposition, and fibrosis in the absence of inflammatory infiltrate. Since these changes are not specific, it seems overzealous to recommend biopsy in the presence of other diagnostic features. Another objective change is the "leafless tree" pattern seen in sialography by Duplessis (1956) and Hasler (1982).

The literature presents differing figures on the incidence of salivary gland swelling; for instance, over half of a series of 275 patients were reported as being affected by "puffy cheeks" (Mitchell, Matsukami, Eckert, & Pyle, 1985). A more stringent criterion of palpable enlargement was noted in only 8% of a series of 39 bulimic patients by Jacobs and Schneider (1985), although serum amylase was elevated in 62% of these patients. It would seem, therefore, that patients' subjective feeling may precede swelling that is evident to the clinician. This is noteworthy since the puffiness or swelling may be reported by the patient, the anorexic being particularly aware of body "fat." The dentist should be aware of this sign, which may have escaped observation during routine or even specific examination. The evidence suggests that this is not a transient swelling and that it may persist for many years (Hasler, 1982), even after a return to normal eating.

## ORAL COMPLICATIONS OF ANOREXIA AND BULIMIA NERVOSA

### Soft Tissues

Dehydration is a feature common to both anorexia and bulimia nervosa and may result from mechanisms ranging from reduced water intake to erratic vasopressin secretion with diabetes insipidus–like polyuria (Gold, Kaye, Robertson, & Evert, 1983). This dehydration may be exacerbated by the unsupervised use of laxatives and diuretics, with subsequent hypokalemia. The added effect of vomiting in the bulimic will aggravate the electrolyte imbalance. Dehydration causes dryness of the mouth, which may be evident on clinical examination as thick, frothy saliva or visibly dry mucosa. The dry mouth may also be exacerbated by anxiety or depression.

The lips may be cracked and dry, with occasional fissures at the angles (angular cheilitis). The fissured angles are a feature of vitamin B deficiency, and this may be a specific example of perlèche secondary to dietary insufficiency. A common cause of angular cheilitis in dental practice is increased moisture due to deep folds or a licking habit, which in turn predisposes to infection with *Candida albicans*. The possibility of candidal infection should not be overlooked in the anorexic or bulimic patient.

### Intraoral Changes Secondary to Vomiting

Bulimic anorexics and bulimics with sufficient exposure to gastric contents will present a range of oral features suggestive of their condition. The soft tissues may exhibit erythema, especially of the palate, pharynx, and gingiva (Abrams & Ruff, 1986). A distinct erythematous line associated with the marginal palatal gingiva of the maxillary teeth is evident in patients who continue to vomit. This may be accompanied by symptoms of burning or sore mouth and tongue (Harrison, George, & Cheatham, 1984).

The most obvious signs in advanced cases are those involving the teeth. Damage to teeth in patients with eating disorders has been documented in the literature since the 1930s (Bargen & Austin, 1937; Holst & Lange, 1939) and with increasing frequency over the last two decades (Allan, 1969; House, Grisuis, Bliziotes, & Licht, 1981; Andrews, 1982; and many others). Several series of patients with dental complications have been presented (Hellstrom, 1974, 1977; Hurst, Lacy, & Crisp, 1977; Roberts & Li, 1987). The loss of tooth substance may be considered in three progressive stages:

1. Erosion of enamel
2. Erosion and attrition of enamel and dentin
3. Loss of vertical height of tooth

### Erosion of Enamel

The initial changes are subtle and difficult to measure accurately without computerized superimposition imaging techniques. Patients who seek routine dental treatment early in the course of their bulimia are unlikely to arouse the suspicion of the dentist even under the closest clinical scrutiny.

The first observable sign is a replacement of natural tooth surface character with an unnaturally smooth and dull appearance. This is the manifestation of loss of developmental ridges of enamel. As the enamel erosion continues, the more yellow color of the underlying dentin may impart its hue to the affected teeth. This deepening color becomes clinically apparent as the translucency of the ever-thinning enamel reveals the yellowness from the dentin. As the change in teeth becomes noticeable, care must be taken to record the distribution of the changes and thus distinguish vomiting-induced erosion from that from other causes (see Differential Diagnosis of Acid Erosion, following).

The palatal aspect of the maxillary incisors and canines is the area that is most noticeable and the most characteristic of bulimia or rumination. This may be seen with a small mirror and light without special dental equipment. The lingual and palatal surfaces of the posterior teeth are also affected but are more difficult to observe. The occlusal surfaces of the molars and premolars exhibit the increasing yellowness of the underlying dentin. The cusps become blunted, and the depth of the occlusal fissures is reduced as the height of the adjacent cusps decreases. As the enamel loss becomes measurable, any amalgam fillings begin to protrude from the tooth surface (Andrews, 1982), and the unsupported edges may become chipped and irregular or highly burnished (see Figure 5.1). This is not the only cause of high fillings since certain formulations of silver amalgam combined with moisture contamination at the time of placement cause subsequent expansion.

Dental caries was reported by Hellstrom (1974) to be more common in "anorexia" (she used this term to include bulimics), but these findings were not substantiated in subsequent studies using more sophisticated caries measurement techniques (Roberts & Li, 1987; Greenwood, O'Reilly, O'Riordan, & Linden, 1988). Many of Hellstrom's patients were on a high carbohydrate diet, and thus the caries incidence may have been independent of the vomiting behavior.

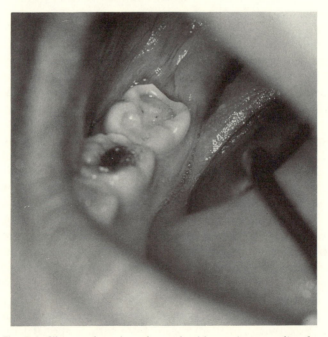

Fig. 5.1. Silver amalgam in molar tooth with margins protruding from the surrounding enamel, which has been eroded by many years of vomiting. Note also the exposed dentin on the surface of the molar tooth without the filling.

Some cases may also display erosion on the lingual surfaces of the mandibular teeth, and the labial and buccal surfaces. This distribution is evident in dietary causes of enamel erosion, thereby making it an unreliable indicator of vomiting or regurgitation except in the presence of lingual, palatal, and occlusal involvement, usually of a more advanced degree.

Attempts to correlate the duration of the bulimia with the degree of enamel loss have so far proved unreliable. Hellstrom (1977) found a significant positive correlation between the duration of vomiting and degree of erosion, but Roberts and Li (1987) found that only 33% of bulimic patients showed lingual erosion of the maxillary anterior teeth. This was a markedly lower incidence than in the Swedish study, and the surprisingly low number was attributed to oral hygiene and rinsing after vomiting. Jones and Cleaton-Jones (1989) concluded that erosions on the palatal surfaces of maxillary anterior teeth and buccal surfaces of maxillary canines, premolars, and incisors make the diagnosis of bulimia likely.

### Erosion and Attrition of Enamel and Dentin

Eventually the enamel is perforated and the underlying dentin is exposed (see Figure 5.2). As previously mentioned, the length of time of admitted bulimic behavior does not correlate well with the degree of tooth loss; this stage seems to take several years, typically about seven. When fresh dentin is exposed by the dental drill, it is easily distinguished from enamel. This is not necessarily the case in bulimia, where the smoothness resulting from the combination of erosion and attrition produces a highly glazed, eburnized surface that does not yield a textural distinction to a dental probe. Since the translucency of the very thin enamel will also fail to maintain a color distinction between the two calcified tissues, even an experienced dentist may, on occasion, be in some doubt. This is of therapeutic importance because enamel provides bond strength higher than dentin when restoration with bonded composite resins is intended. Continuing improvements of dentin-bonding agents are increasing the bond strength between composite resin and tooth, but to date enamel is a more reliable bonding surface.

The dentin when exposed, unlike enamel, retains the capacity in the vital tooth to undergo limited adaptation to the new environment. Dentin is a tubular, calcified structure with patent tubules containing cellular processes of the odontoblasts. The odontoblasts occupy the periphery of dental pulp, and their processes radiate from the pulpal surface of the dentin extending in the tubules to near the amelodentinal junction. When the dentin is exposed, the tubules calcify, and the resulting sclerotic dentin

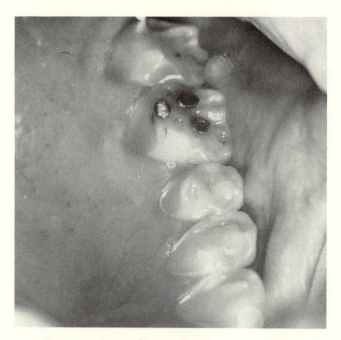

Fig. 5.2. Complete loss of enamel on the palatal and occlusal surfaces of teeth. The molar tooth with the fillings exhibits dentin erosion where the usually convex surface has now become concave. The premolar teeth have lost the definition of their palatal cusps.

is more calcified and harder than normal dentin. The mechanism of calcification is unclear, but the tubules cease to be penetrable by dye, and thus presumably protect the vitality of the pulp. If the attrition, or other cause of loss of tooth substance such as caries, progresses slowly, then a protective layer of new dentin is deposited by the odontoblasts in advance of the destruction, and the vitality of the pulp is maintained at the expense of the volume of the pulp chamber. Eventually, however, the combination of bulimic erosion and attrition may breach the dentin and expose the pulp, which induces its necrosis (see Figure 5.3). This process usually occurs with considerable pain. At this point the definition of the angular and marginal ridges of the incisor teeth is destroyed and the palatal surface is entirely concave.

### Loss of Vertical Height of Teeth

As the anterior teeth become thinner, the incisal edges become sharper. The labial enamel is thin and unsupported, and its prismatic structure

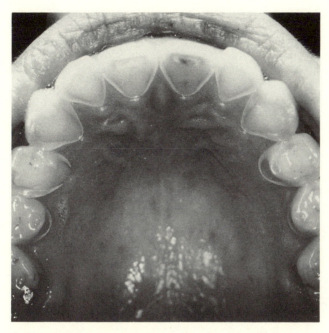

Fig. 5.3. A dark spot on the palatal surface of a central incisor tooth represents the site of perforation of the wall of the pulp chamber, with subsequent necrosis of the dental pulp.

predisposes to many microfractures during normal function. This leads to a ragged incisal edge that wears away quickly, and the tooth may be reduced to one half or one third of its original crown height (see Figure 5.4). A concurrent change affects the occlusal surfaces of the maxillary and mandibular molars and premolars. If the enamel at the peak of the cusp is breached, there is a differential rate of occlusal attrition between the peripheral enamel and central dentin. The dentin wears more quickly and creates a crater within the cusp, giving the appearance of a volcano. As the reduction in height continues, the cusp itself disappears to leave a cupping of the occlusal surface representing the site of more rapid loss of dentin. In those teeth bearing amalgams the proud margins of the fillings may be easily seen. When all the occlusal enamel is lost, the exposed dentin will offer much less resistance to attrition from normal occlusal function. Bruxism may be a contributory factor in tooth wear, but while it is assumed to be responsible for excessive occlusal wear in patients without acid erosion, it may not be correct to assume that all bulimics exhibiting

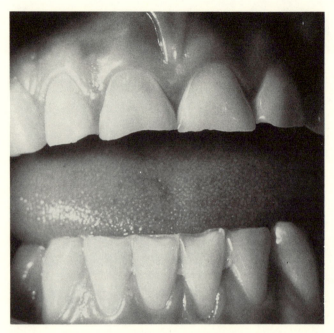

Fig. 5.4. Erosion and attrition have caused loss of about half of original crown length of the maxillary central incisor teeth.

this feature must also be diagnosed as bruxing. Carni (1981) has pointed out, however, that the anxiety felt by bulimics may find expression in bruxism.

The effect of gross tooth loss is an overclosure of the bite, which in the general population may predispose to temporomandibular joint disorders and angular cheilitis. It might be expected that at least some bulimics with severe tooth loss would be similarly afflicted. There may also be an appearance of an anterior open bite (Stege, Visco-Dangler, & Rye, 1982).

## SYMPTOMS ASSOCIATED WITH ACID EROSION OF TEETH

### Thermal Sensitivity

The term "thermal sensitivity" is used widely in the dental literature in relation to erosion due to bulimia nervosa. The pulp contains nerve fibers that transmit pain but are unable to provide proprioception or recognition of thermal changes. Heat or cold is subjectively felt as poorly localized pain. In normal teeth the insulation provided by enamel, dentin, or properly lined fillings will usually protect the individual from discomfort during eating, drinking, or inhaling cold air. To appreciate thermal sensitivity one should try to recall from childhood days the effects of sinking one's lower incisors into a block of ice cream. In childhood the pulps are larger, not having been reduced by the slow deposition of dentin associated with normal aging, and there is correspondingly less insulation provided by the smaller lower incisors. In advanced erosion the decreased thickness of tooth between the mouth and the pulp gives this same sensation with much milder and brief stimuli, such as drinking hot and cold liquids or breathing through the mouth on a winter morning. Eventually the discomfort of this pain may nudge an unwilling bulimic patient to seek dental help. This sensitivity is usually felt by the most severely affected teeth and is therefore distributed over the anterior maxilla.

## Pulpitis

Although pulpitis has been subjected to various classifications, the most useful for therapeutic purposes is simply (a) reversible or (b) irreversible. Dental caries is the most common cause of pulpitis and may be present coincidentally in a bulimic patient, but thermal stimuli, if sufficiency frequent and prolonged, can also induce a pulpitis. Pulpitis can be distinguished from thermal sensitivity by the persistence of pain that may last from several minutes to over a half hour after removal of the stimulus. There is no distinct duration that will permit a confident change of diagnosis from reversible to irreversible pulpitis, but certain additional features will suggest that pulp death is unavoidable. These are the following:

1. The pain lasts for "hours" after stimulation, although the patient's claim of "hours" may best be treated as a subjective rather than a chronological measurement.
2. Heat or cold provokes a much more distressing pain than the dull ache of reversible pulpitis.
3. The pain may start spontaneously.
4. Lying down may exacerbate the pain.

Acid-eroded teeth may exhibit the full range of symptoms of pulpitis.

**Pulpal Necrosis**

The pain of pulpitis may subside spontaneously as pulp necrosis intervenes. Pulp necrosis may be asymptomatic and progress to a chronic periapical infection (periapical granuloma) with minimal symptoms, or evolve to a periapical abscess. An abscess may succeed pulp necrosis within days or, more commonly, exacerbate from a periapical granuloma months or even years after the death of the pulp. Whatever the history, the acute periapical abscess is characterized by severe pain with exquisite sensitivity to pressure on the affected tooth. This is usually accompanied by malaise and fever. The pain may subside if drainage occurs or can be established surgically.

Pulpal necrosis may also occur as a result of direct attrition and erosion of the dentin until the dental pulp is exposed (Figure 5.3). In this event the open pulp chamber or the different color of the reparative dentin that ineffectively protected the pulp may be seen. Since any of these reactions is more usually seen as a sequel to dental caries, oral examination is required to rule out that possibility. If the affected tooth is to be retained, it must be treated by filling its root canal(s).

## REVIEW OF HISTORY AND EXAMINATION

When the dental evidence suggests that bulimia or a regurgitation habit is a probable diagnosis, the dentist may wish to review the history with the inclusion of more pointed questions about the following:

1. History of weight loss and/or gain over past year
2. Exercise habits
3. Use of laxatives, diuretics, or other medications with or without prescription
4. Occupation and hobbies, e.g., ballet dancing, long-distance running, or weight training
5. Amenorrhea and age of menarche
6. Cold intolerance
7. Constipation, diarrhea

Patients' clothing may be loose and baggy in their attempt to disguise thinness or, in the case of some bulimics, their overweight condition.

The problem for the dentist lies not in identifying the need for an expanded history but in encountering a recalcitrant historian. Most dentists do not have specific training in interviews of this nature, yet they are unlikely to recruit the help of those with psychiatric, psychological, or other counseling expertise unless they are successful in having the patient acknowledge the condition and be prepared to seek such help. In severe cases the urgency may require medical intervention, yet the patient may remain unwilling to cooperate. Studies suggest that there is a place for a cooperative effort between dentists and the health care team (Simmons, Grayden, & Mitchell, 1986; Howat, Varner, & Wampold, 1990) and that although it may be relatively simple for the psychiatrist to persuade the patient to seek dental help, the converse may not be true. This problem has not received much attention in the literature, but the following guidelines are suggested:

The dentist should adopt a more assumptive attitude during history taking—for example, *"How often* are you troubled with vomiting?" Patients who admit to vomiting may then try to minimize both the frequency and the duration of vomiting. Thus "twice a day" should be clarified as to whether this means vomiting twice or two prolonged sessions of vomiting. Patients may also deny vomiting but admit to reflux, regurgitation, rumination, indigestion, hiatus hernia, or something similar. Another example of assumptive questioning concerns the use of laxatives; thus the question *"How often* do you take laxatives?" may be less likely to elicit prompt denial than "Do you take laxatives?" Again, if patients admit to the use of laxatives, they may minimize the dose; thus, "one packet or box" should be clarified as to its size.

The objectives in taking the history should be clearly defined by the dentist as follows:

1. To reach a provisional diagnosis, which must be confirmed by a psychiatrist who may also assist with any necessary medical intervention
2. To establish the trust and maintain the continued cooperation of the patient leading to psychiatric and medical consultations
3. To complete the necessary dental treatment (v.i.)

At this point the dentist may bear sole responsibility for persuading the patient to seek further treatment. The tone during the history taking should be sympathetic and nonjudgmental. The patient should not be badgered and must feel comfortable that confidences will be maintained, particularly if the patient is afraid of parental reproach. The dentist will probably not accomplish this immediately, and it may take months. Some patients may be more forthcoming than others, and the differences in attitude between bulimics and anorexics will require modifications to the approach. This phase of the dentist/patient relationship is the most critical for those patients who have not been referred by psychiatrists or other qualified counselors.

## DIFFERENTIAL DIAGNOSIS OF ACID EROSION OF TEETH

The demonstration of erosion of teeth in itself is not prime facie evidence of bulimia. The other major causes of enamel erosion may be classified as (a) dietary, (b) industrial, and (c) gastrointestinal. The primary distinguishing feature between endogenous and exogenous acids is that the latter will cause erosion on the labial and buccal surfaces of teeth more rapidly than on the palatal (Ten Bruggen Cate, 1968), although the changes in the posterior occlusal surfaces may be similar in appearance to those seen in bulimia (Smith & Knight, 1984). There is a wide array of dietary acids that, when consumed excessively, may erode teeth. Many drinks, especially fruit juices and carbonated beverages, have pH measurements in the 2.1 to 4.3 range (Eccles & Jenkins, 1974), with carbonated cola drinks around 2.7 (Clark, Woo, Silver, Swelt, & Grisdale, 1990). The acidity of certain carbonated soft drinks and fruit juices as measured by intraoral telemetry by Infeld (1983) was found to be sufficient to cause reduced pH of dental plaque and oral fluid, and he concluded that acid-containing sweetened beverages may promote erosion and dental caries in humans if frequently consumed. Grenby, Mistry, and Desai (1990) found that acids in drinks caused dissolution of calcium and phosphate from enamel more quickly in vitro than any acid generated by microbial fermentation of sugars. It is significant that Smith and Knight (1984) presented a subgroup of patients in their series who admitted to anorexia but not bulimia nervosa and included a large proportion of citrus fruits in their limited diet. Therefore, signs of dietary erosion without bulimic patterns of tooth loss do not necessarily rule out anorexia nervosa.

As in bulimic erosion, in dietary erosion the apparent time of exposure to excessive acids has been found to vary widely, and Eccles and Jenkins (1974) reported a case in which severe lesions were produced in 3 months by the consumption of large quantities of oranges and grapefruit as part of a diet. Females aged 20 to 29 were the largest group in their series. This suggests that the psychiatric factors involved in certain cases of dietary erosion may be related to those involved in anorexia nervosa.

Many potentially erosive "dietary" elements are available, and it is not surprising that increasing numbers of more unusual examples are being reported. Amongst these are chronic ingestion of ascorbic acid (Passon & Jones, 1986; Hayes, 1989), salicylates (Tanchyk, 1986), hydrochloric acid administered in the treatment of achlorhydria (Eccles & Jenkins, 1974) and acid in wine (Schuurs, Abraham-Inpijn, Von Straalen, & Sastrowizoto, 1987). Thus wine tasters might be considered to be at occupational rather than dietary risk. A specific form of cocaine intake has also been documented by Krutchkoff, Eisenberg, O'Brien, and Ponzillo (1990) where the drug is placed on the gingiva usually because of damage to the nasal mucosa. The acid used in preparing the cocaine extract is activated by the saliva and then erodes the adjacent teeth.

**Industrial/Occupational Risk**

There are many potential industrial causes of dental erosion, some of which were identified by Ten Bruggen Cate (1968). Of these, the most afflicted occupation was battery formation workers, 50 percent of whom exhibited progressing erosion due to the sulphuric acid used in battery manufacture (nitric and sulphuric acids) and sanitary cleanser manufactures (acid sodium sulphate). An accidental case of acid erosion was caused by improper management of a gas-chlorinated swimming pool and a resultant pH of 2.7 (Centrewell, Armstrong, Funkhauser, & Elzay, 1986). The affected individuals were competitive swimmers who spent considerable time in the water. The risk of acidic swimming pool water has also been pointed out by Gabai, Fattal, Rahamin, and Gedalia (1988). There are many potential sources of environmental acid, and a detailed occupational history or other detective work may be required to reveal the origin of certain cases.

**Gastrointestinal Disorders**

Endogenous acid may cause dental erosion without the presumption of bulimia. There may be individuals who bear the stigma of bulimic erosion but who do not conform to the typical population group. Alcoholics, apart from the direct effect of acid in wine, frequently expose teeth to regurgitated stomach contents secondary to gastritis (Smith & Knight,

1984; Simmons & Thompson, 1987). This effect may well be exacerbated by its nocturnal pattern—the salivary flow being at its lowest at night—and by the dehydration caused by the alcohol itself (Smith & Robb, 1989). The resulting erosion mimics bulimia, and the alcoholic may share the same secretive tendencies as the bulimic patient, again testing the dentist's tactfulness. The gastrointestinal disorders known to produce increased acid, such as reflux esophagitis and duodenal ulcer, are associated with dental erosion. However, patients with cholecystectomy and alkaline reflux or those with gastric ulcers and normal gastric secretions have not been found to lose tooth enamel (Jarvinen, Meurman, Hyvarinen, Rytomaa, & Murtomaa, 1988).

## CONSIDERATIONS FOR DENTAL TREATMENT OF THE SEVERELY ERODED DENTITION

The objectives of dental treatment may be divided into the following phases:

1. Stopping destruction caused by acid erosion and encouraging remineralization
2. Arresting occlusal attrition due to loss of enamel
3. Short-term dental rehabilitation
4. Long-term dental rehabilitation

### STOPPING DESTRUCTION CAUSED BY ACID EROSION

When vomiting is still a frequent and uncontrollable compulsion, the patient may protect the teeth by the insertion of a specially constructed tooth guard made of flexible thermoplastic material. Sports guards bought and moulded by the patient may also be used to cover the teeth during vomiting. Chemical neutralization may be aided by the sprinkling of sodium bicarbonate or magnesium hydroxide inside the guard. Immediately after vomiting, the stomach acid may be neutralized by sodium bicarbonate or magnesium hydroxide rinse, the patient taking care to rinse the dorsum of the tongue, which may act as a reservoir of regurgitated stomach acid.

The use of a protective cover for the teeth should be encouraged only when the patient has not yet begun or remains refractory to psychotherapy. In a series of 10 consecutive patients referred from nutritional counselors or psychiatrists, I noted that all refused the offer of a tooth guard. They feared that this would represent a license to resume their bulimic behavior. On the other hand, of eight patients who were previously undiagnosed and untreated, six accepted the offer of a tooth guard. It seems a wise precaution for the dentist to consult the psychiatrist or counselor in individual cases before prescribing such a device. To those patients who have yet to seek counseling, the dentist should emphasize the temporary nature of this barrier to stomach acid and that it is not an acceptable alternative to behavior modification.

The role of toothbrushing in the prevention of acid erosion must be understood by the patient. After an acid attack there is a partly reversible surface demineralization of the enamel rods. At this point the enamel rods are fragile and more likely to be permanently destroyed by the mechanical action of the toothbrush. If the acidity is neutralized, remineralization will occur, thus permitting at least partial recovery of the mechanical strength of the surface enamel. Toothbrushing should therefore be delayed until a few hours after a purging session, but mouthwashing should be begun immediately (Roberts & Tylenda, 1989). If diet analysis shows a high content of fruits, it is worth noting that fruit acids, notably malic, tartaric, and citric, predispose the enamel calcium for complexing by citrate (Infeld, 1983). Toothbrushing should therefore be avoided during the period immediately following the eating of raw fruit. A measure in common use in regular preventive dentistry regimens is the use of topical sodium fluoride as a means for increasing acid resistance of dental hard tissues and decreasing root sensitivity. Fluoride may be administered as a daily rinse of 0.05% neutral sodium fluoride, as a direct application of 1.1% neutral sodium fluoride or 0.04% stannous fluoride gel in a custom-made dental tray, and through the regular use of fluoridated toothpaste. The application of topical fluoride is important in its conventional use as a caries prevention agent, particularly in bulimics who may still binge on foods containing refined carbohydrates. This is also true of anorexics during high-calorie therapy. The stannous fluoride may induce remineralization of the recently eroded tooth surfaces in much the same way as it does in early carious lesions (Harrison et al., 1984).

### Arresting Occlusal Attrition

The loss of occlusal tooth substance on the posterior teeth due to endogenous and exogenous acids has been described. When dentin is exposed, the rate of wear is accelerated because dentin is less dense and lower in mineralization than enamel. In patients who have a concomitant habit of bruxism, the effects of attrition are even more destructive. This attrition will continue, even in the rehabilitated patient, unless the teeth are restored with materials able to withstand occlusal function. The excessive occlusal wear also causes increased closing of the bite, which in turn can predispose to angular cheilitis. Unfortunately, the tooth-colored composites that bond to teeth do not possess the same wear resistance as some more conventional materials such as silver amalgam, porcelain, or gold alloys. If teeth have been extensively restored in the past, the fillings may lend themselves to modifications or replacement by a filling material and cavity design that offer increased wear resistance. In teeth without existing fillings, it is suggested that composites be used as a temporary measure to protect the occlusal surface. This will allow for the construction of a balanced, functional occlusion that will stop further wear and acid erosion while the patient's psychiatric needs are addressed.

The functional demands for a balanced occlusion may be treated as less urgent by the patient than the dental sensitivity of the maxillary anterior teeth and concern for deteriorating cosmetic appearance resulting from shortened tooth length. Any pain that arises from a necrotic tooth apex or a dying pulp is usually more acute, and endodontic treatment must be started to prevent acute infection. The thin, ragged teeth may be insulated by the addition of composite material to the palatal surface. The loss of enamel also represents a decrease of potential bond strength to composite material, and while materials that bond to dentin are improving, none exhibits the reliability of a resin-enamel bond. There is usually sufficient peripheral enamel at the mesial, distal, incisal, and cervical margins to allow at least a temporary application of composite resin. The mandibular incisors are often in close occlusal relationship with the palatal surfaces of the maxillary teeth, and application of the protective composite depends on space created by the restoration of the original occlusal height of the posterior teeth.

## Short-Term and Long-Term Dental Rehabilitation

The labial surface of the maxillary incisors may be improved by the application of composite resin by bonding. This yields a satisfactory medium-term result. Over time, however, composites do wear, and the junction of the material to natural tooth may become stained. Although there is no clear-cut progression to long-term measures, a long-lasting result is more likely when the materials used are aesthetic, resist wear, and are compatible with easy maintenance of oral hygiene. Long-term dental treatment frequently requires laboratory-cast restorations such as porcelain or gold onlays, porcelain laminate veneers, or full crowns.

A modification of a crown using cast-gold palatal surfaces has been described by Boksman, Gratton, Burgoyne, and Plotzke (1986). The disadvantage of anterior crowns is that they tend to be more opaque than laminates and, as the gingivae recede with age, the crown margin is exposed to reveal an unsightly line. In addition, their preparation requires further tooth destruction.

There is general agreement in the literature that full crowns should not be constructed until the bulimic behavior stops. There is good reason for this, although I have seen two cases with almost every remaining tooth crowned with porcelain bonded to metal. In these cases, one patient was still bothered by vomiting (although she was 40 years old), but the crown margins were subgingival and the teeth appeared to be protected from acid erosion. This is not a reason to support the routine placement of full crowns to act as a barrier to acid in the unreformed bulimic, since gingival recession may eventually expose root surface, which will become eroded. The other disadvantages are that preparing teeth for crowns is in itself destructive, and financial limitations may encourage patients to proceed piecemeal with treatment while allowing other teeth to become more damaged in the meantime.

Dental treatment for the bulimic is necessarily a prolonged program, progressing through the stages outlined above and always being delivered in the context of the patient's psychiatric progress. The compassion and patience of the dentist are as important as technical skill. Close cooperation with the other health care workers is necessary to maintain a balanced approach to therapy and dental treatment that is appropriate to the state of bulimic symptoms. With timely dental treatment, however, the patient may be able to claim, "I am escaped with the skin of my teeth" (Job 19:20).

## REFERENCES

Abrams, R. A., & Ruff, J. C. (1986). Oral signs and symptoms in the diagnosis of bulimia. *American Dental Association Journal, 113*, 761–764.

Allan, D. M. (1969). Dental erosion from vomiting: A case report. *British Dental Journal, 126*, 311–312.

Andrews, F. F. H. (1982). Dental erosion due to anorexia nervosa with bulimia. *British Dental Journal, 152*, 89–90.

Askevold, F. (1983). The diagnosis of anorexia nervosa. *International Journal of Eating Disorders, 2*, 39–43.

Bargen, J. A., & Austin, L. T. (1937). Decalcification of teeth as a result of obstipation with long continued vomiting: Report of a case. *Journal of the American Dental Association and The Dental Cosmos, 24*, 1271.

Bassiouny, M. A., & Pollack, R. L. (1987). Esthetic management of perimolysis with porcelain laminate veneers. *Journal of the American Dental Association, 115*, 412–417.

Batsakis, J. G., & McWhirter, J. D. (1972). Non-neoplastic diseases of salivary glands. *American Journal of Gastroenterology, 57*, 226–247.

Boksman, L., Gratton, D. R., Burgoyne, A. R., & Plotzke, O. B. (1986). The treatment of perimolysis using resin bonded etched metal onlays. *Quintessence International, 17*, 69–74.

Brady, W. F. (1980). The anorexia nervosa syndrome. *Oral Surgery, 50*, 509–516.

Carni, J. D. (1981). The teeth may tell: Dealing with eating disorders in the dentist's office. *Journal of Massachusetts Dental Association, 30*, 80–86.

Centrewell, B. S., Armstrong, C. W., Funkhauser, L. S., & Elzay, R. P. (1986). Erosion of dental enamel among competitive swimmers at a gas-chlorinated swimming pool. *American Journal of Epidemiology, 123*, 641–647.

Clark, D. C., Woo, G., Silver, J. G., Swelt, D., & Grisdale, J. C. (1990). The influence of frequent ingestion of acids in the diet on treatment of dentin sensitivity. *Journal of the Canadian Dental Association, 56*, 1101–1103.

Duplessis, D. J. (1956). Parotid enlargement in malnutrition. *South African Medical Journal, 302*, 700–703.

Eccles, J. D., & Jenkins, W. G. (1974). Dental erosion and diet. *Journal of Dentistry, 2*, 153–159.

Gabai, Y., Fattal, B., Rahamin, E., & Gedalia, I. (1988). The effect of pH levels in swimming pools on enamel of human teeth. *American Journal of Dentistry, 1*, 241–243.

Garfinkel, P. D., & Garner, D. M. (1982). *Anorexia nervosa: A multidimensional perspective*. New York: Brunner/Mazel.

Gold, P. W., Kaye, W., Robertson, G. L., & Evert, M. (1983). Abnormalities in plasma and cerebrospinal fluid arginine vasopression in patients with anorexia nervosa. *New England Journal of Medicine, 308*, 1117–1123.

Greenwood, A. M., O'Reilly, R., O'Riordan, W. J., & Linden, G. J. (1988). The oral and dental manifestations of bulimia nervosa compared with those of anorexia nervosa. *Irish Dental Association Journal, 34*, 26–28.

Grenby, T. H., Mistry, M., & Desai, T. (1990). Potential dental effects of infants' fruit drinks studied in vitro. *British Journal of Nutrition, 64*, 273–283.

Harrison, J. L., George, L. A., & Cheatham, J. L. (1984). Therapies for a reduction of dental destruction resulting from the manifestations of bulimia nervosa. *Texas Dental Journal, 101*, 12–15.

Hasler, J. F. (1982). Parotid enlargement: A presenting sign in anorexia nervosa. *Oral Surgery, 52*, 567–573.

Hayes, G. L. (1989). Typical/atypical tooth erosion—a case report. *Texas Dental Journal, 106*, 13–15.

Hellstrom, I. (1974). Anorexia nervosa—odontologisk problem. *Swedish Dental Journal, 67*, 253–269.

Hellstrom, I. (1977). Oral complications in anorexia nervosa. *Scandinavian Journal of Dentistry, 85*, 71–76.

Holst, J. J., & Lange, F. (1939). Perimolysis: Contribution towards genesis of tooth wasting from non-mechanical causes. *Acta Ondontologica Scandinavia, 1*, 36–48.

House, R. D., Grisuis, R., Bliziotes, M. M., & Licht, J. M. (1981). Perimolysis: Unveiling the surreptitious vomiter. *Oral Surgery, 51*, 152–155.

Howat, P. M., Varner, L. M., & Wampold, R. L. (1990). The effectiveness of a dental/dietitian team in the assessment of bulimic dental health. *Journal of the American Dietetic Association, 90*, 1099–1102.

Hurst, P. S., Lacy, J. M., & Crisp, A. H. (1977). Teeth, vomiting and diet: A study of the dental characteristics of seventeen anorexia nervosa patients. *Postgraduate Medical Journal, 53*, 298–305.

Infeld, T. N. (1983). Identification of low caries risk dietary components in monographs in oral science V:II (pp. 165–174). Basel, New York: Karger.

Jacobs, M. B., & Schneider, J. A. (1985). Medical complications of bulimia: A prospective evaluation. *Quarterly Journal of Medicine, 54*, 177–182.

Jarvinen, V., Meurman, J. H., Myvarinen, H., Rytomaa, I., & Murtomaa, H. (1988). Dental erosion and upper gastrointestinal disorders. *Oral Surgery, Oral Medicine, Oral Pathology, 65*, 298–303.

Jones, R. R., & Cleaton-Jones, P. (1989). Depth and area of dental erosions and dental caries in bulimic women. *Journal of Dental Research, 68*, 1275–1278.

Katsilambros, L. (1961). Asymptomatic enlargement of the parotid glands. *Journal of the American Medical Association, 178*, 513.

Kriens, O., Schmidt, H., Anders, D., & Horms, D. (1975). Sialadenose bei einem Jungen mit Anorexia Nervosa. *Deutsche Zahnärtzliche Zeitschrift, 30*, 547–551.

Krutchkoff, D. J., Eisenberg, E., O'Brien, J. E., & Ponzillo, J. J. (1990). Cocaine induced dental erosions [Letter]. *New England Journal of Medicine, 322*, 408.

Levin, P. A., Falko, J. M., Dixon, K., Gallup, E. M., & Saunders, W. (1980). Benign parotid enlargement in bulimia. *Annuals of Internal Medicine, 93*, 827–829.

Mitchell, J. E., Matsukami, D., Eckert, E. D., & Pyle, R. L. (1985). Characteristics of 275 patients with bulimia. *American Journal of Psychiatry, 142*, 482–485.

Moshang, T. Jr., & Utiger, R. D. (1977). Low triiodothyranine euthyroidism in anorexia nervosa. In R. Vigersky (Ed.), *Anorexia nervosa* (pp. 263–270). Raven Press.

Passon, J. C., & Jones, G. K. (1986). Atypical dental erosion: A case report. *Gerodontics, 2*, 77–79.

Roberts, M. W., & Li, S. H. (1987). Oral findings in anorexia nervosa and bulimia nervosa: A study of 47 cases. *American Dental Association Journal, 115*, 407–410.

Roberts, M. W., & Tylenda, C. A. (1989). Dental aspects of anorexia and bulimia nervosa. *Paediatrician, 16*, 178–184.

Schuurs, A. H., Abraham-Inpijn, L., Von Straalen, J. P., & Sastrowizoto, S. H. (1987). An unusual case of black teeth. *Oral Surgery, Oral Medicine and Oral Pathology, 64*, 427–431.

Sheldon, J. H. (1939). Anorexia nervosa. *Proceedings of the Royal Society of Medicine, 32*, 738–741.

Simmons, M. S., Grayden, S. K., & Mitchell, J. E. (1986). The need for psychiatric dental liaison in the treatment of bulimia. *American Journal of Psychiatry, 143*, 783–784.

Simmons, M. S., & Thompson, D. C. (1987). Dental erosion secondary to ethanol-induced emesis. *Oral Surgery, Oral Medicine, Oral Pathology, 64*, 731–733.

Smith, B. G. N., & Knight, J. K. (1984). A comparison of patterns of tooth wear with aetiological factors. *British Dental Journal, 157*, 16–19.

Smith, B. G. N, & Robb, N. D. (1989). Dental erosion in patients with chronic alcoholism. *Journal of Dentistry, 17*, 219–221.

Stege, P., Visco-Dangler, L., & Rye, L. (1982). Anorexia nervosa: Review including oral and dental manifestations. *American Dental Association Journal, 104*, 648–652.

Tanchyk, A. P. (1986). Prevention of tooth erosion from salicylate therapy in juvenile rheumatoid arthritis. *General Dentistry, 34*, 479–480.

Ten Bruggen Cate, H. J. (1968). Dental erosion in industry. *British Journal of Industrial Medicine, 25*, 249–266.

Walsh, B. T., Croft, C. B., & Katz, J. L. (1981–82). Anorexia nervosa and salivary gland enlargement. *International Journal of Psychiatric Medicine, 11*, 255–261.

# 6

# *Neurotransmitter, Neuropeptide, and Neuroendocrine Disturbances*

### David S. Goldbloom
M.D., FRCP(C)
### Sidney H. Kennedy
M.D., FRCP(C)

There is a broad spectrum of neurophysiological changes associated with eating disorders. Alterations in neurotransmitters and neuropeptides, neuroendocrine axes, and metabolism have been documented in both anorexia nervosa (AN) and bulimia nervosa (BN). Many of these disturbances, in fact, represent a profound upset of normal bodily functions. Although the recommended treatment for both disorders invariably involves a multidimensional approach, many of the above disturbances remit with nutritional rehabilitation.

Dr. Kennedy acknowledges support from the Ontario Mental Health Foundation. Donna Dunlop, M.A., provided excellent editorial and technical support.

## NEUROTRANSMITTERS

Over the last 30 years, the study of neurotransmitter activity in psychiatric disorders has been the dominant heuristic model for biological investigation. As such, it can be criticized for oversimplification and inaccessibility. As regards the former, diseases are often viewed simplistically in terms of "too much" versus "not enough" of a neurotransmitter. As to the latter, the activity of neurotransmitters in the central nervous system must, because of technical limitations and ethical requirements, be measured by peripheral and indirect means. Despite these constraints, a body of knowledge has evolved implicating neurotransmitter abnormalities in major psychiatric disorders such as depression and schizophrenia.

What is known of neurotransmitter abnormalities in AN and BN? In addition to the limitations already mentioned in applying this model, there exists a further confounding factor in the eating disorders: the known effect of weight and nutritional disturbances on the levels of neurotransmitters themselves (Shaw & Garfinkel, 1990). The few studies that have included longitudinal follow-up of eating disorder patients well after recovery have documented some persistent neurotransmitter disturbances (Kaye, Jimerson, Lake, et al., 1985), but even here the subjects were noted to have some degree of ongoing psychopathology in terms of eating behavior and body image disturbance or physiopathology. Fifty percent of this "recovered" sample were still amenorrheic, which subsequently raises the question of the definition of recovery. Furthermore, it is critical for longitudinal studies to address state-versus-trait issues in biological abnormalities. Long-term follow-up studies of AN patients have, nevertheless, firmly established that, as a group, these patients are vulnerable to a variety of psychiatric disorders, such as major depressive illness and anxiety disorders, whether their AN was active or quiescent (Toner, Garfinkel, & Garner, 1986). Neurotransmitter abnormalities have been extensively implicated in mood and anxiety disorders to which not only eating disorder patients, but also their families, are vulnerable (Kassett, Gershon, Maxwell, et al., 1989). Finally, neurotransmitters play a critical role in the regulation of appetitive behavior in the hypothalamus (Leibowitz & Shor-Posner, 1986). Disturbances in such neurotransmitters may serve to perpetuate these frequently chronic disorders (Garfinkel & Kaplan, 1985).

## Norepinephrine

Norepinephrine (NE) levels are assessed centrally via cerebrospinal fluid (CSF) measurement of NE or its principal metabolite, 3-methoxy-4-hydroxyphenylglycol (MHPG), or peripherally via urinary or plasma levels of MHPG. These are essentially static measures, as contrasted with neuro-endocrine provocation studies, and abnormal levels are thought to reflect alterations in neurotransmitter turnover. Even central measures via CSF are at some distance from hypothalamic and other limbic sites of interest.

It is well established in AN that urinary excretion of MHPG is decreased in the context of emaciation (Gross, Lake, Ebert, et al., 1979; Riederer, Toifl, & Kruzik, 1982). The specificity of this measure for AN, however, is unclear as it is highly correlated with the amount of body fat in both normal women and those with AN (Johnston, Leiter, Burrow, et al., 1984). This may be understood clinically as an adaptive response to starvation by decreasing nutrient requirements. In addition, levels of MHPG increase with weight restoration, indicating state dependency (Abraham, Beumont, Cobin, et al., 1981). A further confounding variable in this measure may be the coexistence of depression, which lowers MHPG, as documented by Biederman, Herzog, Rivinus, et al. (1984). In contrast, in the CSF, NE and MHPG levels are not different from those of controls in emaciated AN subjects, but are surprisingly lower than levels of controls in long-term weight-recovered AN subjects (Kaye, Ebert, Raleigh et al., 1984a; Gerner, Cohen, Fairbanks, et al., 1984). This longitudinal finding is supported by plasma MHPG data (Kaye, et al., 1985), and more recent studies cast some doubt on a simple equation of weight loss with decreased NE levels (Lesem, George, Kaye, et al., 1989). One study has demonstrated a correlation between triiodothyronine ($T_3$) levels and urinary MHPG in AN and BN, suggesting that the starvation process, rather than the degree of weight loss, may be a critical variable (Philipp, Eckert, Tuschl, et al., 1990).

At a dynamic level of assessment, feeding serves as a useful clinical test of sympathetic nervous system reactivity. NE levels rise in response to a meal and facilitate thermogenesis. In AN, the NE response to a meal, as measured in plasma, is blunted compared to the response in controls (Pirke, Riedel, Tuschl, et al., 1988), which may serve an adaptive function. In neuroendocrine dynamic models of NE activity using clonidine to stimulate $\alpha_2$-adrenoreceptors, AN patients do not demonstrate a different growth hormone response from controls (Brambilla, Lampertico, Sali, et al., 1987).

In BN, decreased plasma levels of NE at rest (Kaye, Gwirtsman, Lake, et al., 1986) after short-term stabilization of bulimic behaviors and a blunted rise in the plasma NE concentration on standing (Pirke, Pahl, Schweiger, et al., 1985) have been documented. Consistent with decreased NE activity, BN patients displayed decreased blood pressure and heart rate compared to controls (Kaplan, Garfinkel, Warsh, et al., 1989a; Kennedy & Heslegrave, 1989). Clonidine provocation studies in these patients, however, were not associated with abnormal growth hormone responses. A broader study of NE in BN indicates an increased NE response to food compared to that in controls, and a trend toward lower CSF NE levels after short-term behavioral stabilization (Kaye, Gwirtsman, George, et al., 1990a). This low CSF NE finding has been confirmed elsewhere (Kaye, Ballenger, Lydiard, et al., 1990b). Dynamic study of NE employing iso-proterenol as a β-adrenergic stimulus in short-term stabilized BN patients and controls revealed increased sensitivity of the BN population to the chronotropic effects (George, Kaye, Goldstein, et al., 1990).

In summary, there appears to be underactivity of NE pathways in both AN and BN. This may translate into lowered heart rate and blood pressure in both disorders and may even have implications for the development of amenorrhea as well. The origins of this underactivity, as well as its complex relationship to mood, weight, nutritional chaos, neuroendocrine disturbance, and trait factors await elucidation.

## Serotonin

Serotonin (5HT) has been the subject of intense scrutiny in AN and BN over the last decade (Goldbloom, 1987; Goldbloom & Garfinkel, 1990). The rationale for this inquiry stems from three independent sources: the implication of central 5HT in a wide array of psychiatric disorders that have some clinical overlap with AN and BN (Van Praag, Kahn, Asnis, et al., 1987), the role of 5HT in the regulation of appetitive behaviors (Leibowitz & Shor-Posner, 1986), and the ability of dieting behavior per se to alter brain 5HT activity via precursor availability in women, but not in men (Anderson, Parry-Billings, Newsholme, et al., 1990).

In AN, two longitudinal studies of patients, in emaciated states and after weight recovery, indicate that the main 5HT metabolite in CSF, 5-hydroxyindoleacetic acid (5-HIAA), increases with weight recovery (Kaye, et al., 1984a; Kaye, Gwirtsman, George, et al., 1988a). This suggests that lowered 5HT activity in AN is a state-dependent phenomenon of starvation and/or weight loss. Peripheral measures of precursor availability for 5HT synthesis, reflected by the ratio of tryptophan to large neutral amino acids (TRP/LNAA), have been normal at baseline (Kaye, Ebert, Gwirtsman, et al., 1984b), but delayed in dynamic testing with a food provocation test (Schweiger, Warnhoff, Paul, et al., 1986). Neuroendocrine strategies for dynamic assessment of 5HT function using a TRP stimulus or a postsynaptic 5HT receptor agonist, m-chlorophenylpiperazine (m-CPP), have revealed a blunted prolactin response (Brewerton, Brandt, Lessem, et al., 1990) or a blunted growth hormone response (Goodwin, Shapiro, Bennie, et al., 1989). These are different from the neuroendocrine abnormalities associated with 5HT in acute dieting in healthy women (Anderson et al., 1990), but may reflect adaptation to chronic starvation.

In BN, disturbances in 5HT activity are less likely to reflect the confounding factor of starvation and emaciation, although nutritional chaos and a historically relative underweight state may persist. Reduced levels of CSF 5-HIAA in weight-restored bulimic anorexics compared with weight-restored restricting anorexics and healthy controls suggest an enduring decrease in 5HT activity (Kaye et al., 1984b). While a follow-up study failed to replicate this finding in a population of normal weight BN subjects (Kaye et al., 1990b), an inverse correlation has been demonstrated between frequency of bingeing and CSF 5-HIAA (Jimerson, Lesem, Kaye, et al., 1988). Peripheral measures of 5HT in BN include abnormal platelet 5HT uptake (Goldbloom, Hicks, & Garfinkel, 1990b), altered platelet tritiated-imipramine binding (Marrazziti, Macchi, Rotondo, et al., 1988), low platelet monoamine oxidase (MAO) activity (Hallman, Sakurai, Oreland, et al., 1990), and normal TRP/LNAA ratios (Lydiard, Brady, O'Neil, et al., 1988).

In a study of patients bingeing in a laboratory setting, an increase in plasma TRP/LNAA (and a presumptive increase in brain 5HT) was associated with a spontaneous cessation of bingeing behavior (Kaye, Gwirtsman, Brewerton, et al., 1988b), suggesting a self-medicating model of restoration of 5HT activity. Neuroendocrine probes using TRP, m-CPP (Brewerton et al., 1990), or the immediate 5HT precursor 5-hydroxytryptophan (5-HTP) (Goldbloom, Garfinkel, Katz, et al., 1990a) have all demonstrated blunting of the prolactin and/or growth hormone responses, compatible with a model of 5HT underactivity.

Peripheral and central measures, both static and dynamic, of 5HT in AN and BN suggest important contributions from starvation and weight loss, as well as bingeing behavior. There may exist, however, beyond this trait, factors connecting 5HT dysfunction with some of the other clinical features of these disorders (depression, impulsivity, substance abuse, suicidality, obsessionality) that are overrepresented among these patients and their families.

## Dopamine

Despite a significant literature implicating dopamine (DA) in regulation of feeding behavior (Leibowitz & Shor-Posner, 1986), it has received relatively little attention in eating disorders. In AN, CSF studies of the main DA metabolite, homovanillic acid (HVA), show either that it increases with refeeding (Kaye et al., 1984a) or that it is positively correlated with body weight (Gerner et al., 1984), but that it is not different from controls. Urinary HVA has been reported as either low (Riederer et al., 1982) or normal (Johnston et al., 1984) in AN patients.

Studies of CSF HVA in weight-restored AN patients who also had BN showed no differences between them and healthy controls (Kaye et al., 1984b). This has been replicated among BN subjects at a normal body weight, with the additional finding of an inverse correlation between binge frequency and CSF HVA levels (Kaye et al., 1990b).

Each of the three neurotransmitters reviewed displays a striking plasticity in the context of abnormal eating behavior, from the availability of precursors through the acute modulatory effect of binge eating, thus observing state-trait distinctions and complicating parallels to other psychiatric disorders. The demonstrated efficacy of antidepressant medications in BN, even in the absence of coexistent depression, may relate to their effects on these neurotransmitters in the hypothalamic regulation of hunger and satiety.

## Opioids

The identification of opiate receptors within the central nervous system (Pert & Snyder, 1973) was immediately followed by evidence of the potential role of endogenous opioids in the regulation of feeding (Holtzman, 1974). A controlled study of CSF total opioid activity in AN, as measured by radioreceptor assay, revealed increased activity in emaciated subjects compared with the same subjects after weight restoration (Kaye, Pickar, Naber, et al., 1982). This increased activity was postulated to serve a protective function via diminution of metabolic requirements in the context of starvation. Separate studies, employing a radioimmunoassay to measure the specific opioid β-endorphin in CSF, detected normal or low levels in AN subjects (Gerner & Sharp, 1982; Kaye, Berrettini, Gwirtsman, et al., 1987a). Increased opioid activity in AN has been hypothesized to underlie an autoaddictive model of the disorder (Marrazzi & Luby, 1986) and has generated trials of opiate antagonists of a case report nature (Luby, Marrazzi, & Kinzie, 1987). Plasma β-endorphin is elevated in AN subjects versus controls (Panerai, Cavagnini, Invitti, et al., 1986; Melchior, Rigaud, Colas-Linhart, et al., 1990), but the relationship between peripheral and central measures of opiate levels is unexplained.

In BN, attention has focused on plasma β-endorphin measurement. Controlled studies have generated contradictory results of increased (Fullerton, Swift, Getto, et al., 1986) and decreased (Waller, Kiser, Hardy, et al., 1986) levels of plasma β-endorphin compared to controls. It is evident that the act of vomiting may account for β-endorphin elevation (Fullerton, Swift, Getto, et al., 1988). In the CSF, β-endorphin levels appear to be linked, as well, to disease activity. In acutely ill BN subjects, levels are the same as in controls, while hospitalization and abstinence from BN behaviors in these subjects led to a marked reduction in CSF β-endorphin (Gwirtsman, Kaye, Berrettini, et al., 1990).

The study of opioids in eating disorders indicates that with these, as with the monoamines, starvation, bingeing, and purging behavior have a significant impact on measurement and obscure putative trait disturbances. Nevertheless, clinical trials of opiate antagonists have been pursued with little benefit under double-blind, placebo-controlled conditions (Mitchell, Christenson, Jennings, et al., 1989). The opioid dynorphin, with its high affinity for kappa opioid receptors, may play a significant role in food intake and may itself be subject to nutritional regulation (Smith & Lee, 1988). To date, its role in eating disorders has not been studied.

Other neuroregulators of feeding behavior, such as neuropeptide YY (Berrettini, Kaye, Gwirtsman, et al., 1988) and cholecystokinin (CCK) (Geracioti & Liddle, 1988), have been investigated in AN and BN; again, the pervasive changes in weight and feeding behaviors in these subjects are associated with abnormal levels of these substances. CCK is a satiety-promoting agent in a variety of species. Among 24 BN patients compared to well-matched healthy controls, the plasma CCK response to a fixed-load meal was blunted and associated with lower subjective ratings of satiety. For a subgroup of these patients, successful treatment of their BN with antidepressants was associated with improvement in CCK responses and satiety ratings (Geracioti & Liddle, 1988).

Indeed, what is striking is how few of the multiple neural regulators of appetitive behavior are immune to disruption in the context of AN and/or BN. A unitary or cohesive model of etiology or pathogenesis has yet to emerge from this data, or to be integrated with the important psychological disturbances of these disorders. A more humble perspective allows an understanding of the biological disturbances that may explain the perpetuation of these often chronic disorders (Garfinkel & Kaplan, 1985), as well as contribute to the neuroendocrine and metabolic manifestations.

## NEUROENDOCRINE DISTURBANCES

Over 40 years ago, Pincus and Hoagland (1950) described the role of hormones as symbolic markers of psychophysiological responses. Since then, neuroendocrine challenge testing has been a valuable strategy in defining endocrine disturbances in major psychiatric disorders (Carroll, Feinberg, Greden, et al., 1981; Gold, Chousos, Kellner, et al., 1984) and has led to speculation that altered hypothalamic peptides, including thyrotropin-releasing hormone (TRH) (Loosen & Prange, 1980) and corticotropin-releasing factor (CRF) (Gold, Loriaux, Roy, et al., 1986a; Gold, Gwirtsman, Avgerinos, et al., 1986b), may be causally linked to psychiatric disorders.

Neuroendocrine abnormalities are of interest in AN and BN for two main reasons. First, disturbances in several hypothalamic-pituitary axes are associated with starvation and metabolic dysregulation. These abnormalities may play a role in perpetuating both the psychological and behavioral disturbances found in AN or BN. Repeated evaluations of these indices during relapse and remission may help to elucidate which, if any, "trait" abnormalities persist beyond "the starved state." Second, on a more practical level, the detection of neuroendocrine abnormalities may have direct treatment implications. For example, while it may be beneficial to replace estrogen in chronically amenorrheic women as a preventive measure in combating osteoporosis, it would be inappropriate to supplement the compensatory low thyroid condition found in AN. In the following section, the most significant abnormalities in each of the hypothalamic-pituitary-end organ axes are discussed.

## Hypothalamic-Pituitary-Ovarian Axis

Amenorrhea is an essential feature of AN (American Psychiatric Association, 1987). Menstrual irregularities are also common in BN (Pyle, Mitchell, Eckert, et al., 1981; Fairburn & Cooper, 1982; Cantopher, Evans, Lacey, et al., 1988). Frisch and McArthur (1974) linked onset and maintenance of regular menstrual function in women to a critical level of fat storage, and resumption of menses may require a somewhat higher "critical level" (Frisch, 1977).

Treasure, Gordon, King, and colleagues (1985a) and Treasure, Wheeler, King, and colleagues (1988), in a series of elegantly performed studies, demonstrated how pelvic ultrasonography findings and plasma levels of reproductive hormones are related during weight restoration in AN. Hypogonadotrophic hypogonadism is associated with amorphous ovaries in the severely underweight state and resembles the prepubertal profile in which luteinizing hormone (LH) and follicle stimulating hormone (FSH) pulsations are absent (Boyar & Katz, 1977). As weight gain proceeds, an augmented secretion of FSH parallels the growth of multifollicular ovaries, followed by an elevation in LH associated with the development of a dominant follicle. Within 1 month, this latter stage is accompanied by restoration of menstrual function in 50% of patients (Russell & Treasure, 1989). According to Wakeling and associates (1977), it is this last stage of recovery that may be delayed beyond the resumption of normal weight. Also at this stage, a trial of clomiphene therapy may be justified in the presence of persistent amenorrhea to induce ovulation through its estrogen receptor blocking effects (Marshall & Fraser, 1971).

Males with AN are also hypogonadal, with associated impotence and decreased libido. Decreased levels of urinary testosterone occur both in underfed AN (Beumont, Beardwood, & Russell, 1972) and in "volunteer starvation" males (Copeland, 1985). As in women, an exaggerated response of LH to luteinizing hormone releasing hormone (LHRH) occurs in AN men during the phase of intermediate weight loss (Crisp, Hsu, Chen, et al., 1982).

In BN, low progesterone levels during the luteal phase have been associated with menstrual irregularities, which may be caused by intermittent dieting and binge eating (Pirke, Fichter, Schweiger, et al., 1987a). Low basal LH levels (Pirke et al., 1987a), and an exaggerated LH response to LRH, have also been reported in BN (Kiriike, Nishiwaki, Nagata, et al., 1988; Levy, Dixon, Malarkey, et al., 1989).

For further discussion of the clinical implications of these disturbances on menstrual function and fertility, see Chapter 8.

## Hypothalamic-Pituitary-Adrenal Axis

Elevated plasma cortisol values have been consistently reported in AN (Garfinkel, Brown, Stancer, et al., 1975; Boyar, Hellman, Roffwarg, et al., 1977; Walsh, Katz, Levin, et al., 1978; Casper, Chatterton, Davis, et al., 1979) and return to normal with weight restoration (Treasure, Wheeler, Safieh, et al., 1985b; Kennedy, Brown, McVey, et al., 1991). Several mechanisms are associated with this hypercortisolism, including an elevated cortisol production rate relative to body weight (Walsh, Katz, Levin, et al., 1981) and delayed cortisol metabolism (Boyer & Katz, 1977; Doerr, Fichter, Pirke, et al., 1980).

Although hypercortisolism also occurs in protein-calorie malnutrition (PCM) (Rao, Sri Kantia, & Gopalan, 1968; Smith, Bledsoe, & Chketri, 1975), it is also associated with a normal or decreased rate of cortisol production (Beitins, Kowarski, Migeon, et al., 1975; Doerr et al., 1980), which increases with weight gain.

Similarities and differences between AN and PCM have also been reported following perturbations to the hypothalamic-pituitary-adrenal (HPA) axis. Dexamethasone fails to suppress cortisol secretion in low weight AN subjects (Gerner & Gwirtsman, 1981), in PCM subjects (Alleyne & Young, 1967), and in normal volunteers following brief diet-induced weight loss (Berger, Pirke, Doerr, et al., 1983; Mullen, Linsell, & Parker, 1986). A substantial number of weight-restored AN patients continue, however, to display cortisol nonsuppression (Gwirtsman & Gerner, 1981), again suggesting that weight loss alone does not explain all abnormalities in the HPA axis. On the other hand, adrenal stimulation with exogenous adrenocorticotrophic hormone (ACTH) produces an exaggerated cortisol response in AN (Warren & Vande Wiele, 1973), but not in PCM (Rao et al., 1968; Smith et al., 1975). Finally, with the development of synthetic corticotrophin-releasing factor (CRF), it has been possible to evaluate the integrity of the HPA axis. In at least two studies (Gold et al., 1986b; Hotta, Shibash, & Masurd, 1986), an intact negative feedback system from pituitary to adrenal levels was demonstrated in AN; elevated CRF levels in the cerebrospinal fluid of low weight and weight-restored AN patients have also been reported (Hotta et al., 1986; Kaye, Gwirtsman, & George, 1987b).

Overall, these findings suggest that, in addition to weight-related changes in the HPA axis, further dysregulation at the hypothalamic level occurs in AN, and this likely involved hypersecretion of CRF (Gold et al., 1986b; Hotta et al., 1986).

Although BN patients have been less extensively investigated, they also have been found to show disturbed HPA activity. Elevated nocturnal cortisol levels have been documented in some (Kennedy, Garfinkel, Parienti, et al., 1989), but not all (Walsh, Roose, Katz, et al., 1987a) reports; cortisol nonsuppression following dexamethasone has been reported in 20% to 67% of BN patients (Musisi & Garfinkel, 1985; Hudson, Pope, Jonas, et al., 1983; Kaplan et al., 1989b). Gold and colleagues (1986b) also reported normal ACTH and cortisol responses to CRF in bulimic patients compared to controls. Several factors may influence these findings in BN. First, about one third of BN patients have previously been diagnosed as having AN. Second, although BN patients may be in a statistically average weight range, they may actually be underweight compared to their premorbid weight range, and in a metabolically unstable state. Third, there is a high rate of comorbidity between BN and mood disorders (Hudson, Laffer, Pope, et al., 1982; Piran, Kennedy, Garfinkel, et al., 1985) in which similar HPA axis disturbances have been recognized. Finally, concerns about purging led Walsh, Sing, Cooper and colleagues (1987b) to assess plasma dexamethasone levels in BN patients. They found a positive relationship between plasma dexamethasone levels and suppression status. This suggests that in some instances "nonsuppression" may be related to partial or absent absorption of the dexamethasone, rather than to any inherent axis dysregulation.

## Thyroid Axis

Bradycardia, hypothermia, dry skin, hair loss, and delayed deep tendon reflexes are clinical findings common to AN and hypothyroidism. These changes are generally found in states of starvation, however, and reflect a state of hypometabolism rather than hypothyroidism (Moshang & Utiger, 1977).

Levels of thyroxine ($T_4$) tend to be within the low normal range (Miyai, Yamamoto, Azukizawa, et al., 1975; Brown, Garfinkel, Jeuniewic, et al., 1977), while triiodothyronine ($T_3$) levels are decreased (Croxson & Ibbertson, 1977; Moshang & Utiger, 1977). This low $T_3$ state is associated with an elevation in reverse $T_3$ (Leslie, Isaacs, & Gomez, 1978), a finding also noted in experimentally induced starvation (Vagenakis,

Burger, Portmay, et al., 1975), and in other systemic illnesses (Chopra & Smith, 1975). The normal conversion of $T_4$ to $T_3$ appears to be diverted to reverse $T_3$ as a peripheral adaptation to starvation (Portnoy, Obrian, & Bush, 1974) and may be closely linked to the hypersecretion of cortisol also found in AN, since administration of $T_3$ normalizes the half-life of cortisol (Boyar & Katz, 1977).

In most instances baseline TSH levels are within normal limits (Brown et al., 1977; Moshang & Utiger, 1977), although a minority of AN patients demonstrate elevated TSH levels (Matsubayashi, Tamai, Uehata, et al., 1988). There is also both a delayed and occasionally blunted TSH response to exogenous thyrotropin-releasing hormone (TRH) (Miyai et al., 1975; Casper & Frohman, 1982; Kiyohara, Tamai, Karibe, et al., 1987). Similar responses have been demonstrated in some (Fichter, Pirke, & Holsboer, 1984), but not all, studies involving healthy starving subjects (Portnoy et al., 1974; Vagenakis et al., 1975).

In summary, evidence of reduced thyroid function in AN is closely tied to starvation and low weight, but the persistence of a delayed TSH response to TRH, even after weight restoration, may reflect longer term alterations in metabolic status.

In BN, levels of $T_3$ and $T_4$ are within the normal range (Gwirtsman, Roy-Byrne, & Yager, et al., 1983; Mitchell & Bantle, 1983), as are baseline TSH levels (Gwirtsman et al., 1983), although there are contradictory reports involving the TSH response to TRH. In several reports (Gwirtsman et al., 1983; Norris, O'Malley, & Palmer, 1985) blunted responses occurred, while others (Kaplan et al., 1989b) reported normal responses to TRH stimulation.

## OTHER NEUROENDOCRINE DISTURBANCES

### Growth Hormone Axis

Basal levels of growth hormone (GH) are increased in starvation, and normalize with restoration of nutrition even before actual weight gain (Brown et al., 1977; Phillips, 1986). During the acute phase of AN there is an exaggerated response to growth hormone–releasing factor (GRF) (Brambilla, Ferrari, Cavagnini, et al., 1989) that is not attenuated by the hyperglycemic conditions known to attenuate the GRF response in normals (Rolla, Andreoni, & Bellitti, 1990). Clonidine, an $\alpha_2$-adrenergic agonist, increases GH and reduces cortisol in normals (Lal, Tolis, Martin, et al., 1975) and in both AN (Brambilla et al., 1989) and BN (Kaplan et al., 1989a), suggesting that these aspects of $\alpha_2$-adrenergic function are not altered in AN or BN.

Evidence from animal studies links GRF to stimulation of food intake (Vaccarino, Bloom, Rivier, et al., 1985; Vaccarino, Feifel, Rivier, et al., 1988), so it is possible that the supersensitive GH response to GRF in AN is indicative of diminished endogenous GRF activity (Kennedy, Goldbloom, & Vaccarino, 1992).

## Melatonin

Melatonin (MT) is secreted by the pineal gland mainly in darkness and under noradrenergic control. It also provides an index of circadian rhythm. Both normal (Kennedy et al., 1989; Kennedy, Brown, Garfinkel, et al., 1990a; Bearn, Treasure, Murphy, et al., 1988) and elevated levels of MT (Brambilla, Fraschini, Esposti, et al., 1988) have been reported in AN, although those patients with concomitant depression show lower levels than nondepressed AN or BN patients (Kennedy et al., 1989; Kennedy et al., 1990a). It is probable that acute starvation, and not low weight, accounts for the elevation in MT levels (Brown, Chik, & Ho, et al., 1989; Kennedy, Brown, & Garfinkel, 1990b).

The past decade has seen a surge of interest in the neurotransmitter and neuroendocrine disturbances associated with BN. This has complemented previous reports on the abnormal findings in AN, many of which represent the state-dependent consequences of starvation and weight loss. The next challenge in understanding BN is to clarify the relationship between these neurotransmitter and neuroendocrine disturbances and abnormalities of energy metabolism (see Chapter 7).

## REFERENCES

Abraham, S. F., Beumont, P. J. V., Cobin, D. M., et al. (1981). Catecholamine metabolism and body weight in anorexia nervosa. *British Journal of Psychiatry, 138*, 244–247.

Alleyne, G. A. O., & Young, V. H. (1967). Adrenocortical function in children with severe protein calorie malnutrition (PCM). *Clinical Science, 33*, 189–200.

American Psychiatric Association. (1987). *Diagnostic and statistical manual of mental disorders* (rev. 3rd ed.). Washington, DC: Author.

Anderson, I. M., Parry-Billings, M., Newsholme, E. A., et al. (1990). Dieting reduces plasma tryptophan and alters brain 5-HT function in women. *Psychological Medicine, 20,* 785–791.

Bearn, J., Treasure, J., Murphy, M., et al. (1988). A study of sulphatosymelatonin excretion and gonadotrophin status during weight gain in anorexia nervosa. *British Journal of Psychiatry, 152,* 372–376.

Beitins, I. Z., Kowarski, A., Migeon, C. J., et al. (1975). Adrenal function in normal infants and in marasmus and Kwashiorkor. *Journal of Pediatrics, 86,* 302–308.

Berger, M., Pirke, K. M., Doerr, P., et al. (1983). Influence of weight loss on the dexamethasone suppression test. *Archives of General Psychiatry, 40,* 585–586.

Berrettini, W. H., Kaye, W. H., Gwirtsman, H., et al. (1988). Cerebrospinal fluid peptide YY immunoreactivity in eating disorders. *Neuropsychobiology, 19,* 121–124.

Beumont, P. J. V., Beardwood, D. J., and Russell, G. F. M. (1972). The occurrence of the syndrome of anorexia nervosa in male subjects. *Psychological Medicine, 2,* 216–231.

Biederman, J., Herzog, D. B., Rivinus, T. M., et al. (1984). Urinary MHPG in anorexia nervosa patients with and without concomitant major depressive disorder. *Journal of Psychiatric Research, 18,* 149–160.

Boyar, R. M., Hellman, L. D., Roffwarg, H., et al. (1977). Cortisol secretion and metabolism in anorexia nervosa. *New England Journal of Medicine, 296,* 190–193.

Boyar, R. M., & Katz, J. L. (1977). Twenty-four hour gonadotropin secretory patterns in anorexia nervosa. In R. A. Vigersky (Ed.), *Anorexia nervosa* (pp. 271–276). New York: Raven Press.

Brambilla, F., Fraschini, F., Esposti, G., et al. (1988). Melatonin circadian rhythm in anorexia nervosa and obesity. *Psychiatry Research, 23,* 267–276.

Brambilla, F., Ferrari, E., Cavagnini, F., et al. (1989). Alpha 2 receptor sensitivity in anorexia nervosa: GH response to clonidine or GHRH stimulation. *Biological Psychiatry, 25,* 256–264.

Brambilla, F., Lampertico, M., Sali, L., et al. (1987). Clonidine stimulation in anorexia nervosa: Growth hormone, cortisol, and beta-endorphin responses. *Psychiatry Research, 20,* 19–31.

Brewerton, T. D., Brandt, H. A., Lessem, M. D., et al. (1990). Serotonin in eating disorders. In E. F. Cociaaro & D.I. Murphy (Eds.), *Serotonin in major psychiatric disorders* (pp. 155–184). Washington, DC: American Psychiatric Press.

Brown, G. M., Chik, C. L., Ho, A. K., et al. (1989). Effects of food restriction on pineal function. In R. J. Reiter & S. F. Pang (Eds.), *Advances in pineal research* (pp. 87–92). New York: Libbey and Co.

Brown, G. M., Garfinkel, P. E., Jeuniewic, N., et al. (1977). Endocrine profiles in anorexia nervosa. In R. A. Vigersky (Ed.), *Anorexia nervosa* (pp. 123–135). New York: Raven Press.

Cantopher, T., Evans, C., Lacey, J. H., et al. (1988). Menstrual and ovulatory disturbance in bulimia. *British Medical Journal, 297*, 836–837.

Carroll, B. J., Feinberg, M., Greden, J. F., et al. (1981). A specific laboratory test for the diagnosis of melancholia. *Archives of General Psychiatry, 38*, 15–22.

Casper, R. C., Chatterton, R. T., Davis, J. M., et al. (1979). Alterations in serum cortisol and its binding capacities in anorexia nervosa. *Journal of Clinical Endocrinology and Metabolism, 49*, 406–411.

Casper, R. C., & Frohman, L. A. (1982). Delayed TSH release in anorexia nervosa following injection of thyrotropin releasing hormone (TRH). *Psychoneuroendocrinology, 7*, 59–68.

Chopra, I. J., & Smith, S. R. (1975). Circulating thyroid hormones and thyrotropin in adult patients with protein-calorie malnutrition. *Journal of Clinical Endocrinology and Metabolism, 40*, 221–227.

Copeland, P. M. (1985). Neuroendocrine aspects of eating disorders. In S. W. Emmett (Ed.), *Theory and treatment of anorexia nervosa and bulimia: Biomedical, sociocultural and psychological perspectives* (pp. 51–72). New York: Brunner/Mazel.

Crisp, A. H., Hsu, L. K. G., Chen, C. N., et al. (1982). Reproductive hormone profiles in male anorexia nervosa before, during and after restoration of body weight to normal: A study of 12 patients. *International Journal of Eating Disorders, 1*, 3–9.

Croxson, M. S., & Ibbertson, H. K. (1977). Low serum triiodothyronine ($T_3$) and hypothyroidism in anorexia nervosa. *Journal of Clinical Endocrinology and Metabolism, 44*, 167–174.

Doerr, P., Fichter, M., Pirke, K. M., et al. (1980). Relationship between weight gain and hypothalamic pituitary adrenal function in patients with anorexia nervosa. *Steroid Biochemistry, 13*, 529–537.

Fairburn, C. G., & Cooper, P. J. (1982). Self-induced vomiting and bulimia nervosa: An undetected problem. *British Medical Journal, 284*, 1153–1155.

Fichter, M. M., Pirke, K. M., & Holsboer, F. (1984). Weight loss causes neuroendocrine disturbances: Experimental study in healthy starving subjects. *Psychiatry Research, 17*, 61–72.

Frisch, R. E. (1977). Food intake, fatness, and reproductive ability. In R. A. Vigersky (Ed.), *Anorexia nervosa* (pp. 149–161). New York: Raven Press.

Frisch, R. E., & McArthur, J. W. (1974). Menstrual cycles: Fatness as a determinant of minimum weight for height necessary for their maintenance or onset. *Science, 185*, 949–951.

Fullerton, D. T., Swift, W. J., Getto, C. J., et al. (1986). Plasma immunoreactive beta-endorphin in bulimics. *Psychological Medicine, 16*, 59–63.

Fullerton, D. T., Swift, W. J., Getto, C. J., et al. (1988). Differences in the plasma beta-endorphin levels of bulimics. *International Journal of Eating Disorders, 7,* 191–200.

Garfinkel, P. E., Brown, G. M., Stancer, H. C., et al. (1975). Hypothalamic-pituitary function in anorexia nervosa. *Archives of General Psychiatry, 32,* 739–744.

Garfinkel, P. E., & Kaplan, A. S. (1985). Starvation-based perpetuating mechanisms in anorexia nervosa and bulimia. *International Journal of Eating Disorders, 4,* 641–665.

George, D. T., Kaye, W. H., Goldstein, D. S., et al. (1990). Altered norepinephrine regulation in bulimia: Effects of pharmacological challenge with isoproterenol. *Psychiatry Research, 33,* 1–10.

Geracioti, T. D., & Liddle, R. A. (1988). Impaired cholecystokinin secretion in bulimia nervosa. *New England Journal of Medicine, 319,* 683–688.

Gerner, R. H., Cohen, D. J., Fairbanks, L., et al. (1984). CSF neurochemistry of women with anorexia nervosa and normal women. *American Journal of Psychiatry, 141,* 1441–1444.

Gerner, R. H., & Gwirtsman, H. E. (1981). Abnormalities of dexamethasone suppression test and urinary MHPG in anorexia nervosa. *American Journal of Psychiatry, 138,* 650–653.

Gerner, R. H., & Sharp, B. (1982). CSF beta-endorphin immunoreactivity in normal, schizophrenic, depressed, manic and anorexic subjects. *Brain Research, 237,* 244–247.

Gold, P. W., Chousos, G., Kellner, C. (1984). Psychiatric implications of basic and clinical studies with corticotrophin-releasing factor. *American Journal of Psychiatry, 141,* 619–627.

Gold, P. W., Gwirtsman, H., Avgerinos, P. C., et al. (1986b). Pathophysiologic mechanisms in underweight and weight corrected patients. *New England Journal of Medicine, 314,* 1335–1345.

Gold, P. W., Loriaux, D. L., Roy, A., et al. (1986a). The CRH stimulation test: Implications for the diagnosis and pathophysiology of hypercortisolism in primary affective disorders and Cushing's disease. *New England Journal of Medicine, 314,* 1329–1335.

Goldbloom, D. S. (1987). Serotonin in eating disorders: Theory and therapy. In P. E. Garfinkel & D. M. Garner (Eds.), *The role of drug treatments for eating disorders* (pp. 124–149). New York: Brunner/Mazel.

Goldbloom, D. S., & Garfinkel, P. E. (1990). The serotonin hypothesis of bulimia nervosa: Theory and evidence. *Canadian Journal of Psychiatry, 35,* 741–744.

Goldbloom, D. S., Garfinkel, P. E., Katz, R., et al. (1990a). The hormonal response to intravenous 5-hydroxytryptophan in bulimia nervosa. *Psychosomatic Medicine, 52,* 225–226.

Goldbloom, D. S., Hicks, L. K., & Garfinkel, P. E. (1990b). Platelet serotonin uptake in bulimia nervosa. *Biological Psychiatry, 28,* 644–647.

Goodwin, G. M., Shapiro, C. M., Bennie, J., et al. (1989). The neuroendocrine responses and psychological effects of infusion of L-tryptophan in anorexia nervosa. *Psychological Medicine, 19,* 857–864.

Gross, H. A., Lake, C. R., Ebert, M. H., et al. (1979). Catecholamine metabolism in primary anorexia nervosa. *Journal of Clinical Endocrinology and Metabolism, 49,* 805–809.

Gwirtsman, H. E., & Gerner, R. H. (1981). Neurochemical abnormalities in anorexia nervosa: Similarities to affective disorders. *Biological Psychiatry, 16,* 991–995.

Gwirtsman, H. E., Kaye, W. H., Berrettini, W. H., et al. (1990). CSF beta-endorphin decreased in abstinent bulimics. Presented at the 143rd annual meeting, American Psychiatric Association, New York City, May 16, 1990.

Gwirtsman, H. E., Roy-Byrne, P., & Yager, J. (1983). Neuroendocrine abnormalities in bulimia. *American Journal of Psychiatry, 140,* 559–563.

Hallman, J., Sakurai, E., & Oreland, L. (1990). Blood platelet monoamine oxidase activity, serotonin uptake and release rates in anorexia and bulimia patients and in healthy controls. *Acta Psychiatrica Scandinavica, 81,* 73–77.

Holtzman, S. G. (1974). Behavioral effects of separate and combined administration of naloxone and d-amphetamine. *Journal of Pharmacology and Experimental Therapeutics, 189,* 51–60.

Hotta, M., Shibash, T., & Masurd, A. (1986). The response of plasma adrenocorticotropin and cortisol to corticotrophin-releasing hormone (CRH) and cerebrospinal fluid immunoreactive CRH in anorexia nervosa patients. *Journal of Clinical Endocrinology and Metabolism, 62,* 319–324.

Hudson, J. I., Laffer, P. S., & Pope, H. G., Jr. (1982). Bulimia related to affective disorder by family history and response to the DST. *American Journal of Psychiatry, 139,* 685–687.

Hudson, J. I., Pope, H. G. Jr., Jonas, J. M., et al. (1983). Hypothalamic-pituitary-adrenal axis activity in bulimia. *Psychiatry Research, 8,* 111–117.

Jimerson, D. C., Lesem, M. D., Kaye, W. H., et al. (1988). Symptom severity and neurotransmitter studies in bulimia. *Psychopharmacology, 96,* S, 124.

Johnston, J. L., Leiter, L. A., Burrow, G. N., et al. (1984). Excretion of urinary catecholamine metabolites in anorexia nervosa: Effect of body composition and energy intake. *American Journal of Clinical Nutrition, 40,* 1001–1006.

Kaplan, A. S., Garfinkel, P. E., Walsh, J. J., et al. (1989a). Clonidine challenge test in bulimia. *International Journal of Eating Disorders, 8,* 425–435.

Kaplan, A. S., Garfinkel, P. E., Brown, G. M., et al. (1989b). The DST and TRH test in bulimia nervosa. *British Journal of Psychiatry, 154,* 86–92.

Kassett, J. A., Gershon, E. S., Maxwell, M. E., et al. (1989). Psychiatric disorders in the first-degree relatives of probands with bulimia nervosa. *American Journal of Psychiatry, 146,* 1468–1471.

Kaye, W. H., Ballenger, J. C., Lydiard, R. B., et al. (1990b). CSF monoamine levels in normal-weight bulimia: Evidence for abnormal noradrenergic activity. *American Journal of Psychiatry, 147,* 225–229.

Kaye, W. H., Berrettini, W. H., Gwirtsman, H. E., et al. (1987a). Reduced cerebrospinal fluid levels of immunoreactive proopiomelanocortin related peptides (including beta-endorphin) in anorexia nervosa. *Life Sciences, 41,* 2147–2155.

Kaye, W. H., Ebert, M. H., Gwirtsman, H. E., et al. (1984b). Differences in brain serotonergic metabolism between nonbulimic and bulimic patients with anorexia nervosa. *American Journal of Psychiatry, 141,* 1598–1607.

Kaye, W. H., Ebert, M. H., Raleigh, M., et al. (1984a). Abnormalities in CNS monoamine metabolism in anorexia nervosa. *Archives of General Psychiatry, 41,* 350–355.

Kaye, W. H., Gwirtsman, H. E., Brewerton, T. D., et al. (1988b). Bingeing behaviour and plasma amino acids: A possible involvement of brain serotonin in bulimia nervosa. *Psychiatry Research, 23,* 31–43.

Kaye, W. H., Gwirtsman, H. E., George, D. T., et al. (1987b). Elevated cerebrospinal fluid levels of immunoreactive corticotrophin-releasing hormone in anorexia nervosa: Relation to state of nutrition, adrenal function and intensity of depression. *Journal of Clinical Endocrinology and Metabolism, 64,* 203–208.

Kaye, W. H., Gwirtsman, H. E., George, D. T., et al. (1988a). CSF 5-HIAA concentrations in anorexia nervosa: Reduced values in underweight subjects normalize after weight gain. *Biological Psychiatry, 23,* 102–105.

Kaye, W. H., Gwirtsman, H. E., George, D. T., et al. (1990a). Disturbances of noradrenergic systems in normal weight bulimia: Relationship to diet and menses. *Biological Psychiatry, 27,* 4–21.

Kaye, W. H., Gwirtsman, H. E., Lake, C. R., et al. (1986). Noradrenergic disturbances in normal weight bulimia. Presented at the 139th annual meeting, American Psychiatric Association, Washington, DC, May 12, 1986.

Kaye, W. H., Jimerson, D. C., Lake, C. R., et al. (1985). Altered norepinephrine metabolism following long-term weight recovery in patients with anorexia nervosa. *Psychiatry Research, 14,* 333–342.

Kaye, W. H., Pickar, D., Naber, D., et al. (1982). Cerebrospinal fluid opioid activity in anorexia nervosa. *American Journal of Psychiatry, 139,* 643–645.

Kennedy, S. H., Brown, G. M., Garfinkel, P. E., et al. (1990a) Sulphatoxymelatonin: An index of depression in anorexia nervosa and bulimia nervosa. *Psychiatry Research, 32,* 221–227.

Kennedy, S. H., Brown, G. M., & Garfinkel, P. E. (1990b). Melatonin profiles in anorexia nervosa and bulimia nervosa. *Neuroendocrinology, 12,* 292.

Kennedy, S. H., Brown, G. M., McVey, G., et al. (1991). Pineal and adrenal function before and after refeeding in anorexia nervosa. *Biological Psychiatry, 30,* 216–224.

Kennedy, S. H., Garfinkel, P. E., Parienti, V., et al. (1989). Changes in melatonin but not cortisol levels are associated with depression in patients with eating disorders. *Archives of General Psychiatry, 46,* 73–78.

Kennedy, S. H., Goldbloom, D. S., & Vaccarino, F. J. (1992). New drugs, new directions. In G. H. Anderson & S. H. Kennedy (Eds.), *The biology of feast and famine: Relevance to eating disorders* (pp. 341–356). Toronto: Academic Press.

Kennedy, S. H., & Heslegrave, R. J. (1989). Heart regulation in bulimia nervosa. *Journal of Psychiatry Research, 23,* 267–273.

Kiyohara, K., Tamai, H., Karibe, C., et al. (1987). Serum thyrotropin (TSH) responses to thyrotropin releasing hormone (TRH) in patients with anorexia nervosa and bulimia: Influence of changes in body weight and eating disorder. *Psychoneuroendocrinology, 12,* 21–28.

Kiriike, N., Nishiwaki, S., Nagata, T., et al. (1988). Gonadotropin response to LHRH in anorexia nervosa and bulimia. *Acta Psychiatrica Scandinavica, 77,* 420–426.

Lal, S., Tolis, G., Martin, J. B., et al. (1975). Effect of clonidine on growth hormone, prolactin, luteinizing hormone, follicle stimulating hormone and thyroid stimulating hormone in the serum of normal men. *Journal of Clinical Endocrinology and Metabolism, 41,* 827–832.

Leibowitz, S. F., & Shor-Posner, G. (1986). Hypothalamic monoamine systems for control of food intake: Analysis of meal patterns and macronutrient selection. In M. O. Carruba & J. E. Blundell (Eds.), *Pharmacology of eating disorders: Theoretical and clinical developments* (pp. 29–49). New York: Raven Press.

Lesem, M. D., George, D. T., Kaye, W. H., et al. (1989). State-related changes in norepinephrine regulation in anorexia nervosa. *Biological Psychiatry, 25,* 509–512.

Leslie, R. D., Isaacs, A. J., & Gomez, J. (1978). Hypothalamic-pituitary-thyroid function in anorexia nervosa: Influence of weight gain. *British Medical Journal, ii,* 526–528.

Levy, A. B., Dixon, K. N., & Malarkey, W. B. (1989). Gonadotropin response to LRH in anorexia nervosa and bulimia. *Biological Psychiatry, 26,* 424–427.

Loosen, P. T., & Prange, A. J. Jr., (1980). TRH: A useful look for psychoneuroendocrine investigation. *Psychoneuroendocrinology, 5,* 63–80.

Luby, E. D., Marrazzi, M. A., & Kinzie, J. (1987). Case reports—Treatment of chronic anorexia nervosa with opiate blockade. *Journal of Clinical Psychopharmacology, 7,* 52–53.

Lydiard, R. B., Brady, K. T., O'Neil, P. M., et al. (1988). Precursor amino acid concentrations in normal weight bulimics and controls. *Progress in Neuro-Psychopharmacology and Biological Psychiatry, 12,* 893–898.

Marrazzi, M. A., & Luby, E. D. (1986). An auto-addiction opioid model of chronic anorexia nervosa. *International Journal of Eating Disorders, 5,* 191–208.

Marrazziti, D., Macchi, E., Rotondo, A., et al. (1988). Involvement of serotonin system in bulimia. *Life Sciences, 43,* 2123–2126.

Marshall, J. C., & Fraser, T. R. (1971). Amenorrhea in anorexia nervosa: Assessment and treatment with clomiphene citrate. *British Medical Journal, 4,* 590–592.

Matsubayashi, S., Tamai, H., Uehata, S., et al. (1988). Anorexia nervosa with elevated serum TSH. *Psychosomatic Medicine, 50,* 600–606.

Melchior, J. C., Rigaud, D., Colas-Linhart, N., et al. (1990). Negative allesthesia and decreased endogenous opiate system activity in anorexia nervosa. *Pharmacology, Biochemistry and Behaviour, 35,* 885–888.

Mitchell, J. E., & Bantle, J. P. (1983). Metabolic and endocrine investigations in women of normal weight with the bulimia syndrome. *Biological Psychiatry, 18,* 355–365.

Mitchell, J. E., Christenson, G., Jennings, et al. (1989). A placebo-controlled, double-blind crossover study of naltrexone hydrochloride in outpatients with normal-weight bulimia. *Journal of Clinical Psychopharmacology, 9,* 94–97.

Miyai, K., Yamamoto, T., Azukizawa, M., et al. (1975). Serum thyroid hormones and thyrotropin in anorexia nervosa. *Journal of Clinical Endocrinology and Metabolism, 40,* 334–338.

Moshang, T. Jr., & Utiger, R. D. (1977). Low triiodothyronine euthyroidism in anorexia nervosa. In R. A. Vigersky (Ed.), *Anorexia nervosa* (pp. 263–270). New York: Raven Press.

Mullen, P. E., Linsell, C. R., & Parker, D. (1986). Influence of sleep disruption and calorie restriction on biological markers in depression. *Lancet, ii,* 1051–1054.

Musisi, S. M., & Garfinkel, P. E. (1985). Comparative dexamethasone suppression test measurements in bulimia, depression and normal controls. *Canadian Journal of Psychiatry, 30,* 190–194.

Norris, P. D., O'Malley, B. P., & Palmer, R. L. (1985). The TRH test in bulimia and anorexia nervosa: A controlled study. *Journal of Psychiatry Research, 2,* 215–219.

Panerai, A. E., Cavagnini, F., Invitti, C., et al. (1986). Plasma beta-endorphin and beta-lipotropin in anorexia nervosa. *Advances in Bioscience, 60,* 219–227.

Pert, C. B., & Snyder, S. H. (1973). Opiate receptor: Demonstration in nervous tissue. *Science, 179,* 1011–1014.

Philipp, E., Eckert, M., Tuschl, R. J., et al. (1990). MHPG in urine of patients with anorexia nervosa and bulimia and of healthy controls. *International Journal of Eating Disorders, 9,* 323–328.

Phillips, L. S. (1986). Nutrition, somatomedins and the brain. *Metabolism, 35,* 78–87.

Pincus, G., & Hoagland, H. (1950). Adrenal cortical responses to stress in normal men and in those with personality disorders. *American Journal of Psychiatry, 106,* 641–650.

Piran, N., Kennedy, S. H., & Garfinkel, P. E. (1985). Affective disturbance in eating disorders. *Journal of Nervous and Mental Diseases, 73,* 395–400.

Pirke, K. M., Fichter, M. M., Schweiger, U., et al. (1987a). Gonadotropin secretion pattern in bulimia nervosa. *International Journal of Eating Disorders, 6,* 655–661.

Pirke, K. M., Pahl, J., Schweiger, U., et al. (1985). Metabolic and endocrine indices of starvation in bulimia: A comparison with anorexia nervosa. *Psychiatry Research, 15,* 33–39.

Pirke, K. M., Riedel, W., Tuschl, R., et al. (1988). Effect of standardized test meals on plasma norepinephrine in patients with anorexia nervosa and bulimia. *International Journal of Eating Disorders, 7,* 369–373.

Portnoy, G. I., Obrian, J. T., & Bush, J. (1974). The effect of starvation on the concentration and binding of thyroxine and triiodothyronine in serum and on the response to TRH. *Journal of Clinical Endocrinology and Metabolism, 39,* 191–194.

Pyle, R. L., Mitchell, J. E., & Eckert, E. D. (1981). Bulimia: A report of 34 cases. *Journal of Clinical Psychiatry, 42,* 60–64.

Rao, K. S. J., Sri Kantia, S. G., & Gopalan, C. (1968). Plasma cortisol levels in protein-calorie malnutrition. *Archives of Diseases of Childhood, 43,* 365–367.

Riederer, P., Toifl, K., & Kruzik, P. (1982). Secretion of biogenic amine metabolites in anorexia nervosa. *Clinical Chimica Acta, 123,* 27–32.

Rolla, M., Andreoni, A., & Belliti, D. (1990). Failure of glucose infusion to suppress exaggerated GH response to GHRH in patients with anorexia nervosa. *Biological Psychiatry, 27,* 215–222.

Russell, G. F. M., & Treasure, J. L. (1989). The modern history of anorexia nervosa: An interpretation of why the illness has changed. In L. H. Schneider, S. J. Cooper, K. A. Halmi (Eds.), *The psychobiology of human eating disorders: Preclinical and clinical perspectives* (pp. 13–30). New York: Annals of The New York Academy of Sciences, 575.

Schweiger, V., Warnhoff, M., Paul, J., et al. (1986). Effects of carbohydrate and protein meals on plasma large neutral group acids, glucose, and insulin plasma levels of anorectic patients. *Metabolism, 35,* 938–943.

Shaw, B. F., & Garfinkel, P. E. (1990). Research problems in the eating disorders. *International Journal of Eating Disorders, 9,* 545–555.

Smith, A. P., & Lee, N. M. (1988). Pharmacology of dynorphin. *Annual Review of Pharmacology and Toxicology, 28,* 123–140.

Smith, S. R., Bledsoe, T., & Chketri, M. K. (1975). Cortisol metabolism and the pituitary adrenal axis in adults with protein calorie malnutrition. *Journal of Clinical Endocrinology and Metabolism, 49,* 43–52.

Toner, B. B., Garfinkel, P. E., & Garner, D. M. (1986). Long-term follow-up of anorexia nervosa. *Psychosomatic Medicine, 48,* 520–529.

Treasure, J. L., Gordon, P. A. L., King, E. A., et al. (1985a). Cystic ovaries: A phase of anorexia nervosa. *Lancet, ii,* 1379–1382.

Treasure, J. L., Wheeler, M. J., King, E. A., et al. (1988). Weight gain and reproductive function: Ultrasonographic and endocrine features in anorexia nervosa. *Clinical Endocrinology, 29,* 607–616.

Treasure, J. L., Wheeler, M. J., Safieh, B., et al. (1985b). Anorexia nervosa and the adrenal: The effect of weight gain. *Journal of Psychiatry Research, 19,* 221–225.

Vaccarino, F. J., Bloom, F. E., Rivier, J., et al. (1985). Stimulation of food intake in rats by centrally administered hypothalamic growth hormone-releasing factor. *Nature, 314,* 167–168.

Vaccarino, F. J., Feifel, D., Rivier, J., et al. (1988). Centrally administered growth hormone releasing factor stimulates food intake in free feeding rats. *Peptides, 9* (Suppl. 1), 35–38.

Vagenakis, A. G., Burger, A., Portmay, G. I., et al. (1975). Diversion of peripheral thyroxine metabolism from activating to inactivating pathways during complete fasting. *Journal of Clinical Endocrinology and Metabolism, 41,* 191–194.

van Praag, H. M., Kahn, R. S., Asnis, G. M., et al. (1987). Denosologization of biological psychiatry or the specificity of 5HT disturbances in psychiatric disorders. *Journal of Affective Disorders, 13,* 1–8.

Wakeling, A., De Souza, V. F. A., Beardwood, C. J., et al. (1977). Assessment of the negative and positive feedback effects of administered oestrogen on gonadotrophin release in patients with anorexia nervosa. *Psychological Medicine, 7,* 371–380.

Waller, D. A., Kiser, R. S., Hardy, B. W., et al. (1986). Eating behaviors and plasma beta-endorphin in bulimia. *American Journal of Clinical Nutrition, 44,* 20–23.

Walsh, B. T., Katz, J. L., Levin, J., et al. (1978). Adrenal activity in anorexia nervosa. *Psychosomatic Medicine, 40,* 499–506.

Walsh, B. T., Katz, J. L., Levin, J., et al. (1981). The production rate of cortisol declines during recovery from anorexia nervosa. *Journal of Clinical Endocrinology and Metabolism, 53,* 203–205.

Walsh, B. T., Roose, S. R., Katz, J. L., et al. (1987a). Hypothalamic-pituitary-adrenal-cortical activity in anorexia nervosa and bulimia. *Psychoneuroendocrinology, 12,* 131–140.

Walsh, B. T., Sing, L. E., Cooper, T., et al. (1987b). Dexamethasone suppression test and plasma dexamethasone levels in bulimia. *Archives of General Psychiatry, 44,* 797–800.

Warren, M. P., & Vande Weile, R. L. (1973). Clinical and metabolic features of anorexia nervosa. *American Journal of Obstetrics and Gynaecology, 117,* 435–449.

# 7

# *Alterations in Metabolism and Energy Expenditure in Eating Disorders*

Richard M. Black, PH.D.
Caroline Davis, PH.D.
Sidney H. Kennedy, M.D., FRCP(C)

Although one might argue that the most obvious features of an eating disorder are certain behavioral characteristics, such as the bingeing/purging of bulimia nervosa +(BN) or the rigid refusal to eat and the exercise extremes of anorexia nervosa (AN), there are also disturbances in a broad range of physiological factors. For example, there are substantial alterations in neuropeptide and neuroendocrine function (see Chapter 6), medical and dental complications (Chapters 4 and 5, respectively), and changes in reproductive function (Chapter 8). Most of these physiological changes are secondary to restricted food intake, weight loss, or the purging process utilized by the patient, and they are reversed shortly after the implementation of a nutritionally adequate treatment regimen.

Alterations in metabolism are also seen in patients with eating disorders, and these can be placed into two broad categories: those of a biochemical nature and those related to energy expenditure. In either case, the majority of disturbances may relate to the current state of the patient, while the minority may represent a more fundamental trait that persists following the remission of symptoms.

## BIOCHEMICAL ALTERATIONS

### Insulin, Glucagon, and Glucose

Insulin regulates carbohydrate and amino acid metabolism, thereby maintaining plasma glucose homeostasis (Li & Anderson, 1987). In the postabsorptive state, glucagon secretion stimulates hepatic gluconeogenesis, providing fuel for cell metabolism. Thus, alterations in either insulin or glucagon production and clearance can alter the metabolic response to a meal, and can also change metabolism in the fasting state.

Static measures of plasma insulin, glucose, and glucagon are reduced in AN (Kirrike, Nishiwaki, Nagata, et al., 1990; Kumai, Tamai, Fujii, et al., 1988; Zuniga-Guajardo, Garfinkel, Zinman, et al., 1986), in a manner similar to that observed following weight loss (Unger, Eisentraut, Madison, et al., 1963). In both cases, normalization of these indices occurs with weight restoration (Casper, Davis, & Pandy, 1977; Kanis, Brown, Fitzpatrick, et al., 1974) and so need not be specifically treated in AN.

Response to a dynamic challenge of metabolic functioning through an oral (Kumai et al., 1988) or intravenous (Silverman, 1977) glucose load is impaired in AN. As indicated above, baseline insulin levels are initially below those of controls, but, in response to such a dynamic challenge, rise to abnormally high levels. In addition, plasma glucose levels are significantly elevated after a challenge. Glucagon levels, in contrast, are lower in AN following an oral glucose challenge (Kumai et al., 1988). Impaired glucose tolerance, similar to that seen in AN with an overshoot of insulin secretion (Schweiger, Poellinger, Laessle, et al., 1986), is also seen during starvation (Unger et al., 1963), and in both conditions, glucose tolerance improves with dietary treatment and weight gain (Kumai et al., 1988).

In contrast, BN patients do not display reduced levels of plasma insulin, glucose, and glucagon in the fasting state (Casper, Pandy, & Jaspan, 1988; Hohlstein et al., 1986; Schweiger et al., 1987; Weingarten et al., 1988). There is less of a consensus, however, on the effect of a glucose challenge in BN. Hohlstein, Gwirtsman, Whalen, and associates (1986) and Weingarten, Hendler, and Rodin (1988) reported a normal glucose tolerance in BN patients who did not have any prior history of AN. On the other hand, both Schweiger and colleagues (1987) and Pirke, Schweiger, Laessle, and colleagues (1987) reported an insulin overshoot in response to a glucose load similar to that seen in AN patients and starved controls, though these results may be due in part to a past history of AN in some of the BN patients. However, Casper and colleagues (1988) did not find that a previous diagnosis of AN correlated with poor glucose tolerance in BN. They studied 14 BN patients, four of whom had a past diagnosis of AN, and found normal glucose tolerance in that group.

Two other aspects of insulin metabolism may also be important. These involve insulin secretion/degradation, and changes in receptor sensitivity. There is decreased insulin secretion as measured by C-peptide in both AN (Zuniga-Guajardo, et al., 1986) and BN (Goldbloom, Zinman, Hicks, et al., in press). In addition, there are reports of increased receptor sensitivity in AN associated with an increase in the metabolic clearance of insulin (Zuniga-Guajardo et al., 1986) and an increased sensitivity in BN (Kirrike et al., 1990). However, the potential impact of these changes on glucose homeostasis is not clear.

### Free Fatty Acids, β-hydroxybutyric Acid

When nutrition is inadequate and glycogen stores have been depleted, lipolysis becomes the primary energy-producing process. This results in the release of free fatty acids (FFA) and ketone bodies such as β-hydroxybutyric acid (βHBA) (Pirke et al., 1987). Thus, elevations in plasma FFAs and βHBA can serve as indicators of starvation.

Both FFA and βHBA are elevated in AN (Pahl, Pirke, Schweiger, et al., 1985) and in those suffering from malnutrition (Viteri & Torun, 1980). In both cases, levels rapidly return to normal following implementation of dietary treatment, prior to any significant weight gain (Pahl et al., 1985).

It is unclear whether FFA and βHBA levels are altered in BN. Some have reported elevated levels of these metabolites, suggesting the possibility of an inadequate energy intake (Pirke, Pahl, Schweiger, et al., 1985; Pirke et al., 1987). Others, however, have observed normal FFA and βHBA levels in BN patients (Casper et al., 1988; Goldbloom et al., in press). There is even a report of reduced FFA levels in BN (Weingarten et al., 1988). It is important to note, though, that this reduction was observed following ingestion of a "normal" (cottage cheese and peaches) meal. Since plasma FFA levels can change dramatically following the ingestion of even a small meal (Casper et al., 1988; Weingarten et al., 1988) masking potential differences between patients and controls, these measures must be interpreted with caution.

## ENERGY EXPENDITURE ALTERATIONS: A MODEL FOR EATING DISORDERS

As others in this volume have indicated (see Goldbloom & Kennedy, Chapter 6), there is evidence to suggest that activity in norepinephrine (NE) pathways is reduced in the active phases of both AN and BN. Such a reduction might be expected to have an impact on thermogenesis and energy expenditure, as these processes are positively correlated with, and dependent upon, NE release (for a review, see Jequier, 1986). Decreased NE activity could result in reduced energy expenditure and a consequent weight gain, provided food intake remains constant. Alternatively, reductions in thermogenic activity and energy expenditure could trigger self-enforced intake restrictions in order to prevent weight gain. Some components of energy expenditure are reduced in AN and BN, and these alterations in energy metabolism may represent predisposing, and possibly perpetuating, factors for the development of an eating disorder.

Some patients suffering from either AN or BN report a history of premorbid obesity, as well as a family history of obesity (Garfinkel, Moldofsky, & Garner, 1980). This has a direct bearing on the relationship between eating disorders and energy expenditure, since obesity can develop in two ways (which are not necessarily mutually exclusive). If energy expenditure is normal, excess food consumption may lead to weight gain and the development of obesity. Alternatively, if energy expenditure is reduced, obesity may occur without excess intake. In this case, intake would have to be reduced simply to maintain weight at a "normal" level. In other words, a person would be forced to diet, not to lose weight but rather simply to maintain body weight, as in the model for BN proposed by Tuschl (1990).

A decrease in energy expenditure could result from changes in any or all of its components: resting metabolic rate (RMR), thermic effect of food (TEF), adaptive thermogenesis (AT), and thermic effect of exercise (TEE). The effects of these changes are discussed below.

### Resting Metabolic Rate

#### The Effects of Caloric Restriction on RMR
Fat free mass (FFM), sometimes referred to as lean body tissue, is the primary determinant of RMR. This energy is expended in maintaining the sodium/potassium gradient across cell membranes, tissue maintenance and repair, neural activity, and the mechanical activity of respiratory and

cardiac function. RMR accounts for approximately 95% of resting energy expenditure (Owen, 1988). Although it has been suggested that RMR per unit FFM may vary by as much as 15% between individuals of similar body weight and composition (Durnin, 1983), most consider it to be relatively constant in healthy individuals. RMR decreases with extreme weight loss, and this in turn leads to a decrease in food intake requirements (Viteri & Torun, 1980; for reviews, see Jequier, 1986; Keesey, 1982). Part of this reduction in RMR is a direct result of the loss of metabolically active FFM. In addition, however, there is a reduction in the metabolic activity of the remaining FFM. This can represent a drop of as much as 22% from baseline RMR values (Elliot, Goldberg, & Kuehl, 1989), and translates into a large energy savings for a starved individual. It follows that a reduced RMR would also be an effective means of promoting weight gain when access to food is restored.

These changes in RMR are not restricted to obese subjects experiencing weight loss. Normal weight subjects who lose weight on a calorie-restricted diet also demonstrate reduced energy expenditure that likely occurs through a reduced RMR (Tuschl, Platte, Laessle, et al., 1990). In such instances, the metabolic activity per unit of FFM is reduced by about 15% (Shah, Miller, & Geissler, 1988).

### Increased Exercise, Energy Expenditure, and RMR

Reduction in energy expenditure resulting from weight loss through caloric restriction should be contrasted with weight loss through exercise. Frey-Hewitt, Vranizan, Dreon, and colleagues (1990) found that a 1-year diet program produced a significant decline in RMR per kilogram FFM in moderately overweight men. Subjects who were placed on an exercise regimen, however, while losing a similar amount of weight as those who were dieting without exercise, showed no change in their RMR. This suggests that it is weight loss through calorie restriction without exercise, and not weight loss alone, that leads to a reduction in RMR. Furthermore, it is precisely those who have lost weight through dieting who are most susceptible to weight gain resulting from a lowered RMR.

### Yo-yo Dieting and RMR

Yo-yo dieting—that is, repeated cycles of weight loss followed by weight gain—is a common precursor of eating disorders (Tuschl, 1990), and represents a special case in the relationship between weight loss and energy expenditure. Not only is yo-yo dieting associated with increases in blood pressure (Brownell, Greenwood, Stellar, et al., 1986) and insulin resistance (McCarger, Clandinin, Fawcett, et al., 1988), but there is a tendency to lose less weight with repeated cycles (Beeson, Ray, Coxon, et al., 1989—see endnote). Furthermore, animal models of yo-yo dieting indicate that after each successful weight loss, the rate of weight gain increases significantly (Grand & Millar, 1990). This increased rate of weight gain following successive cycles of weight loss has also been observed in humans (Heyman, Young, Fuss, et al., 1991).

There are two mechanisms underlying these changes in a person's ability to lose weight and maintain that loss, both of which result in a reduced RMR. First, increases in lipogenesis and feeding efficiency (i.e., the number of calories that can be extracted from a meal) have been observed both in humans (Bray, 1972; Liebel & Hirsch, 1984) and in animals (Contreras & Williams, 1989) during weight cycling. Because of the increased lipogenesis, the new tissue representing the weight regained has a higher percentage of metabolically inactive fat than the tissue lost, thereby reducing RMR despite a return to the prediet weight. Furthermore, dieting of this nature also leads to an increase in appetite for fats and carbohydrates (McCarger et al., 1988), which may also influence energy expenditure through a reduction in the thermic effect of food (see below).

Secondly, yo-yo dieting can directly reduce RMR per kilogram of FFM with no long-term reduction in weight (Blackburn, Wilson, Kanders, et al., 1989). While this RMR reduction may not manifest itself in the early stages of dieting (Van Sanat, Van Gaal, Van Acker, et al., 1989), once developed it can be maintained not only in the short term (8 weeks) (Elliot et al., 1989), but also in the long term (up to 42 months) (van Dale, Saris, & Hoor, 1990).

In summary, yo-yo dieting can have a significant impact on energy expenditure, both through a reduction in the amount of FFM (without any reduction in overall weight) and a reduction in the metabolic rate of the remaining FFM. Either one of these conditions would require changes in food intake to maintain body weight.

### Changes in RMR in Anorexia Nervosa

The RMR of AN patients has been found to be as much as 51% below values predicted by standard Harris-Benedict equations for energy expenditure (Schoeller, Hnilicka, & Casper, 1990; Vaisman, Rossi, Goldberg, et al., 1988). However, while these equations control for height and weight, they do not control for the amount of metabolically active FFM, and some have suggested that the reduced RMR in AN is due to a reduction in FFM and not a reduction in metabolic activity of the remaining tissue (Melchior, Rigaud, Rosen, et al., 1989). In fact, AN patients often require more calories for weight gain than would be predicted in light of their emaciation, drawing into question conclusions regarding a reduced RMR (Kaye, Gwirtsman, Lake, et al., 1986a; Kaye, Gwirtsman, Obarzanek, et al., 1987b; Newman, Halmi, & Marchi, 1987). It is, however, more likely that increased energy expenditure in components other than RMR (e.g., exercise and adaptive thermogenesis) necessitate the increased food intake for weight gain (see below for a more thorough discussion).

### Changes in RMR in Bulimia Nervosa

Patients in the active phase of AN are obviously underweight. BN patients may also be at a suboptimal weight, even though their weight falls within the average mean for age-matched populations. Typically they report not only premorbid obesity but also a reduced dietary intake prior to the onset of the disorder with swings between weight gain and weight loss, that is, yo-yo dieting. This places them at risk for developing changes in RMR similar to those discussed above.

In a treatment program where binge eating and purging are prohibited, normal weight patients with BN require fewer calories for weight maintenance than do healthy controls (Kaye et al., 1986b; Newman et al., 1985; Sedlet & Ireton-Jones, 1989). This would suggest a decrease in energy expenditure. Similar observations have also been reported for patients with the dual diagnosis of AN and BN (Kaye et al., 1986b; Newman et al., 1987). Furthermore, some studies have documented a reduced RMR in those with BN compared with healthy controls (Devlin, Walsh, Kral, et al., 1990; Obarzanek, Lesem, Goldstein, et al., 1991), RMR being lowest in those most severely ill (Bennett, Williamson, & Powers, 1989; Perkins, McKenzie, & Stoney, 1987).

Recent studies of RMR in symptomatic BN patients have produced some unexpected results. RMR in these patients is not less than that of healthy controls, but rather drops below control values only when bingeing/purging is prohibited (Altemus, Hetherington, Flood, et al., 1991). The authors suggest that bingeing may stimulate NE release, thereby increasing energy expenditure. Thus it may be that bingeing is an effective means of artificially elevating what might otherwise be a subnormal RMR. This might also imply that those who binge/purge most often (the most severely ill) would demonstrate the greatest reductions in RMR when prevented from engaging in this behavior, and so be at greatest risk for weight gain.

Whether the RMR of BN patients returns to control levels following a successful treatment program and full symptom remission is unknown. In view of the tenacity of RMR reduction in other populations experiencing weight loss, decreased energy expenditure may represent a trait-related rather than a state-related phenomenon in BN, persisting for a long period of time after symptom remission. These alterations in energy expenditure should be considered not only when refeeding programs are being developed, but also when patients are being counseled on long-term weight gain and weight maintenance.

### *Thermic Effect of Food*

TEF is the energy cost of digestion and is triggered by NE release. The reduction in NE seen in AN and BN could be expected to produce a reduction in TEF and therefore reduce energy expenditure. The plasma NE response to a meal is reduced both following weight loss (Jequier & Schultz, 1985) and in AN (Pirke, Riedel, Tuschl, et al., 1988). Although TEF has also been reported to decrease following a similar challenge in weight loss subjects (Jequier & Schutz, 1985), we are unaware of published reports of TEF and AN.

TEF has been reported as normal in BN patients abstinent from bingeing and purging while undergoing treatment (Obarzanek, Lesem, Goldstein, et al., 1991). However, recent data shows that TEF is reduced in symptomatic BN patients (i.e., patients currently bingeing and purging through vomiting), and only normalizes with treatment (Black, Kennedy, Kaplan, et al., submitted).

The magnitude of the TEF also depends upon the macronutrient content of the food consumed. Protein produces a response approximately 3 times greater than that seen following the consumption of carbohydrates (Belko, Barbier, & Wong, 1986; Karst, Steiniger, Noak, et al., 1984). Fat consumption, on the other hand, results in essentially no TEF (Karst et al., 1984). These differences could be important in light of the shift in appetite towards consumption of carbohydrates and fats, often observed in those who are yo-yo dieting (McCarger et al., 1988) and in those with BN (Walsh, 1988). This suggests that the dieting pattern that generally precedes the development of BN not only may reduce RMR but also may lead to a choice of foods with a low thermic effect, reducing energy expenditure even further. TEF, nevertheless, returns to normal with weight restoration in normals (Jequier, 1986), and so if reduced in AN or BN would likely represent a state disturbance.

### Adaptive Thermogenesis and the Thermic Effect of Exercise

It is possible that AN patients expend more energy than healthy controls in maintaining body temperature, that is, through adaptive thermogenesis. While fat is reduced to an average of 17% of body weight in AN patients compared to 27% in age-matched female controls, the surface area per unit of weight increases, and both of these changes increase heat loss through the skin (Shizgal, 1985; Vaisman et al., 1988). An increase in AT may contribute to the increased caloric requirements for weight gain in AN patients that are often noted at the beginning of treatment (Kaye et al., 1986a,b; Newman et al., 1987).

There is no significant reduction in body fat or body weight in BN patients. As is the case with controls, their body fat averages about 29% of total body weight (Devlin et al., 1990). Although no studies of AT have been conducted in BN patients, one could predict that energy expended in AT would not be above control values, and would not have an impact on clinical considerations of caloric requirements for weight stabilization.

Energy can also be expended through exercise. Intense physical activity, as noted in clinical reports of AN, has been shown to increase energy expenditure to the level of healthy controls, despite a reduced RMR (Schoeller et al., 1990).

### THE ROLE OF EXERCISE IN AN AND BN

### Associations Between Exercise and Eating Disorders

A paradoxical aspect of eating disorders is the observation that many patients display high levels of physical activity despite severe weight loss. In fact, episodic hyperactivity has been listed as a secondary diagnostic criterion for anorexia nervosa in earlier classifications (Feighner, Robins, Guze, et al., 1972). Estimates of the number of eating-disordered patients classified as excessive exercisers have varied from 33% to 75% (Kron, Katz, Gorzynski, & Weiner, 1978; Crisp, Hsu, Harding, & Hartshorn, 1980; Long & Smith, 1990), and appear to exceed, by a substantial amount, that which is found in the general female population (Davis, 1991). In the clinical literature, this aberrant behavior is frequently noted, but is generally not emphasized. Most clinicians and researchers have concluded that anorectics engage in assiduous physical activity for the sole purpose of expending unwanted calories (e.g., Bruch, 1982; Garfinkel & Goldbloom, 1988), and that exercise is "simply . . . another weapon in the arsenal dedicated to rigid weight control" (Garner, Rockert, Olmsted, et al., 1985, p. 517). In fact, the revised third edition of the *Diagnostic and Statistical Manual of Mental Disorders* states that the observed weight loss among anorectics is "usually accomplished by reduction in total food, often with extensive exercising" (American Psychiatric Association, p. 65). A recent publication reviews the complex relationship between eating disorders and exercise (Yates, 1991).

### Activity-Induced Anorexia—An Animal Model for AN?

Nevertheless, there are some who believe that physical activity occupies a more central and causal role in the etiology of eating disorders, and the impetus for this idea has come primarily from the evidence of activity-induced anorexia in animals (Routtenberg, 1968; Epling, Pierce, & Stefan, 1983; Epling & Pierce, 1984; Pierce, Epling, & Boer, 1986). Well-controlled laboratory studies with rats and mice have shown that for these animals the process of self-starvation requires both the opportunity to engage in locomotor activity and the presence of dietary restriction, and that a positive relationship exists between degree of exercise and the severity of weight loss. Two processes seem to be operating in this starvation chain:

1. Restricted food intake increases physical activity levels up to some limiting value when activity eventually declines. Epling and associates (1983) explain the survival value of this behavior in that in times of food scarcity, increased activity enhances the likelihood of the organism locating food.
2. Strenuous physical activity serves to suppress appetite. However, the relationship between activity and food intake is probably not linear, and the negative component is only the first phase of an overall U-shaped function (Levitsky, 1974; Tokuyama, Saito, & Okuda, 1982; Epling & Pierce, 1988, for a review). It seems that the positive arm of the U fails to develop when the availability of food is restricted, or when the level of physical activity increases exponentially.

Epling and his colleagues (Epling at al., 1983; Epling & Pierce, 1988) present the case for a human analogue of the activity-induced anorexia found in rodents. They argue that sociocultural exigencies can initiate a state of food restriction (e.g., dieting to lose weight), which can then cause an increase in physical activity if the opportunity to exercise is available. Deprivation-induced activity will further suppress appetite, and so the weight loss cycle begins. Although this is an interesting notion, there are several factors that mitigate its relevance for the understanding of anorexia nervosa. For example, the strength of their argument rests on the assumption that the relationship between activity and appetite is reciprocal. Specifically, they maintain that food intake is reduced following exercise, and that in the face of food restriction, physical activity increases—an interaction that is spiraling and self-perpetuating. The first claim appears to be well supported if exercise is excessive and strenuous (e.g., Karvonen, Saarela, & Votila, 1978; Brouns, Saris, & Ten Hoor, 1986), and can be explained by the increase in core body temperature, and by the evidence that moderately high intensity exercise stimulates the release of the opioid peptide β-endorphin that dampens or suppresses appetite (Sforzo, 1988). However, the second proposition, that hyperactivity develops during a period of severe food restriction and energy deficit, is not only counterintuitive, but inconsistent with the evidence that people subject to imposed starvation are typically lethargic and show reductions in physical activity (Keys, Brozek, Henschel, Mickelson, & Taylor, 1950; Nisbett, 1972). In addition to these criticisms. Mrosovsky (1983, 1984) makes the very important point that because anorexia nervosa is a uniquely human disorder, the animal analogy can offer no explanation for the numerous "cognitive aggressors" like feelings of inadequacy and body image distortion that appear to motivate self-imposed starvation, and that do constant battle with the body's "physiological defenders," which are essentially intact. Mrosovsky concludes that the utility of animal models lies only in their ability to elucidate some of the physiological aspects of the disorder, for example, the increases in CRH and activity of the hypothalamic-pituitary axis (Burden, White, & Martin, 1991; Gold, Gwirtsman, Avgerinos, et al., 1986).

## Clinical Evidence for Activity-Induced Food Restriction

In addition to extrapolations from the animal research, there is some clinical evidence that indicates a causal link from exercise to disturbed eating. Reports show that a number of patients with anorexia nervosa were extremely physically active well before they ever dieted or lost weight (Kron, et al., 1978; Katz, 1986). These reports imply that exercise is not always a consequence of weight preoccupation, and may actually contribute to its development and even to clinical eating disorders. Katz (1986) offers a psychological explanation for the temporal primacy of exercise. He suggests that diligent exercising may foster weight and diet concerns in certain susceptible individuals because the initial weight loss that often accompanies regular physical activity elicits certain social reinforcers that, in turn, may lead to a narcissistic interest in physical appearance. It is also reasonable to assume that a serious commitment to sport and exercise will inevitably focus attention on the relationship between weight and maximal performance.

Some recent research has examined the relationship between exercise and weight and dietary concerns among groups of nonclinical women. Using structural equation modeling to analyze the data, it was found that the degree of physical activity participation had positive and direct effects on weight preoccupation for a group of exercising women. However, the reverse was not the case. That is, weight preoccupation did not predict the level of exercising (Davis & Dionne, 1990; Davis, Fox, Cowles, Hastings, & Schwass, 1990). These results are consistent with the clinical reports that avid exercising may be an antecedent factor in the development of anorexia nervosa.

Some have argued against a causal model and suggest instead that intense exercising—in particular, long distance running—and anorexia nervosa may be symptomatic of a common psychopathology (Yates, Leehey, & Shisslak, 1983; Yates, 1987). Both groups, it is argued, experience an obsession concerning physical perfection. The obligatory exerciser is driven by the pursuit of physical effectiveness, and the anorectic by the pursuit of physical attractiveness. However, it is fair to say that although this point of view is intuitively appealing, there are several detractors who maintain that obligatory runners are not psychologically similar to women with eating disorders (Blumenthal, O'Toole, & Chang, 1984; Weight & Noakes, 1987; Nudelman, Rosen, & Leitenberg, 1988).

## The Dependence Model for Eating Disorders

Szmukler and Tantam (1984) proposed a novel approach to the psychiatric classification of eating disorders, in which they likened AN to a dependence disorder. Others have also concluded that eating disorders may be forms of addiction (Feldman & Eysenck, 1986; De Silva & Eysenck, 1987). Interestingly, many have made similar claims about excessive exercising, and have concluded that this behavior shares several of the core features of a dependence syndrome (Morgan, 1979; Sachs & Pargman, 1984; De Coverley Veale, 1987; Morris, Steinberg, Sykes, et al., 1990). It is possible that the consequences of starvation may be very similar to the consequences of excessive exercise, and both may involve a physiological dependence on the endogenous endorphins secreted in response to bodily stress. Szmukler and Tantam (1984) suggest that anorectics are addicted to starvation, and others have noted that excessive exercisers often induce weight loss by dieting as a means of improving performance. Superficially and behaviorally there may be little to distinguish these two groups.

Following a thorough review of the literature on sport, exercise, and eating disorders, Eisler and le Grange (1990) concluded that the associations between physical activity and anorexia nervosa are probably numerous, and are certain to be complex. It seems likely that anorexia nervosa is not a disorder that manifests a consistent etiology and a predictable constellation of symptoms, but rather that there are a number of different core pathologies that display a behavioral similarity.

## SUMMARY AND CONCLUSION

Metabolic abnormalities exist in AN and BN patients, but most return to normal with nutritional stabilization and weight gain. The resting metabolic rate, which may have become chronically lowered through repeated dieting, is the sole exception and could, therefore, predispose an individual to develop or perpetuate an eating disorder. To date, however, trait disturbances still await confirmation.

Most of these metabolic disturbances seem to be physiological adaptation for energy conservation in the face of food intake restrictions (for example, decreased NE, RMR, and TEF) and should not be targeted for therapy. Rather, these indices can be viewed longitudinally as markers of dietary treatment success.

Considerable controversy exists regarding the role of exercise in the eating disorders. Although increased activity has traditionally been viewed as secondary to disturbances in body image and eating behavior, it may, in some instances, represent a causative factor in the development of AN or BN. Regrettably, there is a scarcity of research that has systematically investigated these issues. Most of the relevant literature is in the form of anecdotal case reports, and the principal difficulty with the few controlled studies lies in the inconsistency of comparison groups across studies, and in the fact that most of the studies have used samples that are too small to make valid inferences.

## ENDNOTES

Although Beeson et al. (1989) report that their subjects lost weight at a consistent rate in successive diets, inspection of the data indicates otherwise. Without exception, all subjects lost significantly less weight during the second diet cycle than during the first, in spite of the fact that the diets were virtually identical, and were implemented for the same period of time (about 450 kcal/d for 8 weeks).

## REFERENCES

Altemus, M., Hetherington, M. M., Flood, M., et al. (1992). Decrease in resting metabolic rate during abstinence from bulimic behavior. *American Journal of Psychiatry, 148*, 1071–1072.

Beeson, V., Ray, C., Coxon, A., et al. (1989). The myth of the yo-yo: Consistent rate of weight loss with successive dieting by VLCD. *International Journal of Obesity, 13*(Suppl. 2), 135–139.

Belko, A. Z., Barbieri, T. F., & Wong, E. C. (1986). Effect of energy and protein intake and exercise intensity on the thermic effect of food. *American Journal of Clinical Nutrition, 43*, 863–869.

Bennett, S. M., Williamson, D. A., & Powers, S. K. (1989). Bulimia nervosa and resting metabolic rate. *International Journal of Eating Disorders, 8*, 417–424.

Black, R. M., Kennedy, S. H., Kaplan, A. N., Levitt, A. J., Allard, J. S., & Anderson, G. H. Alterations in resting metabolic rate and diet induced thermogenesis during treatment for bulimia nervosa. Submitted to *Biological Psychiatry*.

Blackburn, G. L., Wilson, G. T., Kanders, B. S., et al. (1989). Weight cycling: The experience of human dieters. *American Journal of Clinical Nutrition, 49*, 417–424.

Blumenthal, J. A., O'Toole, L. C., & Chang, J. L. (1984). Is running an analogue of anorexia nervosa? An empirical study of obligatory running and anorexia nervosa. *Journal of the American Medical Association, 252*(4), 520–523.

Bray, G. A. (1972). Lipogenesis in human adipose tissue: Some effects of nibbling and gorging. *Journal of Clinical Investigation, 51*, 537–548.

Brouns, F. J. P. H., Saris, W. H. M., & Ten Hoor, F. (1986). Dietary problems in the case of strenuous exertion. *Journal of Sports Medicine, 26*, 306–312.

Brownell, K. D., Greenwood, M. R. C., Stellar, E., et al. (1986). The effects of repeated cycles of weight loss and regain in rats. *Physiology and Behavior, 38*, 459–464.

Bruch, H., (1982). Anorexia nervosa: Therapy and theory. *The American Journal of Psychiatry, 139*(12), 1531–1538.

Burden, V. R., White, B. D., & Martin, R. J. (1991). Adrenal output increases in activity-based anorexia: Possible involvement of the hypothalamic-pituitary-adrenal (HPA) axis. *FASEB Journal, 5*, Abstract 7470.

Casper, R. C., Davis, J. M., & Pandy, G. N. (1977). The effect of nutritional status and weight changes on hypothalamic function tests in anorexia nervosa. In R. A. Vigersky (Ed.), *Anorexia nervosa* (pp. 137–147). New York: Raven Press.

Casper, R. C., & Frohman, L. A. (1982). Delayed TSH release in anorexia nervosa following injection of thyrotropin releasing hormone (TRH). *Psychoneuro-endocrinology, 7*, 59–68.

Casper, R. C., Pandy, G. N., & Jaspan, J. B. (1988). Hormone and metabolic plasma levels after oral glucose in bulimia and healthy controls. *Biological Psychiatry, 24*, 663–674.

Contreras, R. J., & Williams, V. L. (1989). Dietary obesity and weight cycling: Effects on blood pressure and heart rate in rats. *American Journal of Physiology, 256*, R886–R891.

Crisp, A. H., Hsu, L. K. G., Harding, B., & Hartshorn, J. (1980). Clinical features of anorexia nervosa. *Journal of Psychosomatic Research, 24*, 179–191.

Davis, C., & Dionne, M. (1990). *Weight preoccupation and exercise: A structural equation analysis.* Presentation at the Fourth International Conference on Eating Disorders. New York, April.

Davis, C., & Fox, J. (1991). Excessive exercise and weight preoccupation in women (manuscript under review).

Davis, C., Fox, J., Cowles, M., Hastings, P., & Schwass, K. (1990). The functional role of exercise in the development of weight and diet concerns in women. *Journal of Psychosomatic Research, 34*(5), 563–574.

De Coverley Veale, D. (1987). Exercise dependence. *British Journal of Addiction, 82*, 735–740.

De Silva, P., & Eysenck, S. (1987). Personality and addictiveness in anorexic and bulimic patients. *Personality and Individual Differences, 8*(5), 749–751.

Devlin, M. J., Walsh, T., Kral, J. G., et al. (1990). Metabolic abnormalities in bulimia nervosa. *Archives of General Psychiatry, 47*, 144–148.

Durnin, J. V. G. A. (1983). The variability of dietary energy. In J. Kevaney (Ed.), *Energy balance in human nutrition* (pp. 13–23). Dublin: Royal Irish Academy.

Eisler, I., & le Grange, D. (1990). Excessive exercise and anorexia nervosa. *International Journal of Eating Disorders, 9*(4), 377–386.

Elliot, D. E., Goldberg, L., & Kuehl, K. S. (1989). Sustained depression of the resting metabolic rate after massive weight loss. *American Journal of Clinical Nutrition, 49*, 93–96.

Epling, W. F., & Pierce, W. D. (1984). Activity-based anorexia in rats as a function of opportunity to run on an activity wheel. *Nutrition and Behavior, 2*, 37–49.

Epling, W. F., & Pierce, W. D. (1988). Activity-based anorexia: A biobehavioral perspective. *International Journal of Eating Disorders, 7*(4), 475–485.

Epling, W. F., Pierce, W. D., & Stefan, L. (1983). A theory of activity-based anorexia. *International Journal of Eating Disorders, 3*(1), 27–43.

Feighner, J. P., Robins, E., Guze, S. B., et al. (1972). Diagnostic criteria for use in psychiatric research. *Archives of General Psychiatry, 26*, 57–63.

Feldman, J., & Eysenck, S. B. G. (1986). Addictive personality traits in bulimic patients. *Personality and Individual Differences, 7*, 923–926.

Frey-Hewitt, B., Vranizan, K. M., Dreon, D. M., et al. (1990). The effect of weight loss by dieting or exercise on resting metabolic rate in overweight men. *International Journal of Obesity, 14*, 327–334.

Garfinkel, P. E., & Goldbloom, D. M. (1988). Anorexia nervosa and bulimia nervosa (chap. 1.). *Anorexia Nervosa and Bulimia Nervosa: Current Update.* Toronto: Eating Disorders Group, Department of Psychiatry, Toronto General Hospital.

Garfinkel, P. E., Moldofsky, H., & Garner, D. M. (1980). The heterogeneity of anorexia nervosa: Bulimia nervosa as a distinct subgroup. *Archives of General Psychiatry, 37*, 1036–1040.

Garner, D. M., Rockert, W., Olmsted, M. P., et al. (1985). Psychoeducational principles in the treatment of bulimia and anorexia nervosa. In D. M. Garner & P. Garfinkel (Eds.), *Handbook of psychotherapy for anorexia nervosa and bulimia* (pp. 513–572). New York: The Guilford Press.

Gold, P. W., Gwirtsman, H., Avgerinos, P. C., et al. (1986). Abnormal hypothalamic-pituitary-adrenal function in anorexia nervosa: Pathophysiologic mechanisms in underweight and weight corrected patients. *New England Journal of Medicine, 314*, 1335–1342.

Goldbloom, D. S., Zinman, B., Hicks, L. K., et al. (in press). The baseline metabolic state in bulimia nervosa: Abnormality and adaptation. *International Journal of Eating Disorders,* 146.

Grand, T. C., & Millar, J. S. (1990). The effects of intermittent dietary restriction on weight gain and body fat in white-footed mice, *Peromyscus leucopus. Physiology and Behavior, 48*, 221–224.

Heyman, M. B., Young, V. R., Fuss, P., et al. (1991). Effects of underfeeding on energy metabolism and body composition in healthy young men. *FASEB Journal, 5*, Abstract 7421.

Hohlstein, L. A., Gwirtsman, H. E., Whalen, F., et al. (1986). Oral glucose tolerance in bulimia. *International Journal of Eating Disorders, 5*, 157–160.

Jequier, E. (1986). Thermogenesis and its role in metabolism. *Bibliotheca Nutritio et Dieta* (Basel), *39*, 6–12.

Jequier, E., & Schutz, Y. (1985). New evidence for a thermogenic defect in human obesity. *International Journal of Obesity, 9*(Suppl. 2), 1–7.

Kanis, J. A., Brown, P., Fitzpatrick, K., et al. (1974). Anorexia nervosa: A clinical, psychiatric and laboratory study. *Quarterly Journal of Medicine, 43*, 321–338.

Karst, H., Steiniger, J., Noak, R., et al. (1984). Diet-induced thermogenesis in man: Thermic effects of single proteins, carbohydrates and fats depending on their energy amounts. *Annals of Nutrition and Metabolism, 28*, 245–252.

Karvonen, J., Saarela, J., & Uotila, E. (1978). The effect of repeated exercise on appetite in a 24-hour relay race. In G. Ricci & A. Venerando (Eds.), *Nutrition, dietetics and sport*. Rome: Edizioni Minerva Medica.

Katz, J. L. (1986). Long-distance running, anorexia nervosa, and bulimia: A report of two cases. *Comprehensive Psychiatry, 27*(1), 74–78.

Kaye, W. H., Gwirtsman, H. E., Lake, C. R., et al. (1986a). *Noradrenergic disturbances in normal weight bulimia*. Presented at the 139th annual meeting, American Psychiatric Association, Washington, DC, May 12, 1986.

Kaye, W. H., Gwirtsman, H. E., Obarzanek, E., et al. (1986b). Caloric intake necessary for weight maintenance in anorexia nervosa: Nonbulimics require greater caloric intake than bulimics. *American Journal of Clinical Nutrition, 44*, 435–443.

Keesey, R. E. (1982). A set-point theory of obesity. In K. D. Brownell & J. P. Foreyt (Eds.), *Handbook of eating disorders: Physiology, psychology and treatment of obesity, anorexia and bulimia* (pp. 63–87). New York: Basic Books.

Keys, A., Brozek, J., Henschel, A., Mickelson, O., & Taylor, H. L. (1950). *The biology of human starvation*. Minneapolis: University of Minnesota Press.

Kirrike, N., Nishiwaki, S., Nagata, T., et al. (1990). Insulin sensitivity in patients with anorexia nervosa and bulimia. *Acta Psychiatrica Scandinavia, 81*, 236–239.

Kron, L., Katz, J. L., Gorzynski, G., & Weiner, W. (1978). Hyperactivity in anorexia nervosa: A fundamental clinical feature. *Comprehensive Psychiatry, 19*, 433–439.

Kumai, T., Tamai, H., Fujii, S., et al. (1988). Glucagon secretion in anorexia nervosa. *American Journal of Clinical Nutrition, 47*, 239–242.

Levitsky, D. (1974). Feeding conditions and intermeal relationships. *Physiology and Behavior, 3*, 571–573.

Li, E. T. S., & Anderson, G. H. (1987). Dietary carbohydrate and the nervous system. *Nutrition Research, 7*, 1329–1339.

Liebel, R. R., & Hirsch, J. (1984). Diminished energy requirement in reduced obese patients. *Metabolism, 33*, 164–170.

Long, C., & Smith, J. (1990). Treatment of compulsive overexercising in anorexia nervosa: A case study. *Behavioural Psychotherapy, 18*, 295–306.

McCarger, L. J., Clandinin, M. T., Fawcett, D. M., et al. (1988). Short-term changes in energy intake and serum insulin, neutral amino acids, and urinary catecholamine excretion in women. *American Journal of Clinical Nutrition, 47*, 932–941.

Melchior, J. C., Rigaud, D., Rozen, R., et al. (1989). Energy expenditure economy induced by decrease in lean body mass in anorexia nervosa. *European Journal of Clinical Nutrition, 43*, 793–799.

Morgan, W. P. (1979). Negative addiction in runners. *The Physician and Sportsmedicine, 7*(2), 57–68.

Morris, M., Steinberg, H., Sykes, E. A., et al. (1990). Effects of temporary withdrawal from regular running. *Journal of Psychosomatic Research, 34*(5), 493–500.

Mrosovsky, N. (1983). Animal anorexias, starvation, and anorexia nervosa: Are animal models of anorexia nervosa possible? In P. L. Darley, P. E. Garfinkel, D. M. Garner, & D. V. Coscina (Eds.), *Anorexia nervosa: Recent developments in research* (pp. 199–205). New York: Alan R. Liss.

Mrosovsky, N. (1984). Animal models: Anorexia yes, nervosa no. In K. M. Pirke & D. Ploog (Eds.), *The psychobiology of anorexia nervosa*. Berlin Heidelberg: Springer-Verlag.

Newman, M. M., Halmi, K. A., & Marchi, P. (1987). Relationship of clinical factors to caloric requirements in subtypes of eating disorders. *Biological Psychiatry, 22*, 1253–1263.

Nisbett, R. E. (1972). Hunger, obesity and the ventromedial hypothalamus. *Psychological Review, 79*, 433–453.

Nudelman, S., Rosen, J. C., & Leitenberg, H. (1988). Dissimilarities in eating attitudes, body image distortion, depression, and self-esteem between high-intensity male runners and women with bulimia nervosa. *International Journal of Eating Disorders, 7*(5), 625–634.

Obarzanek, E., Lesem, M., Goldstein, D., et al. (1991). Reduced resting metabolic rate in patients with bulimia nervosa. *Archives of General Psychiatry, 48*, 456–462.

Owen, O. E. (1988). Regulation of energy metabolism. In J. M. Kinney, K. N. Jejeebhoy, G. Hill, & O. E. Owen (Eds.), *Nutrition and metabolism in patient care*. Philadelphia: Saunders.

Pahl, J., Pirke, K. M., Schweiger, U., et al. (1985). Anorectic behaviour, mood, metabolic and endocrine adaptation to starvation in anorexia nervosa during in-patient treatment. *Biological Psychiatry, 20*, 874–887.

Perkins, K. A., McKenzie, S. J., & Stoney, C. M. (1987). The relevance of metabolic rate in behavioral medicine research. *Behaviour Modification, 11*, 286–311.

Pierce, W. D., Epling, W. F., & Boer, D. P. (1986). Deprivation and satiation: The interrelations between food and wheel running. *Journal of Experimental Analysis of Behavior, 46*, 199–210.

Pirke, K. M., Pahl, J., Schweiger, U., et al. (1985). Metabolic and endocrine indices of starvation in bulimia: A comparison with anorexia nervosa. *Psychiatry Research, 15,* 33–39.

Pirke, K. M., Riedel, W., Tuschl, R., et al. (1988). Effect of standardized test meals on plasma norepinephrine in patients with anorexia nervosa and bulimia. *International Journal of Eating Disorders, 7,* 369–373.

Pirke, K. M., Schweiger, U., Laessle, R. G., et al. (1987). Metabolic and endocrine consequences of eating behaviour and food composition in bulimia. In J. I. Hudson & H. G. Pope (Eds.), *The psychobiology of bulimia* (pp. 131–143). New York: American Psychiatric Press.

Routtenberg, A. (1968). "Self-starvation" of rats living in activity wheels. *Journal of Comparative and Physiological Psychology, 66*(1), 231–238.

Sachs, M. L., & Pargman, D. (1984). Running addiction. In M. L. Sachs, & G. W. Buffone (Ed.), *Running therapy* (pp. 231–252). Lincoln: University of Nebraska Press.

Schoeller, D., Hnilicka, J., & Casper, R. (1990). *High levels of physical activity in anorexia nervosa patients normalize total energy expenditure.* Abstract, 10th Annual Bristol-Meyers Squibb/Mead Johnson Symposium on Nutrition Research, Toronto, Canada.

Schweiger, V., Poellinger, J., Laessle, R., et al. (1987). Altered insulin response to a balanced test meal in bulimic patients. *International Journal of Eating Disorders, 6,* 551–556.

Schweiger, V., Warnhoff, M., Paul, J., et al. (1986). Effects of carbohydrate and protein meals on plasma large neutral group acids, glucose, and insulin plasma levels of anorectic patients. *Metabolism, 35,* 938–943.

Sedlet, K. L., & Ireton-Jones, C. S. (1989). Energy expenditure and the abnormal eating patterns of a bulimic: A case report. *Journal of American Dietitians Association, 89,* 74–77.

Sforzo, G. A. (1988). Opioids and exercise: An update. *Sports Medicine, 7,* 109–124.

Shah, M., Miller, D. S., & Geissler, C. A. (1988). Lower metabolic rates in post-obese versus lean women: Thermogenesis, metabolic rate and genetics. *European Journal of Clinical Nutrition, 42,* 741–752.

Shizgal, H. M. (1985). Body composition of patients with malnutrition and cancer: Summary of methods of assessment. *Cancer, 55,* 250–253.

Silverman, J. A. (1977). Anorexia nervosa: Clinical and metabolic observations in a successful treatment plan. In R. A. Vigersky (Ed.), *Anorexia nervosa* (pp. 331–340). New York: Raven Press.

Szmukler, G. I., & Tantam, D. (1984). Anorexia nervosa: Starvation dependence. *British Journal of Medical Psychology, 57,* 303–310.

Tokuyama, K., Saito, M., & Okuda, H. (1982). Effects of wheel running on food intake and weight gain of male and female rats. *Physiology and Behavior, 28,* 899–903.

Tuschl, R. J. (1990). From dietary restraint to binge eating: Some theoretical considerations. *Appetite, 14,* 105–109.

Tuschl, R. J., Platte, P., Laessle, R., et al. (1990). Energy expenditure and eating behaviour in healthy young women. *American Journal of Clinical Nutrition, 52,* 81–86.

Unger, R. H., Eisentraut, M., & Madison, L. (1963). The effects of total starvation on the levels of circulating glucagon and insulin in man. *Journal of Clinical Investigation, 42,* 1031–1039.

Vaisman, N., Rossi, M. F., Goldberg, E., et al. (1988). Energy expenditure and body composition in patients with anorexia nervosa. *Journal of Pediatrics, 113,* 919–924.

van Dale, D., Saris, W. H. M., & Hoor, F. T. (1990). Weight maintenance and resting metabolic rate 18–40 months after a diet/exercise treatment. *International Journal of Obesity, 14,* 347–359.

Van Sant, G., Van Gaal, C., Van Acker, K., et al. (1989). Short and long term effects of a very low calorie diet on resting metabolic rate and body composition. *International Journal of Obesity, 13*(Suppl. 2), 87–89.

Viteri, F. E., & Torun, B. (1980). Protein-calorie malnutrition. In R. S. Goodhart & M. E. Shils (Eds.), *Modern nutrition in health and disease* (pp. 697–720). Philadelphia: Lea & Febiger.

Walsh, B. T. (1988). Laboratory studies of eating behavior in bulimia. In B. T. Walsh (Ed.), *Eating behavior in eating disorders* (pp. 177–185). Washington, DC: American Psychiatric Press.

Weight, L. M., & Noakes, T. D. (1987). Is running an analog of anorexia?: A survey of the incidence of eating disorders in female distance runners. *Medicine and Science in Sports and Exercise, 19*(3), 213–217.

Weingarten, H. P., Hendler, R., & Rodin, J. (1988). Metabolism and endocrine secretion in response to a test meal in normal-weight bulimic women. *Psychosomatic Medicine, 50,* 273–285.

Yates, A. (1987). Eating disorders and long-distance running: The ascetic condition. *Integrative Psychiatry, 5,* 201–211.

Yates, A. (1991). *Compulsive exercise and the eating disorders.* New York: Brunner/Mazel.

Yates, A., Leehey, K., & Shisslak, C. (1983). Running—an analogue of anorexia? *New England Journal of Medicine, 308*(5), 251–255.

Zuniga-Guajardo, S., Garfinkel, P. E., & Zinman, B. (1986). Changes in insulin sensitivity and clearance in anorexia nervosa. *Metabolism, 35,* 1096–1100.

# 8

# Menstrual and Reproductive Function in the Eating Disorders

## David S. Goldbloom
### M.D., FRCP(C)

Disturbances in menstrual and reproductive function in eating disorders have been recognized since the case reports of anorexia nervosa (AN) by Sir William Gull that heralded modern recognition of this illness (Gull, 1874). Indeed, more than a century after Gull's description, the presence of primary or secondary amenorrhea remains a mandatory diagnostic criterion for AN (American Psychiatric Association, 1987). The companion disorder bulimia nervosa (BN), in which nutritional chaos features more prominently than emaciation and which often occurs at statistically normal body weights, also features menstrual and reproductive disturbances, as documented in the initial clinical case series reported by Gerald Russell (1979). For the clinician, the recognition of the interface between eating disorders and menstrual and reproductive function is critical from a variety of perspectives—diagnosis of a covert eating disorder; differential diagnosis of amenorrhea, infertility, or complications of pregnancy and child rearing; determination of a healthy body weight for an individual; and avoidance of iatrogenesis through missed diagnosis. For the researcher, the interface also has implications for understanding neuroendocrinology as well as metabolic and nutritional components of menstrual and reproductive function.

The neuroendocrine disturbances relevant to the hypothalamic-pituitary-gonadal axis are discussed elsewhere (Chapter 6). Although the neuroendocrine disturbances associated with amenorrhea in AN and its consequences have been long acknowledged, it is only recently that clinicians have become aware of similar disturbances in BN, even though many BN patients experience amenorrhea (Pirke, Pahl, Schweiger, & Warnhoff, 1985). BN patients with lower body weights demonstrate absence of follicular development, according to neuroendocrine parameters, that leads to menstrual dysfunction, while an impaired luteal phase in terms of progesterone secretion may explain menstrual dysfunction in BN patients at higher body weights (Pirke, Dogs, Fichter, & Tuschl, 1988).

## MENSTRUAL CYCLE AND EATING BEHAVIOR

While it is well known that disturbed eating behavior from any cause can disrupt menstrual function, it is perhaps less well known that the menstrual cycle itself influences appetitive drives. An increase in total caloric intake may occur in the premenstrual phase (Dalvit, 1981), and this increase reflects greater carbohydrate consumption (Dalvit-McPhillips, 1983). More recent and sophisticated laboratory studies of eating behavior in larger series of normal female subjects have confirmed a relationship between menstrual cycle phase and variation in eating behavior (Lissner, Stevens, Levitsky, Rasmussen, & Strupp, 1988; Bowen & Grunberg, 1990). Several important questions result from this replicated finding: What underlies this relationship? What other associations may coexist with this relationship? What are the clinical implications?

The consumption of carbohydrate is in part under control of serotoninergic mechanisms in the hypothalamus (see Chapter 6). In normal subjects, the availability of tryptophan for serotonin synthesis varies inversely with carbohydrate consumption, suggesting that decreased premenstrual serotonin activity may explain altered eating behavior at that time (Hrboticky, Leiter, & Anderson, 1989). Of note, dieting behavior may further decrease the availability of tryptophan, thus augmenting the menstrually related disturbance in this serotonin precursor (McCargar, Clandinin, Fawcett, & Johnston, 1988; Goodwin et al., 1990). Body image disturbance is also related to menstrual cycle, with greater disturbance reported around the perimenstrual phase (Altabe & Thompson, 1990). This may reflect abdominal bloating from fluid retention, as this area of the body was the focus of greatest disturbance; however, the source of the disturbance was not directly investigated.

In women with premenstrual syndrome (late luteal phase dysphoric disorder, American Psychiatric Association, 1987), a disorder that is itself plagued by definitional difficulties, these menstrual phase-related changes in appetite are even more pronounced and are correlated with irritable and/or depressed mood (Both-Orthman, Rubinow, Hoban, Malley, & Grover, 1988). In women with AN, a discernible effect of menstrual phase on eating behavior has been by definition eliminated. However, in BN evidence exists for a premenstrual exacerbation in the frequency of binge-eating episodes (Price, Torem, & DiMarzio, 1987; Gladis & Walsh, 1987). A more precise relationship between eating disorders and premenstrual syndrome awaits more rigorous prospective study.

Finally, a relationship exists between menstrual cycle disturbances and disturbed eating attitudes that fail to meet syndromal criteria for AN or BN. Among women with psychometric evidence of disturbed eating attitudes but without diagnosable AN or BN on clinical interview, there is frequently a history of secondary amenorrhea of significant duration (66.7%) or oligomenorrhea (26.7%) compared to a control population (Kriepe, Strauss, Hodgman, & Ryan, 1989). The degree of weight fluctuation historically appears as an important determinant of menstrual status. However, within a population selected for leanness by virtue of occupation or interest (runners, dancers, and models), abnormal eating attitudes but not body mass or exercise are significantly associated with menstrual dysfunction; this implies that nutritional as well as body weight factors—particularly the disturbed nutritional behaviors characteristic of eating disorders—may explain abnormal menstrual patterns (Rippon, Nash, Myburgh, & Noakes, 1988).

Recently, a survey of women presenting at an endocrine clinic with menstrual dysfunction revealed an association between abnormal eating patterns and polycystic ovary syndrome (PCOS), the latter diagnosed both clinically and ultrasonographically (McCluskey, Evans, Lacey, Pearce, & Jacobs, 1991). Among 152 women with PCOS, 31% were classified as being at medium to high risk of suffering from bulimia nervosa on the basis of a validated self-report questionnaire. However, clinical diagnoses were not systematically confirmed.

## EATING DISORDERS AND REPRODUCTION

The reality that eating disorders affect predominantly women, and primarily during the phase of the life cycle associated with reproduction, has important implications for not only these women but also their families and their physicians.

The presence of AN does not confer absolute protection against conception, even in the context of amenorrhea (Garfinkel & Garner, 1982). It is a clinical recommendation that AN patients delay conception until they have made sustained gains with regard to both body weight and psychological function. What is the evidence for this recommendation?

As part of a long-term follow-up study of 74 women with either the restricting or the bulimic form of AN, retrospective data were obtained on 15 subjects and their 23 pregnancies. The course and outcome of each pregnancy was evaluated according to subtype of AN and whether the AN was still active or in remission at the time of conception (Stewart, Raskin, Garfinkel, MacDonald, & Robinson, 1987). Women in remission from AN gained on average 28 pounds during pregnancy, while restricting AN women gained 15.8 pounds and the three bulimic AN women gained only 5.7 pounds on average. Further, pregnancy was associated with a worsening of the eating disorder symptoms and psychological difficulties. Complications associated with pregnancy and delivery were limited to those women whose eating disorder was active at conception. Finally, APGAR ratings and birth weights of the infants revealed an adverse effect of an active eating disorder. A mean birth weight of 3,592 g for the infants of AN mothers in remission was contrasted with those of 2,744.4 g and 2,362.7 g for the infants of actively restricting AN and actively bulimic AN mothers, respectively. Mean APGAR scores for these same three groups of infants were 8.8, 7.5, and 4.0, respectively. These data provide sobering evidence for the risk of conception during the active phase of AN.

Data from other countries confirm this risk. In England, Treasure and Russell (1988) reported on six emaciated AN women (mean body mass index, 16.8) who conceived at a low body weight. Their average weight gain in pregnancy was 17.6 pounds, and serial fetal ultrasonography revealed diminished growth in the third trimester and an average infant abdominal circumference at birth below the 3rd percentile. Over half this sample of infants was subsequently investigated for poor growth attributed to inadequate feeding. In a long-term Danish follow-up study of 140 women with AN (Brinch, Isager, &

Tolstrup, 1988), in which 50 of these women had given birth to 86 children, perinatal mortality was nearly six times greater and the prevalence of low-birth-weight babies was two times greater than expected rates. Seventeen percent of the infants displayed failure to thrive in the first year of life. In the Netherlands, a report of seven children with growth retardation secondary to underfeeding and possible psychosocial deprivation linked their clinical state with the AN common to all seven mothers (Van Wezel-Meijler & Wit, 1989).

What is the impact of pregnancy per se on attitudes and behaviors characteristic of eating-disordered patients? A survey of 43 American women with AN and BN showed that fears of loss of control of weight and of fetal damage secondary to poor nutrition were virtually ubiquitous (Lemberg & Phillips, 1989). Clearly, these prevalent fears are at odds with each other and leave the pregnant woman with an eating disorder in a state of conflict. Fortunately, in this self-report sample, 70% felt their eating disorder symptoms improved during the pregnancy, although 18.6% described an intensification of bulimic behavior. Eating for someone else rather than for oneself had a permissive effect. Over one third of the sample was eager to resume dieting postpartum; at 1 year postpartum less than one quarter of the sample was asymptomatic in terms of their eating disorder. Less than half the sample had divulged their eating disorder to their obstetrician, underlining the need for a high index of suspicion among clinicians when pregnancy is complicated by poor weight gain. In this postal survey sample, reported maternal mean weight gain during pregnancy and infant birth weight were normal but with a wide range. A more rigorous study of the impact of pregnancy on 50 British women not selected for an eating disorder was conducted via semistructured interview within 3 days postpartum (Fairburn & Welch, 1990). None had an active eating disorder prior to conception, but four had past diagnoses of BN. Half the sample had a clear history of dieting in the past, and this group had more prominent adverse reactions to the weight gain of pregnancy and body shape changes, although some felt that pregnancy allowed them to relinquish their concern with body weight—again, a permissive effect of eating for someone else. A smaller study of the impact of pregnancy on six AN subjects showed that disturbances in body image that were amplified in early pregnancy were mitigated by improvement in eating behaviors and attitudes in later pregnancy (Namir, Malman, & Yager, 1986).

Finally, hyperemesis gravidarum, a well-recognized complication of pregnancy, may be confused with the purging through self-induced vomiting that occurs in patients with eating disorders. A comparison of pregnant women with AN or BN, pregnant women with hyperemesis gravidarum who were not eating disordered, and pregnant healthy controls highlights important differences (Stewart & MacDonald, 1987). The AN and BN women responded poorly to standard interventions in the hospital for hyperemesis gravidarum and had a protracted course of this symptom; they demonstrated significantly less weight gain during pregnancy and lower infant birth weights.

Several case series have documented the consequences of coexistent pregnancy and BN in the absence of concurrent AN. One series consisted of 20 women studied retrospectively (Lacey & Smith, 1987). For almost all subjects, pregnancy was associated with a reduction in binge-eating frequency, and by the third trimester only one quarter of the sample was still binge eating. At 1-year follow-up, however, only one quarter of the total sample had maintained abstinence from bulimic behaviors, and half the sample had experienced a postpartum intensification of BN compared to their preconception state. With regard to the course of the pregnancies, a number of unspecified complications was noted in this uncontrolled survey. With regard to the subjects' behavior with their infants, one third reported binge eating in front of their infants or ignoring them while inducing vomiting. Finally, one third of the subjects expressed concern their infants might be overweight, and several infants were started on weight-losing or carbohydrate-avoidant regimens. A more recent retrospective survey of 38 pregnancies among 20 actively bulimic women featured age-matched healthy controls as well (Mitchell, Seim, Glotter, Soll, & Pyle, 1991). Although there were no statistically significant intergroup differences with regard to weight gain, gestation duration, birth weight of the infants, or pregnancy complications, miscarriage occurred among 39% of the first pregnancies of the BN subjects versus 17% of control subjects' pregnancies. The positive short-term mutative effects of pregnancy on BN have been reported elsewhere (Willis & Rand, 1988) with a high degree of relapse postpartum. Clinicians must recognize the transient nature of such improvement in BN symptoms.

The transgenerational sequelae of BN merit special attention. Two series of young children born to mothers with BN document feeding difficulties, overconcern with weight and shape, and frank neglect (Stein & Fairburn, 1989; Fahy & Treasure, 1989). Thus, obstetricians as well as primary care physicians and pediatricians need to be aware of the effects on children of an eating disorder in the mother.

## INFERTILITY AND EATING BEHAVIOR

Technological advances in reproductive medicine such as in vitro fertilization and hormonal manipulation have assisted many women to overcome infertility. However, these sophisticated techniques should not lead clinicians to overlook underlying reversible causes of infertility.

Several studies of infertile women have revealed findings of relevance to eating disorders and weight preoccupation. In a group of 29 women referred for evaluation of infertility, a variety of prior diagnostic studies of them and their husbands had failed to discover a cause of the reproductive difficulty; however, as a group, these women had a mean body weight that was only 91% of ideal body weight (Bates, Bates, & Whitworth, 1982). One of these women had a past diagnosis of AN. Once low body weight was suggested as the cause of the infertility, 26 of the 29 women accepted a weight gain program as the sole form of treatment. Seventy-three percent of these women proceeded to conceive spontaneously after a mean weight gain of only 8.2 pounds. A second study of 30 women seeking treatment at an infertility clinic examined not only body weight but also psychological attitudes and beliefs characteristic of eating disorders (Allison, Kalvcy, Gilchrist, & Jones, 1988). These women were also classified as ovulatory or anovulatory. Anovulatory women showed a significantly higher drive to be thin on psychological measures, and there was an inverse correlation between percentage of ideal body weight and disturbed attitudes toward body weight and shape.

More recently, a Toronto study featured a more methodologically rigorous approach to the relationship between infertility and eating disorders (Stewart, Robinson, Goldbloom, & Wright, 1990). Consecutive women presenting to two infertility clinics were screened initially via the 26-item Eating Attitudes Test (EAT), a widely used survey instrument (Garner, Olmsted, Bohr, & Garfinkel, 1982). A second questionnaire examined longitudinal weight and menstrual status. Women who scored above well-established threshold scores on the EAT then underwent a semistructured interview with a clinician regarding the diagnosis of an eating disorder. Among 69 consecutive subjects, only three refused to complete the questionnaires—and one of these three later acknowledged ongoing BN. The mean weight of the 66 respondents was 103% of ideal body weight, in contrast to the study cited earlier. Twelve of the 66 women had oligomenorrhea or frank amenorrhea.

Twelve of the 66 women met or surpassed the cutoff score on the EAT. Two additional women acknowledged that despite their low self-report scores they were under treatment for an eating disorder, and a third woman was alleged to have BN by a family member. Thus, 15 of the 66 women raised adequate concern to merit evaluation by clinical interview. Of these 15 women, 11 met criteria of the revised third edition of the *Diagnostic and Statistical Manual of Mental Disorders* (American Psychiatric Association, 1987) for some form of eating disorder—BN (four subjects), AN (one subject), or eating disorder not otherwise specified (six subjects). The latter category describes individuals who meet most but not all of the diagnostic criteria for AN or BN—and, in some measure, reflects the arbitrary nature of the criteria. These prevalence rates exceed those found in the female population at large. The mean percentage of ideal body weight in the eating disorder subgroup was not different from that of infertile women without an eating disorder; however, seven of the 12 women with abnormal menstrual function had coexistent eating disorders. This suggests that infertile women with menstrual dysfunction are at even higher risk for a coexistent—and often undisclosed—eating disorder. Indeed, none of the subjects with eating disorders identified in this study had divulged this problem to their gynecologist at the infertility clinic. At the same time, many of these women expressed concern and guilt over the influence of their eating behavior on their reproductive function.

This study points to the need for primary care physicians and gynecologists to inquire about eating behavior and longitudinal weight fluctuations among women presenting with infertility. The use of a brief, simple screening instrument such as the EAT may facilitate this process. In light of evidence presented earlier in this chapter, the physician may opt, if an eating disorder is present, to ensure that it is well under control before either beginning extensive and invasive infertility investigations or facilitating pregnancy with its attendant risks (Abraham, Mira, & Llewellyn-Jones, 1990). If an active eating disorder is diagnosed in the context of pregnancy, this should be viewed as a high-risk pregnancy. Consideration should be given to hospitalization for monitoring and nutritional rehabilitation. Psychiatric consultation and a multidimensional approach to treatment are indicated.

## CONCLUSIONS

Eating and reproduction are fundamental human behaviors that are linked in both health and disease. Physicians and allied health personnel helping women with eating disorders must recognize the impact of these disturbances on menstrual and reproductive function; similarly, the evaluation of abnormal menses and infertility must include clinical consideration of the disturbed eating behaviors and attitudes of eating disorders. The clinical diagnosis of these disorders demands not only awareness but also sensitivity.

## REFERENCES

Abraham, S., Mira, M., & Llewellyn-Jones, D. (1990). Should ovulation be induced in women recovering from an eating disorder or who are compulsive exercisers? *Fertility and Sterility, 53*, 566–568.

Allison, S., Kalucy, R., Gilchrist, P., & Jones, W. (1988). Weight preoccupation among infertile women. *International Journal of Eating Disorders, 7*, 743–748.

Altabe, M., & Thompson, J. K. (1990). Menstrual cycle, body image, and eating disturbance. *International Journal of Eating Disorders, 9*, 395–401.

American Psychiatric Association. (1987). *Diagnostic and Statistical Manual of Mental Disorders* (3rd ed.—rev.). Washington, DC: Author.

Bates, G. W., Bates, S. R., & Whitworth, N. S. (1982). Reproductive failure in women who practice weight control. *Fertility and Sterility, 37*, 373–378.

Both-Orthman, B., Rubinow, D. R., Hoban, M. C., Malley, J., & Grover, G. N. (1988). Menstrual cycle phase-related changes in appetite in patients with premenstrual syndrome and in control subjects. *American Journal of Psychiatry, 145*, 628–631.

Bowen, D. J., & Grunberg, N. E. (1990). Variations in food preference and consumption across the menstrual cycle. *Physiology and Behaviour, 47*, 287–291.

Brinch, M., Isager, T., & Tolstrup, K. (1988). Anorexia nervosa and motherhood: Reproductional pattern and mothering behaviour of 50 women. *Acta Psychiatrica Scandinavica, 77*, 98–104.

Dalvit, S. P. (1981). The effect of menstrual cycle on patterns of food intake. *American Journal of Clinical Nutrition, 34*, 1811–1815.

Dalvit-McPhillips, S. P. (1983). The effect of the human menstrual cycle on nutrient intake. *Physiology and Behaviour, 31*, 209–212.

Fahy, T., & Treasure, J. (1989). Children of mothers with bulimia nervosa. *British Medical Journal, 299*, 1031.

Fairburn, C. G., & Welch, S. L. (1990). The impact of pregnancy on eating habits and attitudes to shape and weight. *International Journal of Eating Disorders, 9*, 153–160.

Garfinkel, P. E., & Garner, D. M. (1982). *Anorexia nervosa: A multidimensional perspective.* New York: Brunner/Mazel.

.Garner, D. M., Olmsted, M. P., Bohr, Y., & Garfinkel, P. E. (1982). The Eating Attitudes Test: Psychometric features and clinical correlates. *Psychological Medicine, 12,* 871–878.

Gladis, M. M., & Walsh, B. T. (1987). Premenstrual exacerbation of binge eating in bulimia. *American Journal of Psychiatry, 144,* 1592–1595.

Goodwin, G. M., Cowen, P. J., Fairburn, C. G., Parry-Billings, M., Calder, P. C., & Newsholme, E. A. (1990). Plasma concentrations of tryptophan and dieting. *British Medical Journal, 300,* 1499–1500.

Gull, W. W. (1874). Anorexia nervosa. *Transactions of the Clinical Society of London, 7,* 22–28.

Hrboticky, N., Leiter, L. A., & Anderson, G. H. (1989). Menstrual cycle effects on the metabolism of tryptophan loads. *American Journal of Clinical Nutrition, 50,* 46–52.

Kriepe, R. E., Strauss, J., Hodgman, C. H., & Ryan, R. M. (1989). Menstrual abnormalities and subclinical eating disorders: A preliminary report. *Psychosomatic Medicine, 51,* 81–86.

Lacey, J. H., & Smith, G. (1987). Bulimia nervosa: The impact of pregnancy on mother and baby. *British Journal of Psychiatry, 150,* 777–781.

Lemberg, R., & Phillips, J. (1989). The impact of pregnancy on anorexia nervosa and bulimia. *International Journal of Eating Disorders, 8,* 285–295.

Lissner, L., Stevens, J., Levitsky, D. A., Rasmussen, K. M., & Strupp, B. J. (1988). Variation in energy intake during the menstrual cycle: Implications for food-intake research. *American Journal of Clinical Nutrition, 48,* 956–962.

McCargar, L. J., Clandinin, M. T., Fawcett, D. M., & Johnston, J. L. (1988). Short-term changes in energy intake and serum insulin, neutral amino acids, and urinary catecholamine excretion in women. *American Journal of Clinical Nutrition, 47,* 932–941.

McCluskey, S., Evans, C., Lacey, J. H., Pearce, J. M., & Jacobs, H. (1991). Polycystic ovary syndrome and bulimia. *Fertility and Sterility, 55,* 287–291.

Mitchell, J. E., Seim, H. C., Glotter, D., Soll, E. A., & Jacobs, H. (1991). A retrospective study of pregnancy in bulimia nervosa. *International Journal of Eating Disorders, 10,* 209–214.

Namir, S., Melman, K. N., & Yager, J. (1986). Pregnancy in restricter-type anorexia nervosa: A study of six women. *International Journal of Eating Disorders, 5,* 837–845.

Pirke, K. M., Dogs, M., Fichter, M. M., & Tuschl, R. J. (1988). Gonadotrophins, oestradiol and progesterone during the menstrual cycle in bulimia nervosa. *Clinical Endocrinology, 29,* 265–270.

Pirke, K. M., Pahl, J., Schweiger, U., & Warnhoff, M. (1985). Metabolic and endocrine indices of starvation in bulimia: A comparison with anorexia nervosa. *Psychiatry Research, 15*, 33–39.

Price, W. A., Torem, M. S., & DiMarzio, L. R. (1987). Premenstrual exacerbation of bulimia. *Psychosomatics, 28*, 378–380.

Rippon, C., Nash, J., Myburgh, K. H., & Noakes, T. D. (1988). Abnormal Eating Attitudes Test scores predict menstrual dysfunction in lean females. *International Journal of Eating Disorders, 7*, 617–624.

Russell, G. F. M. (1979). Bulimia nervosa: An ominous variant of anorexia nervosa. *Psychological Medicine, 9*, 429–448.

Stein, A., & Fairburn, C. G. (1989). Children of mothers with bulimia nervosa. *British Medical Journal, 299*, 777–778.

Stewart, D. E., & MacDonald, O. L. (1987). Hyperemesis gravidarum and eating disorders and pregnancy. In S. Abraham, & D. Llewellyn-Jones (Eds.), *Eating disorders and disordered eating* (pp. 51–55). Sydney: Ashwood House.

Stewart, D. E., Raskin, J., Garfinkel, P. E., MacDonald, O. L., & Robinson, G. E. (1987). Anorexia nervosa, bulimia, and pregnancy. *American Journal of Obstetrics and Gynecology, 157*, 1194–1198.

Stewart, D. E., Robinson, G. E., Goldbloom, D. S., & Wright, C. (1990). Infertility and eating disorders. *American Journal of Obstetrics and Gynecology, 163*, 1196–1199.

Treasure, J. L., & Russell, G. F. M. (1988). Intrauterine growth and neonatal weight gain in babies of women with anorexia nervosa. *British Medical Journal, 296*, 1038.

Van Wezel-Meijler, G., & Wit, J. M. (1989). The offspring of mothers with anorexia nervosa: A high-risk group for undernutrition and stunting. *European Journal of Pediatrics, 149*, 130–135.

Willis, D. C., & Rand, C. S. W. (1988). Pregnancy in bulimic women. *Obstetrics and Gynecology, 71*, 708–710.

# 9

# The Interaction of Chronic Medical Illness and Eating Disorders

Gary Rodin
M.D., FRCP(C)
Denis Daneman
M.B., B.CH., FRCP(C)
Janet deGroot
M.D., FRCP(C)

It is not surprising that anorexia nervosa, bulimia nervosa, and their partial syndromes have been reported in association with chronic medical disorders such as diabetes mellitus, cystic fibrosis, and inflammatory bowel disease since each of these conditions is relatively common in young women. However, whether this association is purely coincidental or whether certain medical conditions actually predispose to the development or expression of an eating disorder remains controversial. In this chapter we will review only reports in which medical illness precedes or is possibly associated with an eating disorder. Such an association is important because of its implications for the management of the medical condition, and because in some instances it also raises theoretical considerations about the etiology of eating disorders.

A discussion of the methodological problems that beset studies of eating disorders is beyond the scope of this chapter but has recently been addressed in reviews by Shaw and Garfinkel (1990) and by Fairburn and Beglin (1990). Problems in this field include the validity of screening tests and structured interviews employed for diagnostic purposes, and the appropriateness of specified diagnostic criteria in different populations. For example, modifications to the diagnostic criteria may be indicated in the presence of medical conditions such as diabetes mellitus (Rodin & Daneman, 1992). Further, it has been suggested that diagnostic criteria derived from clinical populations are not necessarily appropriate with non-clinical populations (Patton & King, 1991).

## POSTULATED MECHANISMS

There have been repeated suggestions (Ryle, 1936; Dally, 1969; Beumont, Abraham, Argall, George, & Glaunn, 1978) that prior physical illness may increase the vulnerability to anorexia nervosa. In this regard, a recent study (Patton, Wood, & Johnson-Sabine, 1986) revealed that there was more prior physical illness in women with anorexia nervosa than in comparison groups with schizophrenia or general practice controls. We will address the prevalence of eating disorders in specific medical conditions and will examine how eating disorders might be triggered in these circumstances.

Specific mechanisms that might account for more than a coincidental association of eating disorders with medical illness are varied. Confirmation that such mechanisms operate would suggest that the association of eating disorders with certain chronic medical conditions is not merely due to the chance association of the two conditions or to the non-specific stress of a physical illness. It is conceivable that particular characteristics or complications of specific medical disorders or their management may add an additional and specific risk for eating disorders. These include:

1. *Chronic dietary restraint*: There is evidence that chronic dietary restraint (i.e., the regulation of food intake at below normal levels) may be a risk factor for the development or expression of bulimia (Polivy & Herman, 1985; Dolan & Ford, 1991). In this regard, it has been postulated that restrained eaters come to be deficient in their awareness of satiety, and thus may be at risk for disinhibited eating, especially in response to emotional stimuli (Polivy & Herman, 1985; Herman & Polivy, 1988). Chronic dietary restraint may occur either because of the perceived requirements of the treatment regimen of conditions such as diabetes

mellitus or hyperlipidemia, or because food intake provokes specific distressing symptoms. The latter may include postprandial abdominal discomfort or diarrhea with inflammatory bowel disease or the autonomic neuropathy that may be associated with diabetes.

2. *Food preoccupation*: Conditions such as diabetes mellitus, with its disturbance in glucose utilization, and cystic fibrosis, with its associated gastrointestinal malabsorption, both require relatively constant attention to dietary intake. Maintaining a predictable caloric intake with an appropriate balance amongst nutrients is an integral component of the management of diabetes, while maintaining high caloric intake and weight is most important with cystic fibrosis. It has been estimated that children with cystic fibrosis are required to consume 130% to 200% above the recommended daily caloric intake of healthy children (Hubbard, 1985). These daily requirements produce a necessary preoccupation with food. Nevertheless, preliminary data do not suggest that eating disorders are particularly common in cystic fibrosis (Cowen, Rodin, & Levison, 1988).

3. *Weight gain*: Weight gain, which is commonly associated with increased body dissatisfaction and an unsatisfying cycle of dieting and binge eating in young women (Garfinkel et al., 1992), may occur as a result of some medical conditions or their treatment. This effect has been observed after the institution of appropriate insulin therapy for insulin-dependent diabetes mellitus (IDDM) or after the institution of steroid treatment or in a variety of other medical conditions such as inflammatory bowel disease (The DCCT Research Group, 1988). It is likely that weight gain occurs in IDDM both because of the correction of a malnourished state and because of the effect of insulin entering the systemic rather than the portal circulation.

4. *Interference with growth and development*: Chronic physical illness often leads to a failure to thrive in childhood, lack of appropriate growth and weight gain in adolescence, and weight loss in adulthood. This can lead to an undue focus on weight and eating that in a vulnerable individual translates into a pathological pursuit of thinness.

5. *Availability of a potent method of weight loss*: Inadequate treatment of medical conditions such as cystic fibrosis or diabetes mellitus commonly results in weight loss. Individuals with these conditions readily become aware that omission of their daily required medication will produce this effect. The ability to lose weight as a result of medication noncompliance may perpetuate an eating disorder, mask its presence, and contribute to

adverse medical consequences (Rodin, Craven, Littlefield, Murray, & Daneman, 1991).

6. *Effects on psychological functioning and development*: Medical illnesses could predispose to eating disorders via their effects on body image and the sense of self. Indeed, disturbances in the sense of self have been regarded by some as central to eating disorders (Geist, 1989; Goodsitt, 1985). Although there is remarkable resilience and adaptability of the human organism to adverse circumstances, illnesses such as diabetes have been shown to be associated with subtle disturbances in ego development and self-image complexity (Simonds, 1977; Tebbi, Bromberg, Sills, Cukierman, & Piedmonte, 1990). The presence of a physical illness may distort the representation of the self or body image and interfere with the regulation of self-esteem such that the vulnerability to psychological disturbance is increased. Vulnerable individuals may then try to bolster self-esteem by attempting to change their body shape and weight.

7. *Effect on family functioning*: The family or spouse of a chronically ill person may perceive the individual as fragile and in need of protection. This may interfere with age-appropriate attempts for separation and autonomy. Difficulties in separation and autonomy and fears of psychobiological maturity are hypothesized to be critical risk factors for the later development of an eating disorder (Garfinkel & Garner, 1982; Crisp, 1970).

## Medical Conditions with Specific Nutritional Limitations

The most common of these conditions in young women are diabetes mellitus, cystic fibrosis, the hyperlipidemias, and gastrointestinal disorders. Each of these will be addressed separately, although most of the published research in this area has addressed the association between eating disorders and IDDM.

### Insulin-Dependent Diabetes Mellitus

Insulin-Dependent Diabetes Mellitus (IDDM) is one of the most common chronic disorders of childhood and adolescence, affecting 1 in 300 to 600 children by the age of 20 (Drash, 1987). It is now thought to be an autoimmune disease (Atkinson & Maclaren, 1990) that causes pancreatic β-cell destruction and that requires both genetic susceptibility and environmental triggers for its expression. Although IDDM may begin at any age, it presents most commonly in childhood and adolescence. Since eating disorders and IDDM are both relatively common conditions in young women, the coincidental occurrence of these conditions is to be expected. In fact, Marcus and Wing (1990) recently summarized 57 cases reported in the literature of eating disorders associated with IDDM.

Nielsen, Borner, and Kabel (1987) retrospectively reviewed 242 cases of eating disorders treated at Rigshospitalet in Copenhagen and found that IDDM was present in 0.2%, which they considered to be six times that expected on a chance basis. However, the administration of psychometric tests has produced conflicting findings regarding eating and weight psychopathology in IDDM. Some investigators have shown no difference in such psychopathology between women with IDDM and control groups (Wing, Nowalk, Marcus, Koeske, & Finegold, 1986; Robertson & Rosenvinge, 1990), while others (Rosmark et al., 1986; Steel, Young, Lloyd, & MacIntyre, 1989; Striegel-Moore, Nicholson, & Tamborlane, 1991) have reported more disturbances in young women with IDDM. In a longitudinal study, Steel, Lloyd, Young, and MacIntyre (1990) administered the Eating Attitudes Test-40 (EAT-40) to 32 males and 15 females soon after the onset of IDDM and again 12 months later. They found a mean weight gain of 6.9 kg in the females and 8.6 kg in the males, but only the females showed an increased score on the dieting subscale of the EAT and on the drive for thinness subscale of the Eating Disorder Inventory (EDI). Steel et al. (1990) speculated that weight gain after the diagnosis might be a risk factor for body image disturbances and for the development of eating disorders in the young women.

A number of diagnostic surveys based on self-report measures (Rodin et al., 1991; Hudson, Wentworth, Hudson, & Pope, 1985; Powers, Malone, Coovert, & Schulman, 1990; Stancin, Link, & Reuter, 1989) and using clinical interviews (Rodin, Johnson, Garfinkel, Daneman, & Kenshole, 1986, 1987; Steel, Young, Lloyd, & Clarke, 1987) suggest that bulimia and anorexia nervosa are relatively common in young women with IDDM. However, a recent study (Peveler & Fairburn, 1991) in which 175 patients with IDDM were compared to control subjects matched for age and social class using the Eating Disorder Examination (EDE) and the EDI found no difference between diabetic and control subjects on the EDI subscales or in the prevalence of eating disorders based on criteria of the revised third edition of the *Diagnostic and Statistical Manual of Mental Disorders* (DSM-III-R). Controversy persists about the presence and significance of disordered eating in IDDM. It is possible that the diagnostic criteria for eating disorders should be modified in the presence of IDDM because less extreme behavior may have greater metabolic repercussions in IDDM and because insulin omission may be a more prevalent means of inducing weight loss in women with IDDM than either self-induced vomiting or laxative abuse (Rodin et al., 1991).

Eating disorders in IDDM, even those that do not meet DSM-III-R criteria, may still have significant metabolic and medical consequences. Higher glycosylated hemoglobin levels have been found in IDDM patients with eating disorders than in those without (Rodin et al., 1991; Rodin et al., 1986–87; Steel et al., 1987; Fairburn, Peveler, Davies, Mann, & Mayou, 1991; Rodin, Daneman, Johnson, Kenshole, & Garfinkel, 1985). This relative impairment in metabolic control may be attributed to binge eating, to neglect of diabetes management, or to deliberate underdosing with insulin to prevent weight gain. From 12% (Rodin et al., 1991) to 39% (Stancin et al., 1989) of young women with IDDM report such insulin omission, and the majority of those with IDDM and eating disorders also engage in such behavior (Rodin et al., 1991). Indeed, diabetes noncompliance or impaired metabolic control is a common presentation of eating disorders in the diabetes clinic setting.

Eating disorders may be associated with short-term complications of IDDM including ketoacidosis, growth failure, and hypoglycemic seizures. Unfortunately, they also appear to be associated with long-term diabetes-related microvascular complications. Steel et al. (1987) and Colas, Mathieu, and Tchebroutsky (1991) reported a high incidence and early onset of such complications as retinopathy, nephropathy, and neuropathy in young women with IDDM and eating disorders.

### Cystic Fibrosis

Cystic fibrosis (CF), the most common lethal genetic disease among Caucasians in North America, occurs in from 1 in 1,000 to 1 in 2,000 live births (Hodson, 1983; Warwich & Pogue, 1977). This disease affects the exocrine glands of the body and produces maldigestion, causing poor weight gain and delayed growth, particularly with the onset of adolescence. As well, recurrent respiratory infections are common with this condition. Studies that have explored a possible association between CF and eating disorders are limited, since it is only in recent years that CF patients have survived into and beyond adolescence, the typical age of onset of eating disorders. The mean life expectancy of CF is now 30 years in some centers (Medical News, 1984), while median age of survival was only 12 years a few decades ago (Cystic Fibrosis Foundation, 1978).

One case report clearly describes anorexia nervosa and bulimia of 3 years' duration in a 24-year-old woman with CF (Goldbloom, 1988). An earlier survey found that 13 of 108 (12%) CF patients between the ages of 12 and 21 had "atypical eating disorders" (Pumariega, Pursell, Spock, & Jones, 1986). However, methodological limitations in this study include a failure to describe the method of data collection (i.e., whether retrospective or prospective), and which diagnostic system of classification was used. Although it appears that CF patients may have eating difficulties related to the need to consume well above the recommended daily allowance of healthy children (Hubbard, 1985), none in this study had the body image disturbance typical of women with eating disorders and thus did not meet DSM-III-R criteria for an eating disorder. A recent study (Cowen et al., 1988) suggests that eating and weight psychopathology may be even less common in CF patients than in controls. Another study comparing low weight CF patients with age-matched women with anorexia nervosa who were equally malnourished and had similar pubertal delays found that the CF patients did not have the psychopathological features of those with eating disorders (Steiner, Rahimzadeh, & Lewiston, 1990).

Subjective distress regarding physical appearance in CF patients differs from that in women with eating disorders and is related to shortness and to delayed secondary sexual characteristics (Boyle, de Sant'Agnese, Sack, Millican, & Kulczyki, 1986). In one study, these were of greater concern to patients than the frequent chronic cough associated with CF (Strauss & Wellisch, 1980). Further, CF patients are frequently aware of being underweight and of suffering from a chronic, incurable illness that typically has a shortened life expectancy. Maintaining appropriate weight helps diminish morbidity and the risk of recurrent respiratory infections. Despite these stresses, however, there is little evidence of an increased rate of eating disorders in CF. This is fortunate since malnutrition in CF is associated with increased frequency and severity of pulmonary infections, deterioration of pulmonary function, delay in recovery from illness (Roy, Darling, & Weber, 1984), and increased mortality (Gurwitz, Cory, Francis, Crozier, & Levinson, 1979).

### Gastrointestinal Disorders and Hyperlipidemia

Gastrointestinal disorders may simulate anorexia nervosa because weight loss may be a complication or because patients may reduce food intake to avoid abdominal discomfort (see Chapter 2). Conversely, pancreatitis can be mistakenly diagnosed in women with eating disorders since serum amylase may be elevated in eating disorder patients who frequently induce vomiting (Mitchell, Pyle, Eckert, Hatsukami, & Lentz, 1983). However, elevations of serum amylase in this context tend to be less than twofold (Humphries, Adams, Eckfeldt, Levitt, & McClain, 1987), and the amylase is typically salivary, not pancreatic, in origin.

Schoettle (1979) reported a case of a 12-year-old male who presented with food restriction, body image distortion, increased exercise, and abdominal pain. The abdominal pain was at first mistakenly attributed to an eating disorder, although treatment of the pancreatitis resolved both conditions. Presumably, food restriction was provoked or perpetuated because eating produced pain. Similarly, Isaacs, Saunders, Rosen, and Sladen (1986) reported a case in which malnutrition and ascites were mistakenly attributed to an eating disorder instead of to acute pancreatitis with a subsequent pseudocyst. Since alcoholism is relatively common in women with bulimia, clinicians must be alert to the possibility of pancreatitis and other complications of excessive alcohol intake.

In a follow-up study of 21 patients with hyperlipidemic pancreatitis, the five who had repeated, severe relapses of pancreatitis were found to have bulimia according to DSM-III criteria. It may be significant in this regard that the prescribed diet for this condition is of a restrictive nature, in terms of both calorie and fat content. Such dietary restraint, together with the other emotional stressors associated with the illness, may contribute to the development of an eating disorder in that binge eating may provoke pancreatitis (Gavish et al., 1987). The emotional stresses may include the death of relatives with the same condition, and the knowledge that the illness has a high morbidity and mortality but no definitive treatment. Mild chronic pancreatitis is a recognized complication of malnutrition (Pitchumoni, 1973). It has also been reported in association with AN (Nordgren & von Scheele, 1977), resolving with weight gain. Acute pancreatitis has occurred with refeeding of hospitalized AN patients (Keane, Fennell, & Tomkin, 1978; Gryboski, Hillemeiaer, Kocoshis, Anyan, & Seashore, 1980).

Eating disorders have also been reported with other gastrointestinal diseases, such as Crohn's disease. Crohn's disease is a chronic inflammatory disorder of unknown etiology involving the gastrointestinal tract. Clinically there is recurrent inflammatory involvement of intestinal segments with diverse clinical manifestations and an unpredictable course (*Harrison's Principles of Internal Medicine*, 1991).

Two cases of bulimia reported to occur after the onset of Crohn's disease suggest that the stress of the illness and the weight gain associated with corticosteroid treatment may play a role (Meadows & Treasure, 1989). In these cases, weight gain on steroids was associated with a body image disturbance and triggered excessive dieting, weight loss, and, in one case, the use of laxatives. In that case, the laxatives were used to exacerbate the Crohn's disease and thereby to promote weight loss. The self-induced exacerbation of the disease to promote weight loss is similar to the insulin omission that is common in young women with IDDM and eating disorders (Rodin et al., 1991). A case of anorexia nervosa appears to have been precipitated by Crohn's disease following a bout of diarrhea (Hershman & Hershman, 1985). Following surgical management of Crohn's disease, the patient recovered from anorexia nervosa. Likely, the psychological response to Crohn's disease with feelings of helplessness or being out of control may have contributed to the onset of anorexia nervosa.

A variety of gastrointestinal conditions that interfere with food intake or that are associated with weight loss may mimic or exacerbate eating disorders. For example, conditions such as superior mesenteric artery syndrome (SMAS), and the arteriomesenteric compression of the duodenum with delay in the passage of intestinal contents beyond the third part of the duodenum (Altman & Puranik, 1973; Burrington, 1976), have been reported to present as apparent anorexia nervosa (Burrington & Wayne, 1974). In such cases, food is avoided not out of the pursuit of thinness but to control postprandial vomiting and distress (see Chapter 2).

## Other Medical Conditions

Eating disorders have also been reported in association with certain neurological conditions, although the association seems either idiosyncratic or nonspecific. Anorexia nervosa was reported in a patient with a juxtomedullary meningioma (Reiser & Swigar, 1984), a rare tumor affecting 0.001% of the population. It was postulated that the neurological deficits in this patient that led to urinary and fecal incontinence and difficulties with proprioception contributed to an increased need to experience a sense of control in other domains, including eating behavior. Anorexia nervosa has also been reported in association with multiple sclerosis (Touyz, Gertler, Brigham, Somerville, & Beumont, 1988), the most common disease of the nervous system in the northern hemisphere. In this case, the patient reported an irrational fear that eating would "feed" and thereby worsen her neurological condition. The experiences of helplessness and of losing control as a result of the symptoms of multiple sclerosis were also considered to have contributed to the eating disorder in this case.

Damlouji and Ferguson (1985) reported three cases of anorexia nervosa occurring following motor vehicle accidents with head or facial injury requiring hospitalization. All three cases were notable for marked body image distortion. Case reports have appeared that describe AN coincident with Turner's syndrome (Pitts & Guze, 1963), urogenital anomalies (Halmi & Rigas, 1973), and neurofibromatosis (Fitzpatrick, McDermott, May, & Hofeldt, 1983). A young woman, blind since age 2, with a psychiatric history of suicide attempts, developed AN following exposure to women with AN (Yager, Hatton, & Ma, 1986). She displayed typical disturbed weight and shape concerns as well as psychological difficulties measured by the Eating Disorder Inventory. Contributing factors were chaotic family relations and a disturbed sense of self.

Since eating disorders are common, it is not surprising that they have been reported in association with a variety of medical conditions. In some cases, there are specific features of the medical condition or its treatment that act as triggers for the onset of an eating disorder. In a case reported by Black, Hall, Kay, and Hellborn (1965), anorexia nervosa developed apparently in response both to the hypothalamic disturbance in a patient with Cushing's syndrome and to the associated weight gain and body dissatisfaction. A similar case of anorexia nervosa was reported by Katz, Weiner, Kream, and Zumoff (1986) in a woman with Cushing's syndrome who was subsequently found to have a pituitary adenoma. Anorexia nervosa has also been reported in association with Down's syndrome (Syzmanski & Biederman, 1984; Cottrell & Crisp, 1984), and in one such case an associated insulinoma was discovered. It was suggested that some of the psychological symptoms in that case were due to the hypoglycemia caused by the insulin-producing tumor. Anorexia nervosa was also reported in association with the diagnosis and initial treatment of acute lymphocytic leukemia in an 8-year-old girl (Szajnberg, Zalneraitis, Altman, Weisman, & Andrulonis, 1989). Behavioral and family therapy resulted in rapid resolution of the eating disorder in this girl who had also reported conversion symptoms of a neurological nature. Eating disorders have also been reported to occur in patients with connective tissue disease (Kaplan & Katz, 1992; Erman & Murray, 1980). Acne has also been postulated as a risk factor (Lee, Leung, Wing, & Chiu, 1991); it has been postulated that starvation and weight loss, acting through a reduction in androgenic hormones, may lead to a resolution of acne.

## Diagnostic and Therapeutic Implications

Whatever accounts for the association between chronic medical illnesses and eating disorders, there may be important implications for medical management. For example, in diabetes, eating pathology may present as recurrent ketoacidosis due to insulin omission and/or binge eating. The correct diagnosis requires a high index of suspicion and appropriate adjustment of the diagnostic criteria—for example, insulin omission in adolescent girls with diabetes is the major method for weight reduction rather than self-induced vomiting or purging (Rodin et al., 1991). Clinicians involved in the care of young women with diabetes must be sensitized to the possibility that abnormal eating behaviors may be contributing significantly to problems with metabolic control, for example, recurrent ketoacidosis, severe hypoglycemia, and poor metabolic control (Rodin et al., 1991; Rodin et al., 1986–87).

Once a diagnosis of an eating disorder is made in an individual with diabetes or some other chronic medical illness, the therapeutic plan must take into account the realities of both conditions. In practice, this requires that the plan be tailored to meet the needs of the individual patient. A less rigid approach to dietary planning may be all that is required in some young women. In others, such flexibility may actually heighten anxiety because of its perceived impact on metabolic stability. In that case, a more vigorous psychological intervention (e.g., individual or group therapy) may be indicated. There are no controlled studies available that document the efficacy of different treatment approaches with the eating-disordered young woman who has diabetes.

Similarly, in chronic inflammatory bowel disease, pressure to increase food intake may exacerbate abdominal pain and thereby cause further fear of eating. It is beyond the scope of this chapter to detail the management of specific chronic medical disorders or of eating disorders. However, we wish to emphasize that the management of these coexisting conditions requires an individualized approach that takes into account both medical and psychological sequelae.

## CONCLUSIONS

Medical illness or its treatment may act as a nonspecific trigger for the onset of an eating disorder or may coincidentally be associated with it. The multiple losses and stresses associated with a medical disorder and the alterations in bodily appearance that may occur almost certainly account for the timing of the onset of eating disorders in some patients. In other cases, specific aspects of the illness or its treatment may act as triggers for the occurrence or exacerbation of eating pathology. Examples of this include the dietary restraint that is imposed by IDDM or the hyperlipidemias, or the weight gain that may occur as a result of insulin treatment in IDDM, or steroid treatment for a variety of other medical conditions. Weight gain may lead to a cycle of body dissatisfaction, dieting, and binge eating.

Whether there is an increased prevalence of eating disorders in the medically ill is, at present, unsubstantiated, and a variety of methodological problems complicate this assessment. However, eating disorders, particularly if undiagnosed and untreated, certainly may complicate the course of many medical illnesses. This is particularly true with conditions such as IDDM in which meticulous attention to dietary intake is so important for its management. In young women with IDDM, eating pathology and deliberate omission or reduction of insulin dose to lose weight need to be considered as a cause of unexplained poor metabolic control. The detection and treatment of eating disorders, and attention to factors such as weight gain, which may provoke dieting and binge eating, may help to alleviate one cause of distress in patients who are medically ill.

## REFERENCES

Altman, D. H., & Puranik, S. T. (1973). Superior mesenteric artery syndrome in children. *American Journal of Roentgenology, Radium Therapy, and Nuclear Medicine, 118,* 104–108.

Atkinson, M. A., & Maclaren, N. K. (1990). What causes diabetes? *Scientific American, 261,* 62–71.

Beumont, P. J., V., Abraham, S. F., Argall, W. S., George, G. C. W., & Glaunn, D. E. (1978). The onset of anorexia nervosa. *Australian and New Zealand Journal of Psychiatry, 12,* 145–149.

Black, M. M., Hall, R., Kay, D. W. K., & Hellborn, J. R. (1965). Anorexia nervosa in Cushing's syndrome. *Journal of Clinical Endocrinology and Metabolism, 25,* 1030–1034.

Boyle, I. R., de Sant'Agnese, P. A., Sack, S., Millican, F., & Kulczyki, L. L. (1986). Emotional adjustment of adolescents and young adults with cystic fibrosis. *Journal of Pediatrics, 88,* 318–326.

Burrington, J. D. (1976). Superior mesenteric artery syndrome in children. *American Journal of Diseases of Children, 130,* 1367–1370.

Burrington, J. D., & Wayne, E. R. (1974). Obstruction of the duodenum by the superior mesenteric artery: Does it exist in children? *Journal of Pediatric Surgery, 9*, 733–741.

Colas, C., Mathieu, P., & Tchebroutsky, G. (1991). Eating disorders and retinal lesions in Type I (insulin-dependent) diabetic women [Letter to editor]. *Diabetologia, 34*, 288.

Cottrell, D. J., & Crisp, A. H. (1984). Anorexia nervosa in Down's syndrome: A case report. *British Journal of Psychiatry, 145*, 195–196.

Cowen, L., Rodin, G., & Levison, H. (1988). *The vulnerability of adolescents with cystic fibrosis to eating disorders.* Paper presented at the North American CF Conference, Orlando, FL, September.

Crisp, A. H. (1970). Premorbid factors in adult disorders of weight, with particular reference to primary anorexia nervosa (weight phobia). *Journal of Psychosomatic Research, 14*, 1–22.

Cystic Fibrosis Foundation. (1978). *1976 report on survival studies of patients with cystic fibrosis.*

Dally, P. (1969). *Anorexia nervosa.* London: Heinemann.

Damlouji, N. F., & Ferguson, J. M. (1985). Three cases of posttraumatic anorexia nervosa. *American Journal of Psychiatry, 142*, 362–363.

The DCCT Research Group. (1988). Weight gain associated with intensive therapy in the Diabetes Control and Complications Trial. *Diabetes Care, 11*, 567–573.

Dolan, B., & Ford, K. (1991). Binge-eating and dietary restraint: A cross-cultural analysis. *International Journal of Eating Disorders, 10*, 345–353.

Drash, A. (1987). *Clinical care of the diabetic child.* St. Louis: Yearbook Medical Publishers.

Erman, M. K., & Murray, G. B. (1980). A case report of anorexia nervosa and Gaucher's disease. *American Journal of Psychiatry, 137*, 858–859.

Fairburn, C. G., & Beglin, S. J. (1990). Studies of the epidemiology of bulimia nervosa. *American Journal of Psychiatry, 147*, 401–408.

Fairburn, C. G., Peveler, R. C., Davies, B., Mann, J. I., & Mayou, R. A. (1991). Eating disorders in young adults with insulin dependent diabetes mellitus: A controlled study. *British Medical Journal, 303*, 17–20.

Fitzpatrick, J. E., McDermott, M., May, D., & Hofeldt, F. D. (1983). Eruptive neurofibromatosis associated with anorexia nervosa. *Archives of Dermatology, 119*, 1019–1021.

Garfinkel, P., & Garner, D. (1982). *Anorexia nervosa: A multidimensional perspective.* New York: Brunner/Mazel.

Garfinkel, P., Goldbloom, D., Davis, R., Olmsted, M., Garner, D., & Halmi, K. (1992). Body dissatisfaction in bulimia nervosa: Relationship to weight and shape concerns and psychological functioning. *International Journal of Eating Disorders, 11*, 151–161.

Gavish, D., Eisenberg, S., Berry, E. M., Kleinman, Y., Witztum, E., Norman, J., & Leitersdorf, E. (1987). Bulimia. An underlying behavioral disorder in hyperlipidemic pancreatitis: A prospective multi-disciplinary approach. *Archives of Internal Medicine, 147*, 705–708.

Geist, R. A. (1989). Self psychological reflections on the origins of eating disorders. *Journal of the American Academy of Psychoanalysis, 17*, 5–27.

Goldbloom, D. S. (1988). Anorexia nervosa and cystic fibrosis: A case report. *International Journal of Eating Disorders, 7*, 433–437.

Goodsitt, A. (1985). Self psychology and the treatment of anorexia nervosa. In D. M. Garner & P. E. Garfinkel (Eds.), *Handbook of psychotherapy for anorexia nervosa and bulimia* (pp. 55–82). New York: Guilford Press.

Gryboski, J., Hillemeiaer, C., Kocoshis, S., Anyan, W., & Seashore, J. S. (1980). Refeeding pancreatitis in malnourished children. *Journal of Pediatrics, 97*, 441–443.

Gurwitz, D., Cory, M., Francis, P. S., Crozier, D., & Levinson, H. (1979). Perspective in cystic fibrosis. *Pediatric Clinics of North America, 26*, 603–615.

Halmi, K. A., & Rigas, C. (1973). Urogenital malformations associated with anorexia nervosa. *British Journal of Psychiatry, 122*, 79–81.

*Harrison's principles of internal medicine* (12th ed., Vol. 2). (1991). J. D. Wilson, E. Braunwald, K. J. Isselbacher, R. G. Petersdorf, J. B. Martin, A. S. Fauci, & R. K. Root (Eds.), New York: McGraw-Hill.

Herman, C. P., & Polivy, J. (1988). Restraint and excess in dieters and bulimics. In K. M. Pirke, D. Ploog, & W. Vandereycken (Eds.), *The psychobiology of bulimia nervosa*. Heidelberg: Springer.

Hershman, M. J., & Hershman, M. (1985). Anorexia nervosa and Crohn's disease. *British Journal of Clinical Practice, 39*, 157–159.

Hodson, M. E. (1983). Cystic fibrosis in adolescents and adults. *Practitioner, 227*, 1723–1731.

Hubbard, V. S. (1985). Nutritional considerations in cystic fibrosis. *Seminars in Respiratory Medicine, 6*, 308–313.

Hudson, J. I., Wentworth, S. M., Hudson, M. S., & Pope, H. G. Jr. (1985). Prevalence of anorexia nervosa and bulimia among young diabetic women. *Journal of Clinical Psychiatry, 46*, 88–89.

Humphries, L. L., Adams, L. J., Eckfeldt, J. H., Levitt, M. D., & McClain, C. J. (1987). Hyperamylasemia in patients with eating disorders. *Annals of Internal Medicine, 106*, 50–52.

Isaacs, P., Saunders, A. J., Rosen, B. K., & Sladen, G. E. (1986). Anorexia nervosa and pancreatic ascites. *Postgraduate Medical Journal, 62*, 1151–1152.

Kaplan, A. S., & Katz, M. (1992). Eating disorders and connective tissue disease: Etiologic and treatment considerations. *Psychosomatics, 33*, 105–108.

Katz, J. L., Weiner, H., Kream, J., & Zumoff, B. (1986). Cushing's disease in a young woman with anorexia nervosa: Pathophysiological implications. *Canadian Journal of Psychiatry, 31*, 861–864.

Keane, F. B., Fennell, J. S., & Tomkin, G. H. (1978). Acute pancreatitis, acute gastric dilation and duodenal ileus following refeeding in anorexia nervosa. *Israel Journal of Medical Sciences, 147*, 191–192.

Lee, S., Leung, Y. K., Wing, H. F. K., & Chiu, C. C. (1991). Acne as a risk factor for anorexia nervosa in Chinese. *Australian and New Zealand Journal of Psychiatry, 25*, 134–137.

Marcus, M. D., & Wing, R. R. (1990). Eating disorders and diabetes. In C. S. Holmes (Ed.), *Neuropsychological and behavioural aspects of diabetes* (pp. 102–121). New York: Springer-Verlag.

Meadows, G., & Treasure, J. (1989). Bulimia nervosa and Crohn's disease: Two case reports. *Acta Psychiatrica Scandinavica, 79*, 413–414.

Medical News. (1984). Progress continues against cystic fibrosis. *Journal of the American Medical Association, 252*, 2527.

Mitchell, J. E., Pyle, R. L., Eckert, E. D., Hatsukami, D., & Lentz, R. (1983). Electrolyte and other physiological abnormalities in patients with bulimia. *Psychological Medicine, 13*, 273–278.

Nielsen, S., Borner, H., & Kabel, M. (1987). Anorexia nervosa/bulimia in diabetes mellitus: A review and a presentation of five cases. *Acta Psychiatrica Scandinavica, 75*, 464–473.

Nordgren, L., & von Scheele, C. (1977). Hepatic and pancreatic dysfunction in anorexia nervosa: A report of two cases. *Biological Psychiatry, 12*, 681–686.

Patton, G. C., & King, M. B. (1991). Epidemiological study of eating disorders: Time for a change of emphasis. *Psychological Medicine, 21*, 287–291.

Patton, G. C., Wood, K., & Johnson-Sabine, E. (1986). Physical illness: A risk factor for anorexia nervosa. *British Medical Journal, 149*, 756–759.

Peveler, R. C., & Fairburn, C. (1991). *Prevalence of eating disorders in diabetics*. Paper presented at the American Psychiatric Association 144th Annual Meeting, New Orleans, LA, May [Abstract NR 321].

Pitchumoni, C. S. (1973). Pancreas in primary malnutrition disorders. *American Journal of Clinical Nutrition, 26*, 374–379.

Pitts, F. N., & Guze, S. B. (1963). Anorexia nervosa and gonadal dysgenesis (Turner's syndrome). *American Journal of Psychiatry, 119*, 1100–1102.

Polivy, J., & Herman, C. P. (1985). Dieting and bingeing: A causal analysis. *American Psychologist, 40*, 193–201.

Powers, P. S., Malone, J. I., Coovert, D. L., & Schulman, R. G. (1990). Insulin-dependent diabetes mellitus and eating disorders: A prevalence study. *Comprehensive Psychiatry, 31*, 205–210.

Pumariega, A. J., Pursell, J., Spock, A., & Jones, J. D. (1986). Eating disorders in adolescents with cystic fibrosis. *Journal of the American Academy of Child Psychiatry, 25*, 269–275.

Reiser, L. W., & Swigar, M. (1984). Anorexia nervosa masking the diagnosis of spinal meningioma: A case report. *General Hospital Psychiatry, 6*, 289–293.

Robertson, P., & Rosenvinge, J. H. (1990). Insulin-dependent diabetes mellitus: A risk factor in anorexia nervosa or bulimia nervosa? An empirical study of 116 women. *Journal of Psychosomatic Research, 34*, 535–541.

Rodin, G., Craven, J., Littlefield, C., Murray, M., & Daneman, D. (1991). Eating disorders and intentional insulin undertreatment in adolescent females with diabetes. *Psychosomatics, 32*, 171–176.

Rodin, G., & Daneman, D. (1992). Eating disorders and insulin-dependent diabetes mellitus: A problematic association. *Diabetes Care, 15*, 1402–1412.

Rodin, G. M., Daneman, D., Johnson, L. E., Kenshole, A., & Garfinkel, P. (1985). Anorexia nervosa and bulimia in female adolescents with insulin dependent diabetes mellitus: A systematic study. *Journal of Psychiatric Research, 19*, 381–384.

Rodin, G. M., Johnson, L. E., Garfinkel, P. E., Daneman, D., & Kenshole, A. B. (1986–87). Eating disorders in female adolescents with insulin dependent diabetes mellitus. *International Journal of Psychiatry in Medicine, 16*, 49–57.

Rosmark, B., Berne, C., Holmgren, S., Lago, C., Renholm, G., & Sohlberg, S. (1986). Eating disorders in patients with insulin-dependent diabetes mellitus. *Journal of Clinical Psychiatry, 47*, 547–550.

Roy, C. C., Darling, P., & Weber, A. M. (1984). A rational approach to meeting macro- and micronutrient needs in cystic fibrosis. *Journal of Pediatric Gastroenterology & Nutrition, 3*(Suppl. 1), S154–S162.

Ryle, J. A. (1936). Anorexia nervosa. *Lancet, 2*, 893–899.

Schoettle, U. C. (1979). Pancreatitis: A complication, a concomitant, or a cause of an anorexia nervosalike syndrome. *Journal of the American Academy of Child Psychiatry, 18*, 384–390.

Shaw, B. F., & Garfinkel, P. E. (1990). Research problems in the eating disorders. *International Journal of Eating Disorders, 9*, 545–555.

Simonds, J. F. (1977). Psychiatric status of diabetic youth matched with a control group. *Diabetes, 26*, 921–925.

Stancin, T., Link, D. L., & Reuter, J. M. (1989). Binge eating and purging in young women with IDDM. *Diabetes Care, 12*, 601–603.

Steel, J. M., Lloyd, G. G., Young, R. J., & MacIntyre, C. C. A. (1990). Changes in eating attitudes during the first year of treatment for diabetes. *Journal of Psychosomatic Research, 34*, 313–318.

Steel, J. M., Young, R. J., Lloyd, G. G., & Clarke, B. F. (1987). Clinically appar-

ent eating disorders in young diabetic women: Associations with painful neuropathy and other complications. *British Medical Journal, 294,* 859–862.

Steel, J. M., Young, R. J., Lloyd, G. G., & MacIntyre, C. C. A. (1989). Abnormal
eating attitudes in young insulin-dependent diabetics. *British Journal of
Psychiatry, 155,* 515–521.

Steiner, H., Rahimzadeh, P., & Lewiston, N. B. (1990). Psychopathology in cystic
fibrosis and anorexia nervosa: A controlled comparison. *International Journal of
Eating Disorders, 6,* 675–683.

Strauss, G. D., & Wellisch, D. K. (1980). Psychological assessment of adults with
cystic fibrosis. *International Journal of Psychiatry in Medicine, 10,* 265–272.

Striegel-Moore, R. H., Nicholson, T., & Tamborlane, W. (1991). Disordered eat-
ing in girls with insulin-dependent diabetes mellitus. Paper presented at the
American Psychiatric Association 144th Annual Meeting, New Orleans, LA,
May [Abstract NR 312].

Syzmanski, L. S., & Biederman, J. (1984). Depression and anorexia nervosa of persons with Down's syndrome. *American Journal of Mental Deficiency, 89,*
246–251.

Szajnberg, N. M., Zalneraitis, E., Altman, A. J., Weisman, S. J., & Andrulonis,
P. A. (1989). Atypical anorexia nervosa and hysterical symptomatology in a
child with acute lymphocytic leukemia: A case management conference.
*Clinical Pediatrics, 28,* 561–567.

Tebbi, C. K., Bromberg, C., Sills, I., Cukierman, J., & Piedmonte, M. (1990).
Vocational adjustment and general well-being of young adults with IDDM.
*Diabetes Care, 13,* 98–103.

Touyz, S. W., Gertler, R., Brigham, S., Somerville, B., & Beumont, P. J. V.
(1988). Anorexia nervosa in a patient with multiple sclerosis: A case report.
*International Journal of Eating Disorders, 8,* 231–234.

Warwick, W., & Pogue, R. (1977). Cystic fibrosis: An expanding challenge for
internal medicine. *Journal of the American Medical Association, 239,* 2159.

Wing, R. R., Nowalk, M. P., Marcus, M. D., Koeske, R., & Finegold, D. (1986).
Sub-clinical eating disorders and glycemic control in adolescents with Type 1
diabetes. *Diabetes Care, 9,* 162–167.

Yager, J., Hatton, C. A., & Ma, L. (1986). Anorexia nervosa in a woman totally
blind since the age of two. *British Journal of Psychiatry, 149,* 506–509.

# 10

# *Genetic Contributions to Eating Disorders*

## D. Blake Woodside
### M.D., M.SC., FRCP(C)

This chapter will review a topic that has only recently become a focus of study—the role of heritable genetic factors in the etiology of anorexia nervosa and bulimia nervosa. The chapter will briefly review some relevant terminology, critically comment on the literature on genetic factors in anorexia nervosa and bulimia nervosa, and suggest some routes for future investigation.

## REVIEW OF GENETIC METHODOLOGY RELEVANT TO EATING DISORDERS

### Definition of "Genetic" and Family Study Methodology

Many individuals make the understandable error of equating "running in families" with hereditary genetic causation. However, even a cursory examination of this concept demonstrates its inaccuracy. For example, it has been frequently observed that, if one of your parents is a physician, there is a higher chance of you yourself ending up in medical school. A simplistic conclusion from this observation would be that attending medical school is a genetic condition.

The simplest form of genetic study consists of making observations about the relative occurrence of a condition of interest in specific families and comparing the rate in these families with rates in known, comparable populations. This method of studying families has two major variations. If the observations about the families of interest are obtained from each individual separately, this is known as the family study method. If information about the family is obtained by one individual's reporting about other family members, this is known as the family history method. The advantage of the pure family study method is that the reliability of the information collected is thought to be the highest possible. This particular concern is highly relevant in the study of psychiatric disorders, where there are rarely objective physical or laboratory measures to define the diagnosis. The disadvantages of this method relate, first, to the enormous amount of work involved in assessing all of the members of an extended pedigree, and second, to the disqualification of information that might be available about deceased or unavailable family members.

By contrast, the major advantage of the family history method is the marked reduction in effort required to assemble information about a specific family. This is balanced by the reduced reliability of the data collected, which will result in some amount of under- and misdiagnosis. The degree to which a specific disorder will be underreported varies depending on the nature of the disorder in question. For example, Andreason, Rice, Endicott, Reich, and Coryell (1986), in a study comparing rates of diagnoses using family history and family study methods, showed that there were some differences, as shown in Table 10.1. The addition of a second informant significantly improves the quality of the information collected, at a cost of double the work (Andreason et al., 1986), as shown in Table 10.2.

The choice of which method to use is guided by the goal of the study. Studies collecting data that are to be used for linkage analysis require data of the highest possible reliability. Ideally, each family member should be interviewed by a different clinician expert in the condition of interest, using a structured interview format and taping the interviews for later

TABLE 10.1.
Rates of Illness in Relatives of Probands by Family Study and
Family History Method (Andreason et al., 1986)

| Diagnosis | Rates of Illness (%) | |
|---|---|---|
| | Family Study | Family History |
| Depression | 32.1 | 22.8 |
| Schizophrenia | 0.6 | 0.5 |
| Alcoholism | 15.2 | 13.1 |

TABLE 10.2.
Rates of Illness Using One or Two Informants in Family History
Method (Andreason et al., 1986)

| Diagnosis | Rates of Illness (%) | |
|---|---|---|
| | One Informant | Two Informants |
| Diagnosis | Rates of Illness (%) | |
| | One Informant | Two Informants |
| Depression | 14.9 | 22.8 |
| Schizophrenia | 0.1 | 0.5 |
| Alcoholism | 13.1 | 13.1 |

study (Honer, Bassett, Kopala, & Kennedy, 1990). Needless to say, this ideal is rarely accomplished. Studies aiming to estimate risk or establish familiality of a given condition may be performed by family history method.

Data collected by these methods, when presented as a family study, will typically be compared to some relevant population, usually by one of a variety of regression analytic techniques. A complete discussion of these techniques is beyond the scope of the chapter, but a review of some of the more technical aspects can be found in Matthews and Farewell (1988). Two of the more common of these techniques are the computation of the relative risk of a condition in a population of interest compared to a comparison population and the calculation of an odds ratio. These techniques provide estimations of the chance of an individual in a family of interest developing the condition of interest with specific variables (such as age or gender) held as constants.

**Twin Study Methodology**

Once the familiality of a condition has been established, the next task is to determine what portions of the familiality are due to genetic and to environmental factors. The study of mono- and dizygotic twins has been particularly helpful in this regard. The theory behind such investigations is that comparing monozygotic twins, who are genetically identical, with dizygotic twins, who are simply siblings, should allow for an examination of possible genetic influences. Thus, the demonstration of elevated concordance rates of a given condition in monozygotic twins compared with dizygotic twins has generally been held to indicate at least some degree of genetic heritability for the condition. However, these simple comparisons fail to account for potential differences caused by similarities in parenting or other environmental variables in identical twins. It has been thought that these types of considerations are particularly important for psychiatric illnesses.

An important modification of twin methodology is the adoption study (e.g., Kety, Rosenthal, & Wender, 1975; Kendler & Gruenberg, 1984), where monozygotic twins separated at birth and reared separately are studied. This design has the advantage of eliminating the potential effects of twinning on the incidence of psychiatric illness, and has been used widely where possible. There are potential pitfalls in such a design, such as when adopted twins are reared by biological relatives (aunts, uncles, etc.), but at the present time it is the most rigorous type of twin study available.

## Segregation Analysis and Other Complex Methods of Estimating Mode of Inheritance

Segregation analysis refers to the techniques of demonstrating the presence of a genetic effect by comparing expected rates of the occurrence of disorders to the actual rates in a given population. In its most simple form, this could include observing that one-half of the offspring of an affected individual were affected by the same condition, thus offering up the possibility that the condition was transmitted in a fashion consistent with autosomal dominant inheritance. However, it is unlikely that many psychiatric illnesses are transmitted as simple Mendelian traits: they are more complex, their occurrence affected by both genetic and environmental variables. Such conditions are known as multifactorial. Also, it is possible that many illnesses are determined by more than one gene. These latter types of illnesses are known as polygenic. The analysis of the genetic contributions to these more complex conditions is much more complicated than the analysis of simple single-gene, nonenvironmentally affected conditions.

In recent years, various mathematical techniques have been developed to model the pattern of occurrence of conditions under more complex assumptions about the mode of inheritance (for a review, see Elston & Yelverton, 1975; Lalouel, Rao, Morton, & Elston, 1983). Models have been developed to consider environmental as well as genetic contributions (Eaves, Martin, Heath, & Kendler, 1987; Eaves, 1987). In this type of comparison, the actual distribution of cases in a sample of families is compared to what would have been expected according to the model that has been specified. In these complex segregation analyses, the intent is to demonstrate the effect of a major gene operating in the occurrence of the illness. The importance of such a demonstration is that a major gene effect must be present if more sophisticated methods of genetic analysis, such as linkage analysis, are to be attempted. It is important to be aware that the demonstration of a major gene effect does not identify the location or nature of that gene. These techniques have been successfully employed in the study of affective disorders (Gasperini, Orsini, Bussoleni, Macciardi, & Smeraldi, 1987), alcoholism (Gilligan, Reich, & Cloniger, 1988), and anxiety disorders (Pauls, Bucher, Crowe, & Noyes, 1980).

### Linkage Analysis and Association Studies

The concept of genetic linkage is central to the understanding of more modern genetic analytic techniques. This concept refers to the fact that genes located physically close to one another on a given chromosome will tend to be transmitted together, not being separated by the normal crossing over during meiosis, a special type of cell replication necessary for the formation of gametes. Beyond a certain physical distance, crossing over of maternal and paternal genes between chromosomes derived from an individual's mother and father becomes a random occurrence. The closer together two genes are, the lower the expected rate of such crossing over. Such closely associated genes are said to be linked.

More simple association studies, such as those examining the relationship between human leukocyte antigen (HLA) markers and various illnesses, are actually simplified attempts at demonstrating linkage between known antigenic or enzyme markers and conditions of interest. For example, the location of the HLA locus (human chromosome 6) has been established. If it can be demonstrated that a given HLA haplotype is closely associated with a particular condition, it may be that genes determining the occurrence of the illness are located in close physical proximity to the known location of the HLA genes.

One limitation of this type of analysis has been the relative paucity of known genetic markers against which to test linkage to conditions of interest. Excluding linkage to a single locus, such as the HLA locus, will exclude only a small portion of the genome. More recently, the discovery of specific enzymes that cleave DNA at particular base-pair combinations (restriction enzymes) has allowed for the demonstration that there is unexpected diversity in base-pair sequences that may not affect the expression of a given gene, because of the redundancy of the genetic code. These variations are called polymorphisms, and polymorphisms detected by restriction enzymes are called restriction fragment length polymorphisms (RFLPs; for a review, see Lewin, 1985). A simple, but helpful way to understand these is to consider them as markers, or "signposts" spread out along the genome, and in this respect they are not very much different from the other types of antigenic and enzymatic markers described above. Their value lies in their comparative abundance, thus allowing, in theory, the construction of a genetic "map" of the human genome. Once completed, the construction of such a map would potentially allow for linkage analysis (of suitable data) regarding a given condition against the whole genome. The development of this technology has led to an explosion in the number of mapped genes from 25 in 1973 to over 1,600 in 1989 (Human Gene Mapping 10, 1989).

## REVIEW OF GENETIC FACTORS IN EATING DISORDERS

### Eating Disorders as Distinct Illnesses

Genetic analysis of disease states requires that the traits to be studied be relatively homogeneous, readily identifiable conditions. Anorexia nervosa has been described in the medical literature since 1694 (Morton, 1694). Since 1970, it has been the focus of increasing attention. The diagnostic criteria as proposed by the revised third edition of the *Diagnostic and Statistical Manual of Mental Disorders* (DSM-III-R; American Psychiatric Association, 1987) and the ninth edition of International Classification of Disease (ICD-9) are accepted internationally. Although the specific etiology of this illness remains obscure, it has been demonstrated to have characteristic psychopathology (Garfinkel & Garner, 1982), which can be elicited at clinical interview and measured by specially designed psychometric instruments (Garner, Olmsted, Bohr, & Garfinkel, 1982; Garner, Olmsted, & Polivy, 1983), and its course and outcome have been well described (Russell, 1970; Garfinkel & Garner, 1982).

Bulimia nervosa has been more recently described (Russell, 1979), but its diagnostic criteria have been well delineated (DSM-III-R). While it shares many clinical and psychopathological features with anorexia nervosa, individuals suffering from bulimia nervosa can be reliably distinguished from patients with anorexia nervosa on clinical and psychopathological grounds (Garner, Garfinkel, & O'Shaughnessy, 1985). The precise relationship between anorexia nervosa and bulimia nervosa remains obscure. It has been suggested that bulimia nervosa is a variant of anorexia nervosa (Russell, 1979), a variant of affective illness (Hudson et al., 1987b), or a separate entity (Woodside et al., 1991). The occurrence of both syndromes concurrently, or the occurrence of one syndrome in the presence of historical evidence of the other is unexplained by current theories. Female cases are the overwhelming majority in eating disorders, with males exhibiting the illnesses comparatively rarely. Although sociocultural and psychological factors have been used to explain this phenomenon, why this sex distribution should occur is not definitely known.

While the syndromes appear to be distinct in some regards, serious questions remain as to the precise nature of the relationship between those with anorexia nervosa and bulimia nervosa and the continuum of weight- and shape-preoccupied dieting women in the general population. Importantly, the relationship between these eating disorders and other psychiatric syndromes, particularly affective, anxiety, and substance use disorders, remains controversial. In fact, some investigators have suggested that eating disorders are variants of these other syndromes, quoting high rates of comorbidity between eating disorders and other disorders in probands with eating disorders. For example, estimates of rates of affective disorder in eating disorder probands have ranged widely, from 20% to 100%; this topic is thoroughly reviewed elsewhere (Strober & Katz, 1988). Rates of specific disorders in probands, first-degree relatives, and controls will be reviewed below.

## Rates of Eating Disorders in Families of Eating Disorder Patients

Tables 10.3 through 10.5 summarize the family studies that have been done with eating disorder populations, including only studies using fairly rigorous methodology for assessing relatives and assigning diagnoses, including standardized diagnostic criteria, and a formalized method for obtaining data on other family members. Despite varying methodologies, including marked differences in methods of data collection, diagnosis, and analysis, studies have consistently demonstrated elevated rates of eating disorders in the families of eating disorder probands. Strober, Morrell, Burroughs, Salkin, and Jacobs (1985) examined the first- and second-degree relatives of 60 anorexic and 95 control families by a mixture of family study and family history methods. Most first-degree relatives were interviewed directly; second-degree relatives were interviewed directly, over the phone, or information was collected by family history method. Diagnostic assessment was made according to DSM-III criteria, on a consensus basis between the interviewer (not blind to proband status) and the senior investigator (blind to proband status). Bulimia nervosa was considered to take precedence over anorexia nervosa in the diagnostic hierarchy. Rates of eating disorder diagnoses were computed, as were odds ratios comparing the eating disorders population to the control families. Finally, a multifactorial model of transmission was tested against the data.

Overall, 27% of the anorexia nervosa families contained a second member with an eating disorder. Rates of eating disorder ranged from 10.0% in mothers and sisters to 0.4% in male relatives. The overall rate for female relatives was 9.7%, and for all relatives 5.0%. The risk for a female relative of an anorexia nervosa patient to develop an eating disorder was fivefold that for the control population, a significant difference. The analysis of the multifactorial transmission model reached statistical significance if subclinical cases (partial syndromes) were included. Attempts to determine whether there was specificity of transmission of anorexia nervosa and bulimia nervosa were hampered by the hierarchy adopted for the diagnosis of bulimia nervosa and the young age of the probands (mean = 15.4 years); this is not old enough for the probands to have passed through the age of risk for developing bulimia nervosa (Woodside & Garfinkel, 1992).

Hudson, Pope, Jonas, and Yurgelun-Todd (1983) reported on rates of anorexia nervosa and bulimia nervosa in the first-degree relatives of 14 patients with anorexia nervosa, 55 patients with bulimia nervosa, and 20 patients with anorexia nervosa and bulimia nervosa. Data collected by the family history method showed an overall rate of 5.2% for any eating dis-

TABLE 10.3.
Studies Examining Rates of Eating Disorders in Families of Probands with Eating Disorders

| Study | Proband Diagnosis: (*n*) | Rates in First-Degree Relatives (%) | Rates in Relatives of Controls (%) |
|---|---|---|---|
| Strober et al. (1985) | AN:60 | 9.7 (females) < 1 (males) | 1.0 |
| Hudson et al. (1983) | AN:14, BN:55, AN/BN:20 | 5.2 | NA |
| Gershon et al. (1984) | AN, AN/BN:24 | 3.8–7.3 | 1.1 |
| Hudson et al. (1987) | BN:69 | 4.0[a] | 0 |
| Keck et al. (1990) | Bulimia:50, BN:66 | 4.3[a] 4.4[a] | 0 |

[a]Morbid risk.

order in these first-degree relatives. This study was extended (Hudson et al., 1987a) to 69 probands with bulimia nervosa, and in this extension the morbid risk for eating disorders in first-degree relatives was 4.0%. In a further extension of this study (Keck et al., 1990) that involved comparing rates of illness in the first-degree relatives of probands with DSM-III bulimia ($n = 50$) and DSM-III-R bulimia nervosa ($n = 66$), the morbid risk for eating disorders in the relatives was 4.4% for bulimia nervosa and 4.3% for bulimia. Gershon et al. (1984) reported on the rates of anorexia nervosa and bulimia nervosa in the first-degree relatives of 24 probands, 13 with anorexia nervosa alone, and 11 with anorexia nervosa and bulimia nervosa, information having been collected by a mixture of family study and family history method. Overall rates for eating disorders in the relatives ranged from 2.0% to 7.3%.

In summary, most studies have found anorexia nervosa and bulimia nervosa to be familial; that is, that rates of anorexia nervosa and bulimia nervosa in families of anorexia nervosa and bulimina nervosa probands are elevated compared to control populations.

### Eating and Affective Disorders

The relationship between eating and affective disorders has been studied intensively in recent years. Family studies have been part of this effort, and most have demonstrated elevated rates of depression in first-degree relatives of probands with anorexia nervosa or bulimia nervosa compared to control populations. Strober, Salkin, Burroughs, and Morrell (1982) demonstrated an 8.8% rate of depression in the first-degree relatives of adolescent probands with anorexia nervosa, using methodologies similar to those described above in his other studies. Gershon et al. (1984), in his study described above, demonstrated rates of 10% to 13% for depression in the relatives of his probands. Rivinus and colleagues (1984), studying 40 probands with anorexia nervosa or anorexia nervosa with bulimia nervosa by the family history method, found rates of depression in first-degree relatives of 11% to 22%. These results are similar to those of Biederman and colleagues (1985), who, using methodology like that of Rivinus et al., documented depression in 6% to 25% of first-degree relatives of eating disorders probands.

Hudson et al. (1987a,b) and Keck et al. (1990) have documented rates of 25% to 36% for affective disorder in the first-degree relatives of probands with DSM-III bulimia (1987) and DSM-III-R bulimia nervosa (1990), using family history methods. Herpetz-Dahlman (1988) demon-

TABLE 10.4.
Affective Disorders in Relatives with Eating Disorders

| Study | Proband Diagnosis: (n) | Rates in First-Degree Relatives (%) | Rates in Relatives of Controls (%) |
|---|---|---|---|
| Strober et al. (1982) | AN, AN/BN:70 | 8.8 | None |
| Gershon et al. (1984) | AN, AN/BN:24 | 10–13 | 5.8 |
| Rivinus et al. (1984) | AN, AN/BN:40 | 11–22 | 3.7–8.0[a] |
| Biederman et al. (1985) | AN:38 | 6–25 | 4.7[a] |
| Hudson et al. (1987) | BN:70 | 30–37 | 9.0[a] |
| Herpetz-Dahlman (1988) | AN, BN:45 | 2–13 | NA |
| Logue et al. (1990) | AN, BN, ANBN:132 | 11–16 | 5 |
| Strober et al. (1990) | AN:97 | 5.1–18 | 4.1[b] |
| Keck et al. (1990) | Bulimia:50 BN:66 | 25–30[a] | 9.0[a] |

[a]Morbid risk.
[b]Mixed other psychiatric diagnosis, nondepressed and nonanorexic.

strated rates of 2% to 13% for first-, second-, and third-degree relatives of probands with anorexia nervosa or bulimia nervosa, with information having been collected by a mixture of family history and family study methodology. Logue, Crowe, and Bean (1990) found rates of 11% to 16% for major depression in the first-degree relatives of 23 anorexia nervosa, 57 bulimia nervosa, and 52 anorexia nervosa with bulimia nervosa probands, using a mixture of family study and family history information. However, logistical regression analytic techniques deriving adjusted odds ratios failed to find any significant differences for rates of depression in eating disorders as compared to control families.

These repeated observations, while intriguing, have not generally attempted to control for the equally common observation of high rates of affective disturbance in the probands themselves. Strober, Lampert, Morrell, Burroughs, and Jacobs (1990), in a final report of his 1985 study, stratified his anorexia nervosa subjects into those with and without comorbid depression, and found that elevated rates of depression in first-degree relatives of anorexia nervosa patients occurred only if the proband had comorbid depression. Rates of affective disorder in first-degree relatives of nondepressed anorexia nervosa probands were significantly lower than for the depressed anorexia nervosa probands, and not significantly different from the comparison group or from expected population rates. These results are similar to pilot work done on a much smaller sample by Biederman and colleagues (1984).

In summary, while there is clear evidence of elevated rates of depression in first-degree relatives of probands with anorexia nervosa and bulimia nervosa compared to control populations, these differences appear to be explained by the presence of comorbid depression in a high proportion of probands with anorexia nervosa and bulimia nervosa. The available evidence does not support the notion that eating and affective disorders are manifestations of a common underlying genetic vulnerability.

## Eating Disorders and Substance Use Disorders

Another line of thought has been that various substance use disorders might be related genetically to anorexia nervosa and bulimia nervosa. As has been the case with affective disorders, most studies have documented elevated rates of substance use disorder in the first-degree relatives of anorexia nervosa and bulimia nervosa probands. Rates of substance use disorder in these relatives range from 2% to 21% (Strober et al., 1982; Rivinus et al., 1984; Biederman et al., 1985; Hudson et al., 1987a; Keck et al., 1990; Herpetz-Dahlman, 1988; Logue et al., 1990).

Several additional studies have examined this association in less rigorous ways. Mitchell, Hatsukami, and Eckert (1988) reported a 37% rate of positive family history for substance use disorder in probands with bulimia nervosa. Molgaard, Chambers, Golbeck, Elder, and Ferguson (1989) suggested a significant association between maternal alcoholism and anorexia nervosa; however, the family history information was collected by retrospective chart analysis and is unlikely to be reliable.

**TABLE 10.5.**
**Rates of Alcoholism in First-Degree Relatives of Probands with Eating Disorders**

| Study | Proband Diagnosis: (*n*) | Rates in First-Degree Relatives (%) | Rates in Relatives of Controls (%) |
|---|---|---|---|
| Strober et al. (1982) | AN, AN/BN:70 | 9.9 | None |
| Rivinus et al. (1984) | AN, AN/BN:40 | 11–12 | 0–17.5[a] |
| Biederman et al. (1985) | AN:38 | 5–13[a] | 6.9 |
| Hudson et al. (1987) | BN:70 | 16–20 | 4.8 |
| Herpetz-Dahlman et al. (1988) | AN, BN:45 | 2–19 | NA |
| Logue et al. (1990) | AN, BN, ANBN:132 | 21 | 19 |
| Keck et al. (1990) | Bulimia:50 BN:66 | 12–20[a] | 4.8[a] |

[a]Morbid risk.

In summary, substance use disorders, like affective disorders, appear to aggregate in the families of probands with anorexia nervosa and bulimia nervosa. However, no studies have controlled for the effect of comorbid substance use on the part of the proband.

## Other Conditions

A few studies have examined the relationship between eating and anxiety disorders, generally not showing elevated rates of anxiety disorders in the first-degree relatives of eating disorder probands (Hudson et al., 1987a,b). The study of weight histories in the families of eating disorder patients has been of interest because of the oft-quoted observation that patients with bulimia nervosa have higher premorbid weights than patients with anorexia nervosa (Garfinkel et al., 1982, p. 45; Garfinkel, Moldofsky, & Garner, 1980). Numerous studies have attempted to evaluate the weight histories of relatives of patients with eating disorders, usually demonstrating that there were no differences from control populations (Kalucy, Crisp, & Harding, 1977; Halmi, Struss, & Goldberg, 1978).

## Twin Studies

Many anecdotal case reports have noted the frequent occurrence of anorexia nervosa or bulimia nervosa in pairs of monozygotic (MZ) twins. These reports are well summarized elsewhere (Scott, 1986). A few more recent reports of concordance of bulimia nervosa in small series of twins are provided for reference only (Kaminer, Feingold, & Lyons, 1988; Hsu, Chesler, & Santhouse, 1990). Fichter and Noegel (1990) have also reported on a series of 27 twin pairs where one twin had bulimia nervosa, noting an 83% concordance rate for MZ twins versus 27% for dizygotic (DZ) twins.

The most comprehensive twin study to date is that of Holland, Murray, Russell, and Crisp (1984). In this study of 34 twin pairs and one set of triplets, the MZ concordance rate for anorexia nervosa was 55%, as opposed to the DZ concordance rate of 7%. Treasure and Holland (1988) have reported on an extension of this study to 68 twin pairs, where all twins were rediagnosed according to DSM-III-R criteria, and family history information was collected. In this analysis, MZ concordance rates for anorexia nervosa remained high (45% vs. 6.7% for DZ twins), but the concordance rate for bulimia nervosa MZ twins was not significantly higher than that for bulimia nervosa DZ twins (47.3% vs. 31.5%).

In summary, there is evidence for high MZ concordance rates for anorexia nervosa, but the evidence for this in bulimia nervosa is less definitive.

## Estimates of Heritability

Two attempts have been made to estimate the heritability of anorexia nervosa and bulimia nervosa. Heritability estimates are derived from the application of segregation models to family data; in this manner they are very roughly analogous to determining the percentage of the variance accounted for by a given variable in a regression analysis. Holland, Sicotte, and Treasure (1988) applied such methodology to their twin and family data, arriving at approximately 80% as the estimate of heritability for anorexia nervosa. In a further analysis, path analytic techniques were used to suggest that nearly 75% of the liability to develop anorexia nervosa was heritable, whereas common environmental effects contribute most to the familial clustering of bulimia nervosa. They suggest that the heritable form of eating disorders is young-onset anorexia nervosa without premorbid obesity.

These results are similar to those of Strober et al. (1990), who, using the same analytic techniques as Holland et al. (1988), estimated a heritability of 64% for anorexia nervosa in their sample of young-onset anorexia nervosa probands.

In summary, preliminary evidence about the heritability of anorexia nervosa and bulimia nervosa suggests that anorexia nervosa is more heritable than bulimia nervosa, and that young-onset anorexia nervosa is the most highly heritable condition.

## Other Studies

Anecdotal reports or small studies have occasionally reported associations between anorexia nervosa or bulimia nervosa and Turner's syndrome (for a review, see Scott, 1986; Darby, Garfinkel, Vale, Kirwan, & Brown, 1981) or specific HLA antigens (Biederman et al., 1984; Kiss, Hajek-Rosenmayr, Haubenstock, Wiesnagrotski, & Moser, 1988). The meaning of these observations is unclear.

## SUMMARY OF THE CURRENT STATE OF KNOWLEDGE
## REGARDING GENETIC FACTORS IN EATING DISORDERS

The current evidence clearly supports the notion that anorexia nervosa and bulimia nervosa have a strong familial component. The degree to which this component is due to genetic as opposed to shared environmental influences is much less clear. Evidence that supports a genetic component can be found in the twin work of Holland and associates, and to a lesser extent in the family studies of Strober and associates. However, it is premature to conclude firmly that a genetic factor is operating, at least on the basis of the current evidence.

A related issue is the specificity of any putative genetic factor. Although there is consistent evidence that anorexia nervosa and bulimia nervosa occur in conjunction with affective and substance use disorders, the available evidence suggests that, at least in the case of affective disorders, this is related to the high rates of comorbid depression in the probands. The observation of Strober and colleagues (1990) strongly suggests that the majority of cases of anorexia nervosa and bulimia nervosa cannot be explained by the assumption that they are due to shared liability to affective disorders. It remains possible, however, that there is a subgroup of such patients.

Another related question is whether a hypothetical liability might be specific to either anorexia nervosa or bulimia nervosa, or common to both. This is a variation of the question reviewed above with respect to affective disorders. There is little evidence to address this question. Strober and colleagues (1990) fail to demonstrate specificity of transmission for anorexia nervosa and bulimia nervosa in their family study; however, these results may have been affected by the comparative youthfulness of the population under study. Holland and colleagues' 1988 analysis of their twin data, suggesting different MZ-DZ concordance rates for bulimia nervosa and anorexia nervosa, is the strongest evidence that we have to date to suggest separate liabilities. Again, it is quite possible that there exist subgroups that have either shared or distinct liabilities for anorexia nervosa and bulimia nervosa.

Despite the above, both Holland et al. (1988) and Strober et al. (1990) have been able to demonstrate fairly high estimates of heritability, especially in the young-onset anorexia nervosa group. Both have concluded that if a genetic factor is operating, it is likely to be in this particular group.

One possible way to understand the above findings would be to consider the following model. It is commonly believed that the incidence of bulimia nervosa has increased proportionally more than that of anorexia nervosa since the 1970s. The evidence reviewed here has suggested that anorexia nervosa is more heritable than bulimia nervosa, in at least some cases. If one were to take these observations at face value, some theory would have to be developed to explain them. We know that bingeing, the hallmark symptom of bulimia nervosa, is thought by some investigators to be related to dietary restraint (Polivy & Herman, 1985). If one were to hypothesize a genetic liability toward binge eating as a consequence of dietary restriction, as distinct from the compensatory overeating observed in the general population, it would then make sense to conclude that this liability would be expressed only in the setting of a society or culture where dietary restriction was encouraged. The observation that patients with bulimia nervosa have histories of being heavier than average would fit into this model in that these would be the individuals most likely to be encouraged to diet. In the absence of such cultural pressures, such a liability (toward binge eating) might be dormant, and thus unexpressed. In a culture where such an emphasis was present, most individuals would be equally exposed, and would be expected to respond or not respond within a fairly defined time period. Western culture over the last 30 years has clearly demonstrated just such an increased emphasis on dieting (Garfinkel & Garner, 1982, pp. 100–122). This model would explain both the rapid increase in incidence of bulimia nervosa over recent years, and perhaps also the observation (Woodside & Garfinkel, 1992) that late-onset bulimia nervosa is rare.

There is no clear suggestion as to what might be the genetic liability in anorexia nervosa. However, examination of the nature of the illness might suggest a number of possibilities, including defects in the neuroregulation of satiety and hunger, and personality variables related to cognitive and perceptual disturbances that may contribute to restrained eating in the face of ongoing hunger.

This simplistic picture does not address the issue of how to view individuals who have experienced both syndromes, or of how to explain the relatively high incidence of late-onset anorexia nervosa (Woodside & Garfinkel, 1992). With regard to the first question, it is likely that complex segregation analyses of very large sets of family data may help our understanding. There is preliminary evidence from anorexia nervosa analysis of age-of-onset data (Woodside & Garfinkel, 1992) that would sup port either a single genetic liability for both illnesses, or separate liabilities; there is no evidence to support the concept of a third distinct liability for the combined syndrome.

Studying the second situation, the onset of anorexia nervosa in an older age group, may allow for the elucidation of psychological factors that are protective against the development of anorexia nervosa, if such individuals are found to be carrying the same liability as younger patients.

## DIRECTIONS FOR FUTURE RESEARCH

Further family studies that simply demonstrate the familial nature of anorexia nervosa and bulimia nervosa will be of limited utility. However, large sets of family data, especially if gathered in a methodologically sophisticated fashion, could provide important insights into several areas. These include clarifying the relationship between anorexia nervosa and bulimia nervosa, and, as an extension of the above, providing more detailed information on the precise mode of inheritance of transmissible effects. Present evidence would suggest focusing on patients with young-onset anorexia nervosa as a first step.

Replication of the excellent twin work of Holland et al. is another urgent priority. His results, while compelling, must be duplicated on other populations. Further twin work will also allow for the study of discordant MZ twins, which may clarify environmental and psychological factors that are both protective and predisposing for the development of anorexia nervosa and bulimia nervosa.

Attempts to perform molecular genetic linkage studies are at present premature. Currently, there is no putative site to probe, and screening the entire genome at this stage is certainly premature. However, there is sufficient evidence for a genetic liability that such studies should eventually be performed. Paradoxically, the greatest danger to the eventual carrying out of such studies is probably too much haste now, which would be likely to lead to disappointing results and much discouragement, as has been the case in the study of genetic factors in other psychiatric illnesses, most notably schizophrenia.

In summary, this chapter has selectively reviewed the existing knowledge about the genetics of eating disorders. While there is clear evidence that the disorders are familial, and that there is likely to be a genetic liability in at least some patients, the nature and extent of this liability remain to be elucidated. The next decade may see a considerable increase in our knowledge about these factors through the application of sophisticated genetic epidemiologic and molecular biological techniques.

## REFERENCES

American Psychiatric Association. (1987). *Diagnostic and Statistical Manual of Mental Disorders* (3rd ed.—rev.). Washington, DC: Author.

Andreason, N. C., Rice, J., Endicott, J., Reich, T., & Coryell, W. (1986). The family history approach to diagnosis. *Archives of General Psychiatry, 43*, 421–429.

Biederman, J., Rivinus, T. M., Herzog, D. B., Harmatz, J. S., Shanley, K., & Yunis, E. J. (1984). High frequency of HLA-Bw16 in patients with anorexia nervosa. *American Journal of Psychiatry, 141*, 1109–1110.

Biederman, J., Rivinus, T., Kemper, K., Hamilton, D., MacFayden, J., & Harmatz, J. (1985). Depressive disorders in relatives of anorexia nervosa patients with and without a current episode of nonbipolar major depression. *American Journal of Psychiatry, 142*, 1495–1497.

Darby, P. L., Garfinkel, P. E., Vale, J. M., Kirwan, P. J., & Brown, G. M. (1981). Anorexia nervosa and 'Turner syndrome': Cause or coincidence? *Psychological Medicine, 11*, 141–145.

Eaves, L. J. (1987). Including the environment in models for genetic segregation. *Journal of Psychiatric Research, 21, 639–647.*

Eaves, I. J., Martin, N. G., Heath, A. C., & Kendler, K. S. (1987). Testing genetic models for multiple symptoms. *Behavioural Genetics, 17*, 331–341.

Elston, R. C., & Yelverton, K. C. (1975). General models for segregation analysis. *American Journal of Human Genetics, 27*, 31–45.

Fichter, M. M., & Noegel, R. (1990). Concordance for bulimia in twins. *International Journal of Eating Disorders, 9*, 255–263.

Garfinkel, P. E., & Garner, D. M. (1982). *Anorexia nervosa: A multidimensional perspective.* New York: Brunner/Mazel.

Garfinkel, P. E., Moldofsky, H., & Garner, D. M. (1980). The heterogeneity of anorexia nervosa. *Archives of General Psychiatry, 37*, 1036–1040.

Garner, D. M., Garfinkel, P. E., & O'Shaughnessy, M. (1985). Validity of the distinction between bulimia with and without anorexia nervosa. *American Journal of Psychiatry, 142*, 581–587.

Garner, D. M., Olmsted, M. P., Bohr, Y., & Garfinkel, P. E. (1982). The Eating Attitudes Test: Psychometric features and clinical correlates. *Psychological Medicine, 12*, 871–878.

Garner, D. M., Olmsted, M. P., & Polivy, J. (1983). Development and validation of a multidimensional eating disorder inventory for anorexia and bulimia. *International Journal of Eating Disorders, 2*(2), 15–34.

Gasperini, M., Orsini, A., Bussoleni, C., Macciardi, F., & Smeraldi, E. (1987). Genetic approach to the study of heterogeneity of affective disorders. *Journal of Affective Disorders, 12*, 105–113.

Gershon, E. S., Schreiber, J. L., Hamovit, J. R., Dibble, E. D., Kaye, W., Nurnberger, J. I., Andersen, A. E., & Ebert, M. (1984). Clinical findings in patients with anorexia nervosa and affective illness in their relatives. *American Journal of Psychiatry, 141*, 1419–1422.

Gilligan, S. B., Reich, T., & Cloninger, C. R. (1988). Alcohol-related symptoms in heterogeneous families of hospitalized alcoholics. *Alcoholism: Clinical and Experimental Research, 12*, 671–678.

Halmi, K. A., Struss, A., & Goldberg, S. C. (1978). An investigation of weights in the parents of anorexia nervosa patients. *Journal of Nervous and Mental Disease, 166*, 358–361.

Herpetz-Dahlmann, B. (1988). Affective disorders in the families of patients with anorexia nervosa. *Zeitung fur Kinder und Jugendpsychiatrie, 16*, 14–19.

Holland, A. J., Murray, R., Russell, G. F. M., & Crisp, A. H. (1984). Anorexia nervosa: A study of 34 twin pairs and one set of triplets. *British Journal of Psychiatry, 145*, 414–419.

Holland, A. J., Sicotte, N., & Treasure, J. (1988). Anorexia nervosa: Evidence for a genetic basis. *Journal of Psychosomatic Research, 32*, 561–571.

Honer, W. G., Bassett, A. S., Kopala, L., & Kennedy, J. L. (1990). A genotype-phenotype research strategy for schizophrenia. *Canadian Journal of Psychiatry, 35*, 776–783.

Hsu, L. K. G., Chesler, B. E., & Santhouse, R. (1990). Bulimia nervosa in eleven sets of twins: A clinical report. *International Journal of Eating Disorders, 9*, 275–282.

Hudson, J. I., Pope, H. G., Jonas, J. M., & Yurgelun-Todd, D. (1983). Family history study of anorexia nervosa and bulimia. *British Journal of Psychiatry, 142*, 133–138.

Hudson, J. I., Pope, H. G., Jonas, J. M., Yurgelun-Todd, D., & Frankenburg, F. R. (1987a). A controlled family history study of bulimia. *Psychological Medicine, 17*, 883–890.

Hudson, J. I., Pope, H. G., Yurgelun-Todd, D., Jonas, J. M., & Frankenburg, F. R. (1987b). A controlled study of lifetime prevalence of affective and other psychiatric disorders in bulimic outpatients. *American Journal of Psychiatry, 144*, 1283–1287.

Human Gene Mapping 10. (1989). *Cytogenetics and Cell Genetics, 51*, Vols. 1–4. Basel: Karger.

Kalucy, R. S., Crisp, A. H., & Harding, B. (1977). A study of 56 families with anorexia nervosa. *British Journal of Medical Psychology, 50,* 381–395.

Kaminer, Y., Feingold, M., & Lyons, K. (1988). Bulimia in a pair of monozygotic twins. *Journal of Nervous and Mental Disease, 176,* 246–248.

Keck, P. E., Pope, H. G., Hudson, J. I., McElroy, S. I., Yurgelun-Todd, D., & Hundert, E. M. (1990). A controlled study of phenomenology and family history in outpatients with bulimia nervosa. *Comprehensive Psychiatry, 31,* 275–283.

Kendler, K. S., & Gruenberg, A. M. (1984). An independent analysis of the Danish adoption study of schizophrenia. VI. The relationship between psychiatric disorders as defined by DSM-III in the relatives and adoptees. *Archives of General Psychiatry, 41,* 555–564.

Kety, S. S., Rosenthal, D., & Wender, P. M. (1975). Mental illness in the biological and adoptive families of adopted individuals who have become schizophrenic: A preliminary report based on psychiatric interviews. In R. R. Fieve, D. Rosenthal, & H. Brill (Eds.), *Genetic research in psychiatry* (pp. 147–165). Baltimore: Johns Hopkins University Press.

Kiss, A., Hajek-Rosenmayr, A., Haubenstock, A., Wiesnagrotski, S., & Moser, G. (1988). Lack of association between HLA antigens and anorexia nervosa. *American Journal of Psychiatry, 145,* 876–877.

Lalouel, J. M., Rao, D. C., Morton, N. E., & Elston, R. C. (1983). A unified model for complex segregation analysis. *American Journal of Human Genetics, 35,* 816–826.

Lewin, B. (1985). *Genes II.* New York: John Wiley.

Logue, C. M., Crowe, R. R., & Bean, J. A. (1990). A family study of anorexia nervosa and bulimia. *Comprehensive Psychiatry, 30,* 179–188.

Matthews, D. E., & Farewell, V. T. (1988). *Using and understanding medical statistics* (2nd ed.). Basel: Karger.

Mitchell, J. E., Hatsukami, D., Pyle, R., & Eckert, E. (1988). Bulimia with and without a family history of drug abuse. *Addictive Behaviours, 13,* 245–251.

Molgaard, C. A., Chambers, C. M., Golbeck, A. L., Elder, J. P., & Ferguson, J. (1989). Maternal alcoholism and anorexia nervosa: A possible association? *International Journal of the Addictions, 24,* 167–173.

Morton, N. E., & MacLean, C. (1974). Analysis of familial resemblance III. *American Journal of Human Genetics, 26,* 489–503.

Morton, R. (1694). *Phthisologica: Or a treatise of consumption.* London: S. Smith and B. Walford.

Pauls, D. L., Bucher, K. D., Crowe, R. R., & Noyes, R. (1980). A genetic study of panic disorder pedigrees. *American Journal of Human Genetics, 32,* 639–644.

Polivy, J., & Herman, C. P. (1985). Dieting and bingeing: A causal analysis. *American Psychologist, 40,* 193–201.

Rivinus, T. M., Biederman, J., Herzog, D. B., Kemper, K., Harper, G. P., Harmatz, J. S., & Houseworth, S. (1984). Anorexia nervosa and affective disorders: A controlled family history study. *American Journal of Psychiatry, 141,* 1414–1418.

Russell, G. F. M. (1970). Anorexia nervosa: Its identity as an illness and its treatment. In J. H. Price (Ed.), *Modern trends in psychological medicine.* London: Butterworths.

Russell, G. F. M. (1979). Bulimia nervosa: An ominous variant of anorexia nervosa. *Psychological Medicine, 9,* 429–448.

Schotte, D. E., & Stunkard, A. J. (1987). Bulimia vs bulimic behaviours on a college campus. *Journal of the American Medical Association, 258,* 1213–1215.

Scott, D. W. (1986). Anorexia nervosa: A review of possible genetic factors. *International Journal of Eating Disorders, 5,* 1–20.

Strober, M., & Katz, J. (1988). Depression in the eating disorders: A review and analysis of descriptive, family and biological findings. In D. M. Garner & P. E. Garfinkel (Eds.), *Diagnostic issues in anorexia nervosa and bulimia nervosa.* New York: Brunner/Mazel.

Strober, M., Lampert, C., Morrell, W., Burroughs, J., & Jacobs, C. (1990). A controlled family study of anorexia nervosa: Evidence of familial aggregation and lack of shared transmission with affective disorders. *International Journal of Eating Disorders, 9,* 239–253.

Strober, M., Morrell, W., Burroughs, J., Salkin, B., & Jacobs, C. (1985). A controlled family study of anorexia nervosa. *Journal of Psychiatric Research, 19,* 239–246.

Strober, M., Salkin, B., Burroughs, J., & Morrell, W. (1982). Validity of the bulimia-restrictor distinction in anorexia nervosa. *Journal of Nervous and Mental Disease, 170,* 345–351.

Tenth International Workshop on Human Gene Mapping (HGM-10, 1989). *Cytogenetics and Cell Genetics, 51,* Vols. 1–4.

Treasure, J., & Holland, A. (1988). Genetic vulnerability to eating disorders: Evidence from a twin and family study [Abstract].

Woodside, D. B., & Garfinkel, P. E. (1992). Age of onset in eating disorders. *International Journal of Eating Disorders, 12,* 31–36.

Woodside, D. B., Rockert, W., & Garfinkel, P. E. (1991). Patterns of onset of symptoms in eating disorders [Letter]. *American Journal of Psychiatry, 148,* 950–951.

# 11

# *Medical Management of the Hospitalized Patient*

Sidney H. Kennedy
M.D., FRCP(C)

Colin Shapiro
M.D., PH.D., FRCP(C)

A wide range of treatment approaches to promote weight gain in patients with anorexia nervosa (AN) has been described from as far back as Morton's *Phthisologia: Or a Treatise of Consumptions* (1694). He noted "the convenient rise of Stomack-Medicines, and such as comfort and strengthen the nerves" and recommended "chalybeates, antiscorbutick, cephalic and bitter medicines" (referenced in Bhanji & Newton, 1985). Other more drastic approaches have included prefrontal leucotomy (Sargant, 1951) and electroconvulsive therapy "to unblock the inhibition mechanisms" (Laboucaré & Barres, 1954), as well as various forms of insulin therapies (Dally & Sargant, 1960; Bhanji & Mattingly, 1988). In our opinion no single approach to treatment has superiority over others. Some of the more dramatic physical interventions have flown in the face of the psychological aspects of this disorder.

A hospital admission during the course of AN or bulimia nervosa (BN) can provide a vital opportunity to reverse the acute and potentially life-threatening physical and psychological complications of these disorders,

The authors wish to thank the teams they have worked with at the Programme for Eating Disorders, The Toronto Hospital, and the Professorial Unit, Royal Edinburgh Hospital, respectively. Many of the ideas expressed in this chapter are the result of their collaborative work.

and prepare patients to make better use of subsequent outpatient treatments. This chapter will consider the types of hospital settings that may be used, and will include indications for hospital treatment and the different types of approaches that may be taken during the admission. Specific aspects of the admission, including techniques of refeeding and the role of pharmacotherapies, both nonpsychotropic and psychotropic, will be discussed. Two controversial aspects of hospital management, ethical and practical aspects of involuntary treatment, and the role of exercise in treatment are discussed. Finally, the importance of working within a multidisciplinary team and making connections between the hospital and the community will be emphasized.

## HOSPITAL SETTINGS

Whether treatment is offered in a medical unit, general psychiatric unit, or specialized eating disorder unit, inpatient or day center, is less important than the philosophy and commitment of the staff (Garfinkel & Garner, 1982). There is greater pressure to limit the duration of admission in a general medical unit, so that rapid nutritional and weight restoration is usually the main goal of treatment (Croner, Larsson, Schildt, et al., 1985). Alternatively, treatment on a psychiatric unit should allow equal attention to both physical and psychological aspects of the recovery process. While some have advocated a segregated unit for eating disorder patients, others have developed treatment programs in wards where other psychiatric groups receive treatment.

There has been a gradual shift in treatment resources for eating disorder patients over the past two decades in Toronto. Where previously about 80% of patients seen in consultation were admitted to the hospital for treatment, now approximately 30% of patients seen at the Toronto Hospital Programme for Eating Disorders receive intensive day hospital or inpatient treatment (Kennedy, Kaplan, & Garfinkel, 1992). This reflects both an increased availability of outpatient services and a relative increase in the number of patients who present with the BN syndrome.

It is generally best to differentiate between acute "crisis-driven" admissions and elective admissions to an eating disorder or general psychiatric unit where goals of the admission can be jointly assessed by staff and patient.

## Emergency Admissions

### Metabolic Crises

AN patients, who are reluctant to confront their illness as they continue to lose weight, are often "threatened" with compulsory admission unless their weight increases by a particular amount. Although this is sometimes necessary under life-threatening conditions, it makes forging a "working alliance" between patient and staff much more difficult. Certification and "forced feeding" have been the subject of considerable debate by medical ethicists and are, generally, undesirable.

Acute metabolic crises, often related to the combined effects of semistarvation and the abuse of diuretics, laxatives, or emetics, require emergency treatment. Although more typically associated with AN (Garfinkel & Garner, 1982), fluid and electrolyte disturbances are also commonly found in BN. Mitchell, Pyle, Eckert, and associates (1983) reported metabolic alkalosis in 27%, hypochloremia in 24%, and hypokalemia in 14% of a series of 168 patients with BN. These changes were the result of self-induced vomiting and laxative abuse, while metabolic acidosis occurred in a smaller percentage of subjects and was associated with prolonged fasting and acute diarrhea (Mitchell, Hatsukami, Pyle, et al., 1987).

In general, potassium levels below 2.5 mEq/L associated with pathological electrocardiogram changes, particularly a prolongation of the QT interval and occasionally absence of U waves, require intravenous potassium replacement (see below under Replacement Therapies).

Hypocalcemia is often documented, but clinical evidence is usually initially absent. The reason for this is that an associated hypokalemia may mask the clinical manifestations and that the correction of serum potassium subsequently leads to the unmasking of a positive Chvostek's sign and tetany. One consequence of low serum calcium is the development of osteoporosis, although it is presently unclear how rapidly this may occur in eating disorder patients (Treasure, Russell, Fogelman, et al., 1987). This issue is discussed more fully in Chapter 4.

Phosphate levels are usually normal in patients with AN and BN, but repeated vomiting and the abuse of nonphosphate laxatives can lead to low levels. An abnormality of hypophosphatemia frequently becomes apparent on refeeding anorexic patients when metabolic demands on body phosphate reserves reduce phosphate levels. The consequences include status epilepticus, cardiac abnormalities, and suppression of the hematological system. Recently, respiratory failure consequent to hypophosphatemia has been described (Gustavsson & Eriksson, 1989). Close monitoring of serum phosphate during the early stage of refeeding should be mandatory. A review and synthesis of other metabolic changes in eating disorders is available elsewhere (Turner & Shapiro, 1992), and some aspects are covered in Chapter 7 of this volume.

### Psychiatric Crises

Acute suicidal crises may arise during outpatient or other intensive treatments of AN or BN. Major depression occurs in up to 60% of patients even after eating disorder symptoms are in remission (Toner, Garfinkel, Garner, et al., 1986) and may require inhospital treatment. Under these circumstances, acute psychiatric intervention may be necessary.

## Elective Admissions

By holding a preadmission meeting, the treatment team can evaluate motivation, assess the capacity of the prospective patient to form a therapeutic alliance, and tentatively outline the goals of admission. Different patients require different treatment approaches during admission to the hospital. These may involve (a) diagnostic assessment, (b) refeeding and weight restoration, (c) breaking the binge-purge cycle, and (d) providing support for the chronic patient.

### Diagnostic Assessment

In a minority of patients there is a denial of overconcern with weight and shape and an expressed desire to gain weight. Only by arranging a period of supervised observation can the actual pattern of eating be clarified. This may help to differentiate between AN and other emotional causes of weight loss, such as a conversion disorder in which weight loss is linked to a past traumatic event "resulting in food and digestion assuming symbolic significance" (Garfinkel, Kaplan, Garner, et al., 1983). (See Table 2.1.) In the latter case, the misbeliefs about weight and shape, and a pathological desire to be thin, are absent.

### Refeeding and Weight Restoration

Where other less intense approaches to treatment have failed and body weight is below 70% of a previous healthy weight, a longer term admission is often necessary to reestablish healthy patterns of eating and reverse both the psychological and the physical sequelae of starvation (Garfinkel & Kaplan, 1985).

There are different philosophies regarding the rate of weight gain and the techniques to be used in refeeding patients with AN (Maloney & Farrell, 1980). If the objectives are to restore normal weight, normal body composition, and normal eating, then an avoidance of nasogastric feeding, hyperalimentation, and high calorie foods is parsimonious with these objectives. This will often mean a slower change, particularly in the early stages of refeeding. In general, because there is a concern that exercise might be used as a way of reducing weight, many units will restrict exercise in anorexic patients. So far as we are aware, there are no studies that have examined this in a systematic way, or from a motivational perspective, that is, in assisting patients to return to "normal physiological functioning." The potential links between exercise and eating disorders are discussed further in Chapter 7, and in a recent book (Yates, 1991).

Even patients who appear to have survived on minimal quantities of food before admission to the hospital are invariably able to consume a 1,500 kcal daily diet on admission. Refeeding edema, if it occurs, should be carefully monitored but rarely requires specific treatment. Rarely and only under extreme conditions would diuretics be required, and low-dose thiazide diuretic for 1 to 2 weeks would be the preferred treatment.

"Health food" diets, including vegetarianism, are regarded as an expression of anorexic thinking and are not permitted in many programs. Some units allow a limit of two or three foods that a patient can refuse— mostly as a sign of flexibility (this still allows for a balanced diet ). AN patients occasionally have a pattern of consuming small amounts of carbohydrate and avoiding all protein. For these patients, refeeding edema and vitamin deficiency is a particular concern, and vitamin supplementation should be provided for the short term.

The aim is to facilitate a weight gain of 1 to 1.5 kg (2 to 3 lb) per week, which can be achieved by increasing caloric intake gradually in increments of 300 calories. This is a further reason against treatment in a setting in which time limits are a major consideration. With rapid weight gain in AN patients there is the risk of precipitating bulimia. The body often requires some time to redistribute fat to muscle. If this does not occur, then the caloric intake to maintain body mass needs to be teleologically unreasonably high and provides a basis for binge eating, which may lead to a full BN syndrome. Liquid supplements are used to replace food not taken at regular mealtimes, and may also be preferable when patients require more than 3,000 calories per day to continue gaining weight.

There is no certainty about the correct target weight for each patient (Parry-Jones, 1991). It is reasonable to aim for a return to the premorbid weight at which normal menstrual function occurred in the absence of excessive weight or body shape preoccupation. This generally requires a body mass index greater than 20. A further parameter of normal physiological function is a normal body composition measure (Frisch, 1977; Hannen, Cowen, Freeman, et al., 1990).

In line with reports from other centers (Vandereycken, 1985), we have moved from a fixed to a lenient behavior therapy model in promoting weight gain. Certain guidelines are considered de rigueur. A multidisciplinary team of nursing, medical, occupational therapy, psychology, dietary, and social work staff develop and monitor the treatment plan for each patient. This means starting with a restrictive regimen during which meals, bathroom facilities, and other activities are supervised.

Meal supervision is the responsibility of nursing staff. Patients dine as a group under supervision by a nurse and are expected to complete their meal in 30 minutes. They then remain in a lounge for a further 30 minutes under supervision with restricted access to bathroom facilities during this time. In some instances, video playback of abnormal eating habits such as cutting food into minuscule portions can be helpful. For the first few weeks, high-calorie liquid supplements such as Ensure or Boost are permitted to supplement incomplete meals. After the first month, patients are expected to eat a full range of meals and to select foods from all the major food groups. From the beginning, they join a weekly nutrition group where beliefs about good and bad nutrition, vegetarianism, and energy balance are discussed. Some programs avoid the use of a liquid supplement in all but the most extreme cases, preferring to emphasize normal eating habits.

With each kilogram of weight gain, patients assume additional responsibility for their time in the hospital. They attend more group activities, including food shopping and meal preparation led by the occupational therapist. A specific therapy group also focuses on body image disturbance and provides a forum for patients to deal with changing body shape during treatment.

In keeping with the principle of promoting personal responsibility for recovery as treatment progresses, patients begin to eat meals without staff supervision—eating in the hospital cafeteria or in restaurants. This provides individuals with an opportunity to challenge their "food phobias" and discuss the consequences in various group and individual therapy sessions.

*Nasogastric feeding and hyperalimentation.* Food refusal can pose a major challenge. It also has the effect of limiting interventions by staff in other areas of treatment, such as family or group psychotherapy. On the rare occasion when nasogastric tube feeding is considered necessary, clear goals of tube feeding should be stated in advance. For example, a contract can be made stating that the tube is to be inserted and used up to a specific weight. It will then remain in situ, but normal meals will be offered, and only if meals are not completed will the tube be used to deliver supplementation. At a higher stated weight, the tube will be removed. This circumvents recurrent battles around the removal of the tube before the patient is able to demonstrate control over eating. Nasopharyngeal feeding was first used a hundred years ago, and commercially available diets for nasogastric feeding were first used 50 years ago. In comparison with total parenteral nutrition in which intravenous feeding is used, nasogastric feeding is simpler, less hazardous, and cheaper. We have outlined our view as to the appropriate use of nasogastric feeding, but others hold a more extreme view, suggesting that it should almost never be used. Lucas and Huse (1988) advise against using artificial product or parenteral-feeding and dispute the recommendation for consumption of above-average calorie intake in anorexia patients.

There are a range of commercially available supplements that can be used. The composition of a number of these is listed in an appendix to a chapter discussing enteral parenteral nutrition (Shils, 1988, pp. 1607–1623). In general terms a food supplement high in phosphate and potassium should be used. Whether the source of calories is from a particular food type (carbohydrate, fat, or protein) has not been shown to be critical in the refeeding of anorexic patients.

Complications that can occur with nasogastric feeding include equipment failure, problems of hydration, infection, and aspiration. Too rapid refeeding presents the potential hazards of hypophosphatemia, stomach rupture, duodenal ileus with acute pancreatitis, and fluid overload (Browning, 1977; Keane, Fennel, & Tomkin, 1978). Regular monitoring of electrolytes should be carried out in patients receiving nasogastric feeding.

Further information is available in the review by Krey and Lockett (1986). For most patients, consistent, firm, supportive nursing care obviates the need for tube feeding.

During the past two decades "total" parenteral nutrition (TPN) has provided an alternative method for refeeding. This should be considered only when oral and nasogastric routes are either refused or contraindicated. For example, Hirschman, Rao, and Chan (1977) described the successful use of TPN in an anorexic patient with acute renal failure secondary to acute tubular necrosis, while Maloney and Farrell (1980) and Croner and associates (1985) used TPN to successfully promote weight gain in AN patients who had previously failed to respond to alternative approaches. Nevertheless, TPN continues to be a potentially hazardous treatment. Pertschuk, Forster, Buzby, and Mullen (1981) reported one fatality due to hypophosphatemia in a series of eleven AN patients who received TPN.

Successful delivery of TPN requires detailed understanding of macronutrient and micronutrient requirements during starvation and refeeding, such as described by Baumgartner and Cerda (1990).

### Community Reintegration.

It is our policy to have patients remain as inpatients for at least 2 weeks after they reach the target weight range. During this time, discussion of body image and body shape is encouraged as individuals practice previously avoided activities. Body image distortion usually persists following weight restoration. This is frequently a focus for group psychotherapy, as open groups involve people at various stages of weight gain and maintenance.

Buying new clothes, throwing out or giving away clothes bought in childrens' stores, and risking wearing a bathing suit in a swimming pool are some of the new activities tackled in this phase. Preparing meals and dining with friends and family are encouraged. This is also the first opportunity for patients to reestablish contact with people outside the treatment team, and to reexperience cultural pressures toward thinness, hopefully from a healthier vantage point.

### Breaking the Binge-Purge Cycle

Outpatient psychological (Fairburn, Jones, Peveler, et al., 1991) and pharmacological (Kennedy & Goldbloom, 1991) treatments are the mainstays of treatment for BN. However, for a small minority of BN patients, often people with added psychiatric or physical conditions (e.g., diabetes mellitus), a brief, focused admission to the hospital may provide the structure and resources to reverse this dangerous cycle of food restriction, binge eating, and purging.

During a 4- to 8-week admission, patients are prescribed a balanced meal plan that usually contains 1,800 to 2,400 kcal per day, adjusted to a level at which the urge to binge is substantially reduced and weight restoration can occur. For some individuals, having a period of environmental control, albeit externally imposed, suffices in allowing the reestablishment of internal control.

As well as standard ward therapies, these patients are offered additional "binge exposure with response prevention" (Schmidt & Marks, 1989; Leitenberg, Rosen, & Gross, 1988; Kennedy, Katz, & Garfinkel, 1991). In this setting favorite binge foods are provided for "sampling" under supervision. Binge eating is not permitted and anxiety is often increased in the same way that it is in the in situ treatment of agoraphobic patients. Gradually, with repeated exposure and reduced supervision, over 8 to 10 sessions, the individual samples but does not binge on previously labeled "binge foods" without experiencing an anxiety response. This type of exposure therapy is more acceptable to both patients and staff than prescribed binge eating with response prevention of vomiting (Leitenberg et al., 1988). BN patients are also encouraged to complete tasks such as eating in restaurants and visiting old "binge haunts" while continuing to eat normally during their stay in hospital.

There are important issues to be considered in the inhospital treatment of obese and nonobese bulimic patients (see Chapter 3). The latter more frequently induce vomiting and as a result may have medical consequences different from those of obese bulimics (Hudson et al., 1988). This was confirmed by Mitchell, Pyle, Eckert, and associates (1990), who also noted that the overweight bulimic group binge ate less frequently than normal weight bulimics, but had an increased incidence of laxative abuse. It is likely that individuals with BN have reduced metabolic rates compared to controls and may require a lower caloric intake to maintain energy balance (Devlin, Walsh, Kral, et al., 1990). These observations emphasize that nutritional aspects of intense treatment programs need to be tailored to individual patients.

## *Providing Support for the Chronic Patient*

Longer duration of illness is generally associated with poor outcome in treatment (Herzog, Keller, & Lavori, 1988). For patients who have been more or less continuously ill for over 10 years, coercive hospital treatment with overly ambitious expectations for recovery is rarely successful and may precipitate depression and suicide (Crisp, 1980).

For these individuals, brief time-limited admissions to the hospital on an elective basis are indicated. Modest goals are set during a 4- to 6-week length of stay. These usually involve both an improvement in caloric intake and weight gain. When the date of discharge and not a specific weight is set as the end point, the potential for emotionally draining countertherapeutic struggles is removed, and responsibility for making the best use of this time lies with the patient. We have seen patients achieve *and maintain* limited weight gain following several such admissions, where previously they stayed in hospital longer, gained more weight over the short term, and then lost it upon discharge.

## ROLE OF PSYCHOTHERAPIES

During the early stages of treatment, cognitive distortions common to the disorder may be identified during group and individual therapies. For some patients, psychotherapy of any sort is not helpful, particularly in the early stages of treatment, while for others a more interpretive therapy may develop and continue beyond discharge. Frequently, the main issues in therapy involve enhancing low self-esteem by means other than dieting and weight loss, recognizing appropriate expressions of affect, and promoting autonomy.

Group therapy is also an important component of inpatient treatment where issues of body image, sexual identity, assertiveness, and social skills training are emphasized (Duncan & Kennedy, 1992).

Family therapy can be an important complement to both individual and group treatments, especially for younger patients (Russell, Szmukler, Dave, et al., 1987), and a family assessment is generally considered an essential part of the initial evaluation. One objective of family intervention is to enable family members to understand the illness and the goals of treatment. Families need an opportunity to discuss their often-present feelings of guilt and failure. Family sessions also offer an opportunity to examine communication between family members and may set the scene for further family therapy beyond hospital. Failure to elicit even passive family support is a bad prognostic indicator.

Family or parent support groups can also provide much-needed support for exhausted family members before and during hospital treatment. In many cases a group for parents can help overinvolved parents disengage in a healthy way from their ill daughter. For some, setting the objective of the AN patient not returning home after inpatient treatment allows for a long overdue separation—a "parentectomy"—that both patient and parents sometimes require.

## ROLE OF DRUG THERAPIES

Treatment of an eating disorder in a hospital is more likely than is outpatient treatment to include pharmacotherapy. This may be due in part to greater comorbidity with other psychiatric disorders among hospital patients (Kennedy & Garfinkel, 1989), and may also reflect the more serious nature of the illness.

### Anorexia Nervosa

Probably because of the severity and often refractory nature of AN, virtually every type of somatic treatment available in psychiatry has been advocated. Despite this, there is a surprising paucity of adequately controlled trials of pharmacotherapy and none in which drug therapy offers clinically significant enhancement of the nutritional and behavioral therapies previously described.

The rationales for drug prescribing in AN fall into three categories (a) enhancing food intake and weight gain, (b) dealing with associated psychiatric illness such as major depression, and (c) treating medical complications related mainly to chronic undernutrition and low weight. These will be summarized in order.

#### *Drugs to Promote Food Intake and Weight Gain*

*Neuroleptics.* Neuroleptics were the first psychotropic drugs to be advocated in treating AN (Dally, Oppenheim, & Sargant, 1958). Chlorpromazine (CPZ) induced weight gain through different actions including decreased motor activity, increased water retention, altered carbohydrate metabolism, and dopaminergic blockade in the hypothalamus. Doses of 600 mg to 1,000 mg were evaluated (Dally & Sargant, 1960; Crisp, 1965) and produced substantial adverse effects including marked hypotension and seizures. In a retrospective comparison, those patients who received adjunctive chlorpromazine therapy during hospital treatment displayed no more lasting benefits at a 2-year follow-up than those treated without concomitant drug therapy (Dally & Sargant, 1966). In the last decade two novel antipsychotic drugs were evaluated in double-blind, placebo-controlled trials in Holland. Both pimozide (Vandereyecken & Pierloot, 1982) and sulpiride (Vandereyecken, 1984) offered only marginal benefits over placebo when prescribed in combination with behavior therapy.

Thus, generally disappointing results of clinical trials (including the failure of neuroleptics to substantially alter the near-delusional beliefs about weight and shape), together with substantial adverse effects (such as seizures and hypotension in the short term, and tardive dyskinesia over a longer duration), have resulted in the infrequent use of these drugs with AN patients.

*Cyproheptadine.* Following the recognition that cyproheptadine, an antagonist of serotonin (5HT) and histamine, induced weight gain, several investigators evaluated cyproheptadine in hospitalized AN patients (Vigersky & Loriaux, 1977; Goldberg, Halmi, Eckert, et al., 1979; Halmi, Eckert, LaDu, et al., 1986). In each case, no benefit or only marginal benefit accrued to the group receiving cyproheptadine. It was also noted that the drug seemed to adversely affect eating behavior in those AN patients with bulimic symptoms (Halmi et al., 1986).

*Clonidine.* On the basis of evidence from animal studies that hypothalamic noradrenergic mechanisms increased feeding behavior (Liebowitz, 1983), Casper and colleagues (1987) evaluated the effects of oral clonidine (an α-adrenergic agonist) during refeeding in acute AN. Clonidine altered neither the rate of weight gain nor the perception of hunger or satiety during the study, supporting the concept that disturbances of the central control of hunger or satiety are not the main reason for AN patients refusing to eat.

### Antidepressant and Anxiolytic Agents

Several uncontrolled case studies involving tricyclic antidepressants suggested that improvement in mood preceded or paralleled weight gain in AN (Needleman & Waber, 1977; White & Schnaultz, 1977). However, subsequent controlled trials involving clomipramine (Lacey & Crisp, 1980), and amitriptyline (Biederman, Herzog, Rivinus, et al., 1985; Halmi et al., 1986) revealed no real clinical benefit for those on the tricyclic. Two recent open trials involving the 5HT uptake inhibitor fluoxetine have suggested a role for this drug in AN (Gwirtsman, Guze, Yager, et al., 1990; Weltzin, Kaye, Hsu, et al., 1990), although confirmation under double-blind conditions is required. Monoamine oxidase inhibitors have not been effective in promoting weight gain in patients with AN (Kennedy, Piran, & Garfinkel, 1985).

Surprisingly, despite the acknowledged spectrum of anxiety disorders that accompany AN, there are few, if any, controlled trials involving anxiolytic agents in AN (Andersen, 1987). Where anxiety symptoms appear to inhibit eating, short-acting benzodiazepines such as lorazepam and oxazepam, which are not metabolized in the liver, may be helpful in the short term (Goldbloom & Kennedy, 1988). These are prescribed in low dose, 30 minutes before meals. For BN patients, where the potential for coexistent substance dependence is high (Goldbloom & Hicks, 1988), the avoidance of benzodiazepines is recommended.

### Drugs to Treat Physical Complications

*Prokinetic agents.* Delayed gastric emptying occurs in emaciated AN patients (Robinson, Clarke, & Barrett, 1988) and reverses with refeeding (Rigaud, Bedig, Merrouche, et al., 1988). Although acute intravenous administration of antidopaminergic and cholinergic agents has been reported to accelerate gastric emptying (Dubois, Gross, Ebert, et al., 1979; Stacher, Bergmann, Wiesnagrotzki, et al., 1985), double-blind clinical trials involving oral metoclopramide (Moldofsky, Jeuniewic, Garfinkel, et al., 1977), and domperidone (Craigen, Kennedy, Garfinkel, et al., 1987) have failed to demonstrate significant superiority over placebos. Nevertheless, domperidone may, in individual cases, offer some benefit in the early stages of refeeding.

*Drugs to induce ovulation.* While weight restoration is associated with return of menses in most women with AN, a substantial minority remain amenorrheic. Where pregnancy is a goal, or where osteoporosis is of concern, clomiphene (50 to 100 mg/d for 5 to 7 days) or luteinizing hormone releasing hormone (LHRH; 100 ug given intravenously over 5 hours) may be prescribed.

Patients with chronic AN also have a significantly reduced bone mass due to osteoporosis (Rigotti, Nussbaum, Herzog, et al., 1984), which correlates with hypercortisolism (Biller, Saxe, Herzog, et al., 1989; Newman & Halmi, 1989), and which is not rapidly reversed by recovery (Rigotti, Neer, Skates, et al., 1991). Bone mass may continue to fall after weight gain has recommenced. At this time the benefit of prolonged estrogen administration in women with AN has yet to be reported, although it is reasonable to conclude that adequate nutritional intake, including calcium and vitamin D supplements, and maintenance of normal weight are important aspects of treatment. If the effect of physical change in AN, and the possible negative implications for long-term infertility are emphasized to patients, this can, in some situations, enhance weight gain.

### Replacement Therapies

*Hypokalemia.* Hypokalemia is the most common electrolyte abnormality found in patients with anorexia nervosa. It occurs as a result of starvation, loss of body fluid through diarrhea and vomiting, and abuse of diuretics. The features can be detected on electrocardiogram (EKG) and include prolonged PR intervals, wider QRS, inverted T waves, and the presence of U waves. The daily requirement of potassium is 70 mEq. If blood potassium level is above 3 mEq/L, it is usually sufficient to provide oral supplementation of potassium in the form of a potassium salt taken in tablet form. Such medication can be irritating to the stomach, and it would be usual to spread out the dosage to a four times per day regime. If the serum potassium level is below 2 mEq/L, reasonably rapid infusion of potassium is required. This should usually be done at a rate of 20 mEq/h with EKG monitoring. An intravenous bolus of potassium should never be given as this can cause cardiac arrest. Intravenous infusion can cause venous irritation. One should never given intravenous infusion at a rate greater than 40 mEq/h. The rate of infusion should also be based on how rapid the fall in potassium has been. If it has been more rapid (e.g., massive recent use of diuretics), then a more rapid infusion is appropriate. If the loss of potassium is presumed to have been over a prolonged period, then slower reinfusion of potassium is appropriate. At a blood level between 2 mEq/L and 3 mEq/L, an intravenous infusion should be given, but at a slower rate.

*Hypophosphatemia.* The vast majority of anorexic patients do not have low levels of phosphate when initially admitted to an inpatient unit. Once refeeding commences, there may be a fall in blood phosphate level, particularly in patients who have had a low phosphate diet (e.g., an exclusion of eggs, pulses, cereals, and cola and cereal beverages, in addition to the typically restricted anorexic diet) or who have used nonphosphate laxatives. The drop in phosphate level after feeding has recommenced is not infrequent, but results in severe medical problems in only a small minority of anorexic patients. In these rare individuals, the consequences can be extreme (status epilepticus, cardiac arrhythmias, and hemopoietic suppression). Ensuring a diet rich in phosphate for all patients starting a refeeding program is essential. Those patients whose phosphate levels are particularly low a few days after commencing refeeding can be given phosphate-rich supplementation in the form of phosphate-rich foods or specific phosphate foods (one marketed by Sandoz). The latter can cause diarrhea.

*Trace elements and vitamins.* With regard to trace elements, zinc has attracted most attention, because there are parallels between the symptoms of AN and zinc deficiency (Prasad, Rabrani, Abbasil, et al., 1978). These include weight loss, appetitive changes, and taste disturbances. Although several authors (Casper, Kirschman, Sandstead, et al., 1980; Katz, Keen, Litt, et al., 1987; Humphries, Vivian, Stuart, et al., 1989) have reported reduced levels of zinc in AN patients, others have found no abnormality in zinc levels or taste acuity (Roijen, Worsaae, Zlotnick, et al., 1990). Likewise, despite promising open trials involving zinc supplementation in AN (Bryce-Smith & Simpson, 1984; Safai-Kutti, 1990), evidence of clinical benefit from placebo-controlled trials is still lacking.

Magnesium deficiency may also exist in AN (Hall, Hoffman, Beresford, et al., 1988), particularly in the presence of muscular weakness, paresthesia, and leg cramps. Oral supplementation over several weeks resulted in an improvement of these symptoms. In rare instances, hypomagnesemia may be associated with severe congestive cardiac failure (Fonseca & Havard, 1985) and require intravenous replacement with magnesium sulphate.

Measurements of vitamin status have also yielded somewhat inconsistent findings. Hypercarotenemia is the most consistent finding in AN (Pops & Schwabe, 1968). This can be associated with high levels of retinol (Philipp, Pirke, & Seidle Metal, 1988), despite other vitamin levels being in the borderline normal to low range (Philipp et al., 1988; Van Binsbergen, Odink, Van de Berg, et al., 1988). Routine supplementation is not necessary.

Thus, most drug treatments in AN have failed to substantiate evidence for a specific biological hypothesis about the disorder. Rather, they have played a role in the symptomatic treatment of numerous physical and psychiatric symptoms associated with AN.

### Bulimia Nervosa

In contrast to trials with AN patients, several different antidepressant drug trials involving BN patients have yielded substantial evidence that short-term behavioral improvement occurs (Kennedy & Goldbloom, 1991). In only a few instances have hospitalized patients been included in these trials (Fichter, Leibl, Rief, et al., 1991). The link between BN and mood disorder takes into account common phenomenology (Cooper & Fairburn, 1986; Piran, Kennedy, Garfinkel, et al., 1985), longitudinal vulnerability (Hudson, Pope, Jonas, et al., 1987), and family history

(Kassett, Gershon, Maxwell, et al., 1989), as well as certain neuroendocrine abnormalities (Gwirtsman, Roy-Byrne, & Yager, 1983; Kennedy, Garfinkel, Parienti, et al., 1989). However, this link is considerably more complex than was first thought (Levy, Dixon, & Stern, 1989) and does not adequately address the multifaceted etiology of BN.

A second rationale for prescribing antidepressant agents to patients with BN lies in the known effect of these agents on neurotransmitters implicated in the control of appetitive behavior in the hypothalamus (Morley, Levine, Krahn, et al., 1988; see Chapter 6 this volume). Other neuroregulators such as cholecystokinin (CCK) (Baile & Della Ferra, 1985) and the endogenous opioids (Gosnell, 1987) have also been the subject of investigations.

Several selected tricyclic, monoamine oxidase inhibitor, and selective serotonin reuptake inhibitor antidepressants have been investigated under double-blind conditions in BN. Most attention has been paid to measures of altered frequency in binge eating and considerably less to alterations in cognitive symptoms associated with BN.

As has been stated elsewhere (Kennedy & Goldbloom, 1991), virtually all of these trials suffer from significant methodological shortcomings. Inadequate attention has been paid to the issue of maintenance of change beyond each short-term trial. Nonbehavioral aspects of BN, particularly the cognitive beliefs about weight and shape, have been inadequately evaluated, and comparison of the relative merits of pharmacotherapies, psychotherapies, and their combination are still in their infancy (Mitchell et al., 1990). Of the tricyclics, imipramine and desipramine have been evaluated more than other agents and are prescribed at doses similar to those given to depressed patients. Fluoxetine has also been investigated extensively and may need to be given at a higher dose (60 mg) than the recommended antidepressant dose.

### Other Psychotropic Interventions

Other drugs, including anticonvulsants (Kaplan, Garfinkel, Darby, et al., 1983), lithium (Hsu, Clement, & Sandhouse, 1987), and opiate antagonists (Mitchell, Christenson, Jennings, et al., 1989), have been evaluated under experimental conditions but do not currently have a role in the routine management of BN.

At a practical level, there does appear to be an adjunctive role for antidepressant agents such as fluoxetine or desipramine in treating some BN patients in an inpatient unit, although added side effects in the low body weight anorexic patient with bulimia (AN + BN) may limit an adequate therapeutic trial.

## ETHICAL AND PRACTICAL ASPECTS OF INVOLUNTARY HOSPITALIZATION

When patients with AN reach a weight and nutritional state that are considered to be life threatening, they invariably receive some form of involuntary treatment (Crisp, 1981; Hsu, 1986). Two factors traditionally cited to justify involuntary hospitalization are (a) that starvation results in cognitive impairment and (b) that views on weight and nutrition expressed by the anorexic patient are influenced by distorted beliefs about weight and shape. Nasogastric feeding and hyperalimentation are often required during involuntary hospitalization, although both carry substantial risks when administered to uncooperative patients (Maloney & Farrell, 1980). Such treatment does not bode well for long-term recovery and should be used only when death is a serious possibility.

Although the merits of prolonging life in seemingly treatment-resistant patients with AN have been debated (Hébert & Weingarten, 1991; Kluge, 1991; Goldner, McKenzie, & Kline, 1991), we support the role of repeated refeeding for the chronic patient (Kennedy, Kaplan, & Garfinkel, 1992), recognizing that some patients achieve a moderate quality of life even after many years of chronic illness (Theander, 1985).

## THE ROLE OF EXERCISE IN TREATING AN AND BN

In general terms, the restriction of exercise has been considered a mainstay of treatment, particularly for AN patients during an inpatient admission. The reality is that for many patients this is a core component of their identity and one that can be perceived as normal if separated from the other facets of AN. With an emphasis on normal eating and normal body composition, an acceptance of normal levels of exercise and normal physiological responses to exercise would represent a consistent philosophy. Although in the early stages of any treatment program limitation of exercise is desirable, the reintroduction of exercise can be a facet of treatment. Ideally, such exercise should be social, with a goal other than burning off calories or the shaping of one's body. Involvement in some kind of team or competitive sport where there are built-in constraints to the amount of exercise and where the activity is nonisolating and includes a social component is best.

One of the major fears for many anorexic patients is the possibility that return to normal weight is a prelude to becoming obese. The attention to physiological functioning (mentioned above) gives the therapist the "high ground" in emphasizing that in the underweight anorexic state normal body functioning is disturbed (for example, exercise response, as in heart rate with a standard exercise load) and that this requires correction. One can easily extrapolate this to emphasize that exercise response is abnormal in both obesity and emaciation and that there is an inverted-U shape curve in the relationship between weight and normal body function. The object is to place the individual in the optimum position.

The "threat/promise" of readmission to the hospital as a result of a fall in weight or an excessive weight gain (although the latter virtually never occurs) often removes some of the anxiety associated with the initial struggle to gain weight. The emphasis on exercise toward the end of a treatment program may appear paradoxical, but for many it might, with monitoring, provide an escape from the anorexic position.


## DISCHARGE PLANS

Aspects of daily living need to be considered during treatment. These include changes in housing, enhancement of social skills that have been stunted or lost, and the broader facilitation of both work and leisure identities, which are invariably unbalanced or absent. The involvement of a multidisciplinary team, including social workers, physicians, nurses, occupational therapists, nutritionists, psychologists, and allied professionals is required in this process.


## CONCLUSION

Eating disorders represent a spectrum of psychiatric ill health in which there is a danger of overzealous intervention. A sense of what is achievable needs to be held firmly in mind. The recognition of chronicity in some patients would allow inpatient teams to evolve not only models of coping with acute treatments that require considerable therapeutic optimism but also maintenance treatments for patients who continue to have long-standing deficits.

## REFERENCES

Agras, W. S., Dorian, B., Kirkley, B. G., et al. (1987). Imipramine in the treatment of bulimia: A double-blind controlled study. *International Journal of Eating Disorders,* 6(1), 29–38.

Andersen, A. E. (1987). Uses and potential misuses of antianxiety agents in the treatment of anorexia nervosa and bulimia nervosa. In P. E. Garfinkel & D. M. Garner (Eds.), *The role of drug treatments for eating disorders* (pp. 59–73). New York: Brunner/Mazel.

Baile, C. A., & Della Ferra, M. A. (1985). Central nervous system cholescystokinin and the control of feeding. *Annals of the New York Academy of Sciences, 448,* 424–430.

Barlow, J., Blouin, J., Blouin, A., et al. (1988). Treatment of bulimia with desipramine: A double-blind crossover study. *Canadian Journal of Psychiatry, 33,* 129–133.

Baumgartner, T. G., & Cerda, J. J. (1990). Total parenteral nutrition. In T. M. Bayless (Ed.), *Current therapy in gastroenterology and liver disease* (Vol. 3, pp. 245–255). Philadelphia: B. C. Decker.

Bhanji, S., & Mattingly, D. (1988). *Medical aspects of anorexia nervosa.* London: Wright.

Bhanji, S., & Newton, V. B. (1985). Richard Morton's account of "nervous consumption." *International Journal of Eating Disorders, 4,* 589–595.

Biederman, J., Herzog, D. B., Rivinus, I. N., et al. (1985). Amitripyline in the treatment of anorexia nervosa. *Journal of Clinical Psychopharmacology, 5,* 10–16.

Biller, B. M. K., Saxe, V., Herzog, D. B., et al. (1989). Mechanisms of osteoporosis in adult and adolescent women with anorexia nervosa. *Journal of Clinical Endocrinology and Metabolism, 68,* 548–554.

Browning, C. H. (1977). Anorexia nervosa: Complications of somatic therapy. *Comprehensive Psychiatry, 18,* 399–403.

Bryce-Smith, D., & Simpson, R. I. D. (1984). Case of anorexia nervosa responding to zinc sulphate. *Lancet, ii,* 350.

Casper, R. C., Kirschner, B., Sandstead, H. H., et al. (1980). An evaluation of trace metals, vitamins, and taste function in anorexia nervosa. *American Journal of Clinical Nutrition, 33,* 1801–1808.

Casper, R. C., Schlemmer, R. F., & Javaid, J. I. (1987). A placebo controlled crossover study of oral clonidine in acute anorexia nervosa. *Psychiatry Research, 20,* 249–260.

Cooper, P. J., & Fairburn, C. G. (1986). The depressive symptoms of bulimia nervosa. *British Journal of Psychiatry, 148,* 268–274.

Craigen, G., Kennedy, S. H., Garfinkel, P. E., et al. (1987). Drugs that facilitate gastric emptying. In P. E. Garfinkel & D. M. Garner (Eds.), *The role of drug treatment for eating disorders* (pp. 161–176). New York: Brunner/Mazel.

Crisp, A. H. (1965). A treatment regime for anorexia nervosa. *British Journal of Psychiatry, 112*, 505–512.

Crisp, A. H. (1980). *Anorexia nervosa: Let me be.* London: Plenum Books.

Crisp, A. H. (1981). Therapeutic outcome in anorexia nervosa. *Canadian Journal of Psychiatry, 126*, 232–235.

Croner, S., Larsson, J., Schildt, B., et al. (1985). Severe anorexia nervosa treated with total parenteral nutrition. *Acta Paediatrica Scandinavica, 74*, 230–236.

Dally, P. J., Oppenheim, G. B., & Sargant, W. (1958). Anorexia nervosa. *British Medical Journal, ii*, 633–634.

Dally, P. J., & Sargant, W. (1960). A new treatment of anorexia nervosa. *British Medical Journal, 1*, 1770–1773.

Dally, P. J., & Sargant, W. (1966). Treatment and outcome of anorexia nervosa. *British Medical Journal, ii*, 793–795.

Devlin, M. J., Walsh, B. T., Kral, J. G., et al. (1990). Metabolic abnormalities in bulimia nervosa. *Archives of General Psychiatry, 47*, 144–148.

Dubois, A., Gross, H. A., Ebert, M. H., et al. (1979). Altered gastric emptying and secretion in primary anorexia nervosa. *Gastroenterology, 77*, 319–323.

Duncan, J., & Kennedy, S. H. (1992). Inpatient group therapy. In H. Harper-Giuffre & K. R. McKenzie (Eds.), *Group psychotherapy of the eating disorders.* Washington, DC: American Psychiatric Press. (pp. 149–160).

Fairburn, C. G., Jones, R., Peveler, R. C., et al. (1991). Three psychological treatments for bulimia nervosa. *Archives of General Psychiatry, 48*, 463–469.

Fichter, M. M., Leibl, K., Rief, W., et al. (1991). Fluoxetine versus placebo: A double-blind study with bulimic inpatients undergoing intensive psychotherapy. *Pharmacopsychiatry, 24*, 1–7.

Fonseca, V., & Havard, C. W. H. (1985). Electrolyte disturbance and cardiac failure with hypomagnesaemia in anorexia nervosa. *British Medical Journal, 291*, 1680–1682.

Frish, R. E. (1977). Food intake, fatness, and reproduction ability. In R. A. Vigersky (Ed.), *Anorexia nervosa.* New York: Raven Press.

Garfinkel, P. E., & Garner, D. M. (1982). *Anorexia nervosa: A multidimensional perspective.* New York: Brunner/Mazel.

Garfinkel, P. E., & Kaplan, A. S. (1985). Starvation based perpetuating mechanisms in anorexia nervosa. *International Journal of Eating Disorders, 4*, 651–655.

Garfinkel, P. E., Kaplan, A. S., & Garner, D. M. (1983). the differentiation of vomiting/weight loss as a conversion disorder from anorexia nervosa. *American Journal of Psychiatry, 140*, 1019–1022.

Goldberg, S. C., Halmi, K. A., Eckert, E. D., et al. (1979). Cyproheptadine in anorexia nervosa. *British Journal of Psychiatry, 134*, 67–70.

Goldbloom, D. S., & Hicks, L. (1988). *Eating disorders and alcoholism: Coprevalence.* Presented at 141st American Psychiatric Association Annual Meeting, Montreal. [*New Research, #282*].

Goldbloom, D. S., & Kennedy, S. H. (1988). Drug treatment of eating disorders. In P. E. Garfinkel (Ed.), *Anorexia nervosa and bulimia nervosa.* Kalamazoo: Upjohn.

Goldner, E. M., McKenzie, J. M., & Kline, S. A. (1991). The ethics of forced feeding in anorexia nervosa. *Canadian Medical Association Journal, 144,* 1205–1206.

Gosnell, B. A. (1987). Central structures involved in opioid-induced feeding. *Federation Proceedings, 46,* 163–167.

Gustavsson, C. G., & Eriksson, L. (1989). Case Report. Acute respiratory failure in anorexia nervosa with hypophosphataemia. *Journal of Internal Medicine, 225,* 63–64.

Gwirtsman, H. E., Guze, B. H., Yager, J., et al. (1990). Fluoxetine treatment of anorexia nervosa: An open clinical trial. *Journal of Clinical Psychiatry, 51,* 378–382.

Gwirtsman, H. E., Roy-Byrne, P., & Yager, J. (1983). Neuroendocrine abnormalities in bulimia. *American Journal of Psychiatry, 140,* 559–563.

Hall, R. C. W., Hoffman, R. S., Beresford, T. P., et al. (1988). Hypomagnesemia in patients with eating disorders. *Psychosomatics, 29,* 264–272.

Halmi, K. A., Eckert, E., LaDu, T. J., et al. (1986). Anorexia nervosa: Treatment efficacy of cyproheptadine and amitriptyline. *Archives of General Psychiatry, 43,* 177–181.

Hannan, J., Cowen, S., Freeman, C., et al. (1990). Assessment of body composition in anorexic patients. In S. Yasamura, J. E. Harrison, & K. G. McNeill, et al. (Eds.), *Advances in body composition studies* (pp. 149–154). New York: Plenum Press.

Hebert, P. C., & Weingarten, M. A. (1991). The ethics of forced feeding in anorexia nervosa. *Canadian Medical Association Journal, 144,* 141–144.

Herzog, D. B., Keller, M. B., & Lavori, P. W. (1988). Outcome in anorexia nervosa and bulimia nervosa. A review of the literature. *Journal of Nervous and Mental Disease, 176,* 131–143.

Hirschman, G. H., Rao, D. D., & Chan, J. C. M. (1977). Anorexia nervosa with acute tubular necrosis treated with parenteral nutrition. *Nutrition and Metabolism, 21,* 341–348.

Horne, R. L., Ferguson, J. M., Pope, H. G., et al. (1988). Treatment of bulimia with bupropion: A multicenter controlled trial. *Journal of Clinical Psychiatry, 49*(7), 262–266.

Hsu, L. K. G. (1986). The treatment of anorexia nervosa. *American Journal of Psychiatry, 143,* 573–581.

Hsu, L. K. G., Clement, L., & Santhouse, R. (1987). Treatment of bulimia with lithium: A preliminary study. *Psychopharmacology Bulletin, 23*, 45–48.

Hudson, J. I., Pope, H. G., Jonas, J. M., et al. (1987). A controlled study of lifetime prevalence of affective and other psychiatric disorders in bulimic outpatients. *American Journal of Psychiatry, 144*, 1283–1287.

Hudson, J. I., Pope, H. G., Keck, P. E., et al. (1989). Treatment of bulimia nervosa with trazadone: Short-term response and long-term follow up. *Clinical Neuropharmacology, 12*, (Suppl. 1). 538–546.

Hudson, J. I., Pope, H. G. Jr., Wurtman, J., et al. (1988). Bulimia in obese individuals: Relationship to normal-weight bulimia. *The Journal of Nervous and Mental Disease, 176*, 144–152.

Hudson, J. I., Pope, H. G., Keck, P. E., et al. (1989). Treatment of bulimia nervosa with trazadone: Short-term response and long-term follow up. *Clinical Neuropharmacology, 12* (Suppl. 1), S38–S46.

Hughes, P. L., Wells, L. A., Cunningham, C. J., et al. (1986). Treating bulimia with desipramine: A double-blind, placebo-controlled study. *Archives of General Psychiatry, 43*, 182–186.

Humphries, L., Vivian, B., Stuart, M., et al. (1989). Zinc deficiency and eating disorders. *Journal of Clinical Psychiatry, 50*, 456–459.

Kaplan, A. S., Garfinkel, P. E., Darby, P. L., et al. (1983). Carbamazepine in the treatment of bulimia. *American Journal of Psychiatry, 140*, 1225–1226.

Kassett, J. A., Gershon, E. S., Maxwell, M. E., et al. (1989). Psychiatric disorders in the first-degree relatives of probands with bulimia nervosa. *American Journal of Psychiatry, 146*, 1468–1471.

Katz, R. L., Keen, C. L., Litt, I. F., et al. (1987). Zinc deficiency in anorexia nervosa. *Journal of Adolescent Health Care, 8*, 400–406.

Keane, F. B. V., Fennel, J. S., & Tomkin, G. H. (1978). Acute pancreatitis, acute gastric dilatation and duodenal ileus following refeeding in anorexia nervosa. *Irish Journal of Medical Science, 147*, 191–192.

Kennedy, S. H., & Garfinkel, P. E. (1989). Patients admitted to hospital with anorexia nervosa and bulimia nervosa: Psychopathology, weight gain and attitudes toward treatment. *International Journal of Eating Disorders, 8*, 181–190.

Kennedy, S. H., & Goldbloom, D. S. (1991). Current perspectives on drug therapies for anorexia nervosa and bulimia nervosa. *Drugs, 41*, 367–377.

Kennedy, S. H., Goldbloom, D. S., & Vaccarino, F. J. (1992). New drugs, new directions. In G. H. Anderson & S. H. Kennedy (Eds.), *Biology of feast and famine: Relevance to eating disorders* (pp. 341–356) New York: Academic Press.

Kennedy, S. H., Kaplan, A. S., & Garfinkel, P. E. (1992). Intensive hospital treatments for anorexia nervosa and bulimia nervosa. In P. J. Cooper & A. Stein (Eds.), *Feeding problems and eating disorders*. New York: Harwood Academic Publishers.

Kennedy, S. H., Katz, R., & Garfinkel, P. E. (1991). Inpatient treatment of bulimia nervosa. In G. Racagni, N. Brunello, & T. Fukuda (Eds.), *Proceedings of 5th World Congress of Biological Psychiatry*. Holland: Elsevier (pp. 297–299).

Kennedy, S. H., Piran, N., & Garfinkel, P. E. (1985). Monoamine oxidase inhibitor therapy for anorexia nervosa and bulimia: A preliminary trial of isocarboxazid. *Journal of Clinical Psychopharmacology, 5*, 279–285.

Kennedy, S. H., Garfinkel, P. E., Parienti, V., et al. (1989). Changes in melatonin but not cortisol are associated with depression in eating disorder patients. *Archives of General Psychiatry, 46*, 73–78.

Kennedy, S. H., Piran, N., Warsh, J. J., et al. (1988). A trial of isocarboxazid in the treatment of bulimia nervosa. *Journal of Clinical Psychopharmacology, 8*(6), 391–396.

Kluge, E. H., (1991). The ethics of forced feeding in anorexia nervosa. A response to Hébert and Weingarten. *Canadian Medical Association Journal, 144*, 1121–1124.

Krey, S. H., & Lockett, G. M. (1986). Parenteral nutrition: A comprehensive overview. In S. H. Krey & R. L. Murray (Eds.), *Dynamics of nutrition support: Assessment, implication, evaluation* (pp. 279–328). Norwalk, CT: Appleton-Century Crofts.

Laboucaré, J., & Barres, J. (1954). Les aspects cliniques, pathogéniques et therapeutiques de l'anorexie mentale. *L'Evolution Psychiatrique, 1*, 118–119.

Lacey, J. H., & Crisp, A. H. (1980). Hunger, food intake and weight: The impact of clomipramine on a receding anorexia nervosa population. *Postgraduate Medical Journal, 56*, 79–85.

Leitenberg, H., Rosen, J. C., Gross, J., et al. (1988). Exposure plus response prevention treatment of bulimia nervosa. *Journal of Consulting and Clinical Psychology, 56*, 535–541.

Levy, A. B., Dixon, K. N., & Stern, S. L. (1989). How are depression and bulimia related? *American Journal of Psychiatry, 146*, 162–169.

Liebowitz, S. F. (1983). Hypothalamic catecholamine systems controlling eating behaviour: A potential model for anorexia nervosa. In P. L. Darby, P. E. Garfinkel, & M. Garner (Eds.), *Anorexia nervosa: Recent developments in research* (pp. 221–229). New York: Alan R. Liss.

Lucas, A. R., & Huse, D. N. (1988). Behavioral disorders affecting food intake: Anorexia nervosa and bulimia. In M. E. Shils & V. R. Young (Eds.), *Nutrition in health and diseases* (7th ed., pp. 1450–1457). Philadelphia: Lee and Febiger.

Maloney, M. J., & Farrell, M. K. (1980). Treatment of severe weight loss in anorexia nervosa with hyperalimentation and psychotherapy. *American Journal of Psychiatry, 137*, 310–314.

McCann, U. D., & Agras, W. S. (1990). Successful treatment of nonpurging bulimia nervosa with desipramine: A double-blind, placebo-controlled study. *American Journal of Psychiatry, 147*(11), 1509–1513.

Mitchell, J., & Groat, R. (1984). A placebo-controlled, double-blind trial of amitriptyline in bulimia. *Journal of Clinical Psychopharmacology, 4*(4), 186–193.

Mitchell, P. B., Parker, G. B., & Dwyer, J. M. (1988). The law and a physically ill patient with anorexia nervosa: Liberty versus paternalism. *The Medical Journal of Australia, 148,* 41–44.

Mitchell, J. E.,Christenson, G., Jennings, J., et al. (1989). A placebo controlled double blind crossover study of naltrexone hydrochloride in outpatients with normal weight bulimia. *Journal of Clinical Psychopharmacology, 9,* 94–97.

Mitchell, J. E., Hatsukami, D., Pyle, R. L., et al. (1987). Metabolic acidosis as a marker for laxative abuse in patients with bulimia. *International Journal of Eating Disorders, 6,* 557–560.

Mitchell, J. E., Pyle, R. L., Eckert, E. D., et al. (1983). Electrolyte and other physiological abnormalities in patients with bulimia. *Psychological Medicine, 13,* 173–278.

Mitchell, J. E., Pyle, R. L., Eckert, E. D., et al. (1990). Bulimia nervosa in overweight individuals. *The Journal of Nervous and Mental Disease, 178,* 324–327.

Moldofsky, H., Jeuniewic, N., & Garfinkel, P. E. (1977). Preliminary report on metoclopramide in anorexia nervosa. In R. A. Vigersky (Ed.), *Anorexia nervosa* (pp. 373–375). New York: Raven Press.

Morley, J. E., Levine, A. S., & Krahn, D. D. (1988). Neurotransmitter regulation of appetite and feeding. In B. J. Blinder, et al. (Eds.), *The eating disorders* (pp. 11–19). New York: PMA Publishing.

Morton, R., (1694). *Phthisologia: Or a treatise of consumptions.* London: S. Smith & B. Walford.

Multicentre Group (Fluoxetine Bulimia Nervosa Collaborative Study Group) (1992). Fluoxetine in the treatment of bulimia nervosa: A multicenter placebo-controlled double-blind trial. *Archives of General Psychiatry, 49,* 139–147.

Needleman, H. L., & Waber, D. (1977). The use of amitriptyline in anorexia nervosa. In R. A. Vigersky (Ed.), *Anorexia nervosa.* New York: Raven Press.

Newman, M. M., & Halmi, K. A. (1989). Relationship of bone density to estradiol and cortisol in anorexia nervosa and bulimia. *Psychiatry Research, 29,* 105–112.

Parry-Jones, W. L. L. (1991). Target weight in children and adolescents with anorexia nervosa. *Acta paediatrica Scandinavica, 373*(Suppl.), 82–90.

Pertschuk, H. J., Forster, J., Buzby, G., & Mullen, J. L. (1981). The treatment of anorexia nervosa with total parenteral nutrition. *Biological Psychiatry, 16,* 539–550.

Philipp, E., Pirke, K. M., & Seidle Metal. (1988). Vitamin status in patients with anorexia nervosa and bulimia nervosa. *International Journal of Eating Disorders, 8,* 209–218.

Piran, N., Kennedy, S. H., Garfinkel, P. E., et al. (1985). Affective disturbance in eating disorders. *Journal of Nervous and Mental Disease, 173,* 395–400.

Pope, H. G., Keck, P. E., & McElroy, S. L. (1989). A placebo-controlled study of trazadone in bulimianervosa. *Journal of Clinical Psychopharmacology, 9*(4), 254–259.

Pope, H. G., Hudson, J. I., Jonas, J. M., et al. (1983). Bulimia treated with imipramine: A placebo controlled, double-blind study. *American Journal of Psychiatry, 140*(5), 554–558.

Pops, M. A., & Schwabe, A. D. (1968). Hypercastenemia in anorexia nervosa. *Journal of the American Medical Association, 205,* 533–534.

Prasad, A. S., Rabrani, P., Abbasil, A., et al. (1978). Experimental zinc deficiency in humans. *Annals of Internal Medicine, 89,* 483.

Rigaud, D., Bedig, G., Merrouche, M., et al. (1988). Delayed gastric emptying in anorexia nervosa is improved by completion of a renutrition program. *Digestive Diseases and Sciences, 33,* 919–925.

Rigotti, N. A., Neer, R. M., Skates, S. J., et al. (1991). The clinical course of osteoporosis in anorexia nervosa. *Journal of the American Medical Association, 265,* 1133–1138.

Rigotti, N. A., Nussbaum, S. R., Herzog, D. B., et al. (1984). Osteoporosis in women with anorexia nervosa. *New England Journal of Medicine, 311,* 1601–1606.

Robinson, P. H., Clarke, M., & Barrett, J. (1988). Determinants of delayed gastric emptying in anorexia nervosa and bulimia nervosa. *Gut, 29,* 458–464.

Roijen, S., Worsaae, V., & Zlotnik, G. (1990). Anorexia nervosa and zinc. *Scandinavian Journal of Clinical and Laboratory Investigations, 50,* 105.

Russell, G. F. M., Szmukler, G. I., Dave, C., et al. (1987). An evaluation of family therapy in anorexia nervosa and bulimia nervosa. *Archives of General Psychiatry, 44,* 1047–1056.

Sabine, E. J., Yonace, A., & Farrington, A. J. (1983). Bulimia nervosa: A placebo controlled double-blind therapeutic trial of mianserin. *British Journal of Clinical Pharmacology, 15,* 195S–202S.

Safai-Kutti, S. (1990). Oral zinc supplementation in anorexia nervosa. *Acta Psychiatrica Scandinavica, 82*(Suppl. 361), 14–17.

Sargant, W. (1951). Leucotomy in psychosomatic disorders. *Lancet, II,* 87.

Schmidt, U., & Marks, I. M. (1989). Exposure plus prevention of bingeing versus exposure plus prevention of vomiting in bulimia nervosa. *Journal of Nervous and Mental Disease, 177,* 259–266.

Shils, M. E. (1988). Enteral (tube) and parenteral nutrition support. In M. E. Shils & V. R. Young (Eds.), *Modern nutrition in health and diseases* (7th ed., pp. 1023–1066). Philadelphia: Lee and Febiger.

Stacher, G., Bergmann, H., Wiesnagrotzki, S., et al. (1985). *Anorexia nervosa and bulimia: Delayed gastric emptying accelerated by cisapride* [Abstract]. Presented at the International Symposium on Disorders of Eating Behaviour. Pavia, Italy.

Theander, S. (1985). Outcome and prognosis in anorexia nervosa and bulimia: Some results of previous investigations, compared with those of a Swedish long-term study. *Journal of Psychiatric Research, 19,* 493–508.

Toner, B. B., Garfinkel, P. E., & Garner, D. M. (1986). Long term follow-up of anorexia nervosa. *Psychosomatic Medicine, 48,* 520–529.

Treasure, J. L., Russell, G. F. M., Fogelman, I., et al. (1987). Reversible bone loss in anorexia nervosa. *British Medical Journal, 295,* 474–475.

Turner, M. St. J., & Shapiro, C. M. (1992). The biochemistry of anorexia nervosa. *International Journal of Eating Disorders, 12,* 179–193.

Van Binsbergen, C. J. M., Odink, J., Van de Berg, H., et al. (1988). Nutritional status in anorexia nervosa: Clinical chemistry, vitamins, iron and zinc. *European Journal of Clinical Nutrition, 42,* 929–937.

Vandereycken, W., & Pierloot, R. (1982). Pimozide combined with behaviour therapy in the short-term treatment of anorexia nervosa: A double-blind placebo controlled cross over study. *Acta Psychiatrica Scandinavica, 66,* 445–450.

Vandereycken, W. (1984). Neuroleptics in the short-term treatment of anorexia nervosa: A double blind placebo controlled study with sulpiride. *British Journal of Psychiatry, 144,* 288–292.

Vandereycken, W. (1985). Inpatient treatment of anorexia nervosa: Some research guided changes. *Journal of Psychiatric Research, 19,* 413–422.

Vigersky, R. A., & Loriaux, D. L. (1977). The effect of cyproheptadine in anorexia nervosa: A double blind trial. In R. Vigersky (Ed.), *Anorexia nervosa.* New York: Raven Press.

Walsh, B. T., Gladis, M., Roose, S. P., et al. (1988). Phenelzine vs placebo in 50 patients with bulimia. *Archives of General Psychiatry, 45,* 471–475.

Walsh, B. T., Stewart, J. W., Roose, S. P., et al. (1984). Treatment of bulimia with Phenelzine: A double-blind, placebo-controlled study. *Archives of General Psychiatry, 41,* 1105–1109.

White, J. H., & Schnaultz, N. L. (1977). Successful treatment of anorexia nervosa with imipramine. *Diseases of the Nervous System, 38,* 567–568.

Weltzin, T. E., Kaye, W. H., Hsu, L. K. G., et al. (1990). *Fluoxetine improves outcome in anorexia nervosa.* Presented at the 143rd annual meeting, American Psychiatric Association, New York [New Research NR 497].

Yates, A. Y. (1991). *Compulsive exercise and the eating disorders.* New York: Brunner/Mazel.

# Name Index

239

# Subject Index

Abuse, substance: anorectic, 17, 19*tab*; and binge eating, 44; and eating disorders, 203–204
Acidosis, metabolic, 69, 88*tab*
Acquired immunodeficiency syndrome, 23
Addison's disease, 22
Alkalosis: contraction, 68; hypokalemic, 68; metabolic, 69, 88*tab*, 215
Allergies, 6, 13
Alzheimer's disease, 26, 27
Amenorrhea, 4, 19*tab*, 23, 75, 77, 78, 124, 126, 131, 165, 168, 171
Anemia, 82*tab*, 88*tab*; hemolytic, 70; iron deficiency, 89*tab*
Angular cheilitis, 104
Anorexia nervosa: activity-induced, 154–155; and affective disorders, 201–203; anxiety in, 124; associated illnesses, 17–32; body image in, 4–9; cardiac complications, 73–74, 83*tab*; clinical features, 19*tab*; constipation in, 72; dehydration in, 67–68; dental aspects, 101–119; depression in, 124; diabetes and, x; endocrine complications, 77–80, 85–86*tab*; exercise in, 8–9, 64, 153–157, 229–230; fluid and electrolyte abnormalities, 67; gastric emptying in, 71; gastrointestinal

complications, 70–72, 82*tab*, 182–184; genetic contributors, 193–209; heart rates, 73; hematologic changes, 80, 86*tab*; hypophosphatemia in, 70; impaired taste perception in, 71; laxative abuse in, 8; medical complications, 60–93; medical management, 213–230; metabolic complications, 74–76, 84*tab*, 145–158; neuroendocrine disturbances in, 130–135; neurological complications, 80–81, 87*tab*; neurophysiological changes in, 123–135; oral complications, 104–110; orofacial signs, 103; osteoporosis in, 76; pharmacotherapy in, 52–53, 223–229; and prior physical illness, 177; as psychosomatic illness, 1; pulmonary complications, 72–73, 83*tab*; renal complications, 76–77, 85*tab*; resting metabolic rate in, 150–151; signs of, 66–67; treatment in hospital settings, 214–222; vomiting in, 7; vulnerability to psychiatric disorders, 124; weight history, 1, 3–4
Anticonvulsants, 228
Antidepressants, 31, 52–53, 128, 130, 224–225

Hyperemesis gravidarum, 169–170
Hyperlipidemia, 178, 182–184, 187
Hyperphagia, 24–25. *See also* Binge
  eating; adaptive, 30
Hyperthyroidism, 22, 30
Hypoalbuminemia, 21
Hypocalcemia, 89*tab*, 215
Hypochloremia, 68–69, 215
Hypocholesterolemia, 84*tab*
Hypoglycemia, 6, 13, 22, 74, 186;
  fasting, 84*tab*, 90*tab*; insulin-
  induced, 31, 79
Hypokalemia, 10, 63, 68, 70, 73,
  104, 215
Hypomagnesemia, 69–70, 88*tab*
Hyponatremia, 68, 80
Hypoperistalsis, 68
Hypophosphatemia, 60, 70, 88*tab*,
  215, 226
Hypoproteinemia, 73, 84*tab*, 90*tab*
Hypotension, 10, 22, 66, 67, 73,
  88*tab*, 90*tab*, 223
Hypothalamus, 20, 124
Hypothermia, 10, 133
Hypothyroidism, 13, 133

Iatrogenesis, 13
Infection, associated with weight loss,
  23–24
Infertility, 165, 171–172
Inflammatory bowel disease, 21, 176,
  178, 186
Insulin, 20, 146–147; decreased
  secretion, 74; deficiency, 30;
  delayed clearance, 74; effect on
  hunger, 31; effect on weight, 17;
  neglect, 64; omission, 186, 187;
  underdosing, 50, 181
Ipecac abuse, 7, 10, 12, 72, 76;
  consequences, 61*tab*

Ketoacidosis, 181, 186; diabetic, 74
Klein-Levine syndrome, 28–29

Kluver-Bucy syndrome, 26, 27

Lactose intolerance, 6, 12
Laxatives: abuse of, 8, 12, 19*tab*, 30,
  41, 61*tab*, 62*tab*, 62–63, 215;
  bulk-forming, 8, 11, 72;
  proscribing use of, 11; stimulant-
  types, 8; tolerance to, 63
Leukemia, 23
Leukopenia, 86*tab*
Liposuction, 4
Lithium, 31, 228
Lymphoma, 23

Malabsorption syndrome, 21
Mallory-Weiss syndrome, 71
Malnutrition, 75
Medication. *See also* individual
  medications: associated with binge
  eating, 31; associated with weight
  loss, 24; as treatment in binge
  eating, 52–53
Melatonin, 135
Menstruation, 165–173; amenorrhea,
  4, 19*tab*, 23, 75, 77, 78, 124,
  131, 165; disturbances in, 75, 77,
  78; oligomenorrhea, 4, 167;
  restoration of, 131
Metabolism, 18; accelerated, 20;
  alterations in, 145–158;
  biochemical alterations, 146–147;
  complications in, 74–76; and
  energy expenditure, 145–158; fat,
  70, 74; glucose in, 74; increased,
  23, 50; lowered, 23, 78, 79; resting
  rate, 10, 148–152
Mitral valve prolapse, 13, 73, 83*tab*,
  90*tab*
Monoamine oxidase inhibitors, 31
Mortality, ix; perinatal, 169
Multiple sclerosis, 184

Neurofibromatosis, 185